D0919573

The Great
Television
Heroes

Other Books by Donald F. Glut

THE GREAT MOVIE SERIALS (with Jim Harmon)

THE DINOSAUR DICTIONARY

THE FRANKENSTEIN LEGEND: A TRIBUTE TO MARY SHELLEY AND BORIS KARLOFF

TRUE VAMPIRES OF HISTORY

BUGGED!

Other Books by Jim Harmon

THE GREAT RADIO HEROES

THE GREAT RADIO COMEDIANS

JIM HARMON'S NOSTALGIA CATALOGUE

The Great Television Heroes

by Donald F Glut
and Jim Harmon

Doubleday & Company, Inc.
Garden City, New York
1975

Library of Congress Cataloging in Publication Data

Glut, Donald F
    The great television heroes.

    Includes index.
    1. Television programs—United States.   I. Harmon,
Jim, joint author.   II. Title.
PN1992.3.U5G6   791.45'7
ISBN 0-385-05167-0
Library of Congress Catalog Card Number 72–96238
Copyright © 1975 by Donald F. Glut and Jim Harmon
All Rights Reserved
Printed in the United States of America
First Edition

This book is dedicated to our friends
Bob Clampett,
Shari Lewis,
Buffalo Bob Smith,
Burr Tillstrom,
and their many wonderful characters . . .
and to the real Cisco Kid,
Duncan Renaldo.

Foreword

Where were you on weekday evenings during the late 1940s and early 1950s?

If you were one of the fortunate people in your neighborhood to own one of those new televisions sets, you were probably watching its small screen. Most likely the living room was also crowded with neighbors who had not yet purchased a set, arguing that it would never replace radio or that they were awaiting the arrival of color TV. The screen was probably of an awkward shape—like flat on top and bottom and curved at the sides—or altogether circular. But screen size did not matter in those days. The fact that there were pictures in the living room was all that counted. Never before had there been such a parade of cowboys, puppets, comedians, detectives, prize fighters and baseball stars cavorting in the privacy of one's living room. And, unlike the movies, the entertainment could be switched off or changed by the mere turn of a dial. Best of all, after the purchase of a TV set the shows were *free*.

The medium was crude in that so-called Golden Age of Television. Before the development of video tape, many of the programs were telecast *live*. That means *absolutely* live with every mistake, every forgotten line, every snicker on the face of an emcee not believing in the product he was advertising showing up in thousands of living rooms. Only on live television could actor Tristram Coffin, playing a corpse on a major dramatic anthology show, get up and walk off the set, never realizing that he was on camera all the while.

Sets in early television shows were usually cheap as were the budgets of the programs themselves. Live television hosts spoke into cleverly concealed microphones (bouquets of flowers providing suitable camouflage). Children in "Peanut Galleries" screamed to embarrassed kiddie show moderators that they had to go wee wee. Yet, despite the draw-backs of early TV, it was veritably a virgin medium. There was genuine *excitement* in the old shows regardless of their shortcomings. That is one reason why the early shows, bad as some of them were artistically, have remained fondly in our memories.

This book is about that new and exciting era of television. It was an era when detectives like Rocky King, Mike Barnett and the never seen Plainclothesman solved more crimes with their brains than any latter-day private eye could solve with all the scientific gimmicks now at his disposal. It was an era when people and not "laugh tracks" howled at the zany stars of the situation comedies. It was a time when cowboys led action-packed lives and didn't beat the bad guy to the draw by being able to *talk* faster. This was also an era in which children's television did more than present shows in cartoon animation so limited that the figures barely moved. They were *alive* with entertainment.

We hope to re-create a portion of that wondrous era in this book. Naturally there were countless shows, many of which might have been your favorites, which will not be discussed in these pages. Material on some of our most fondly remembered programs is often scarce. In the case of filmed shows, acquiring the rare footage to view again in the 1970s is often impossible. Live shows that were never filmed at all (in the "kinescope" process by which some live programs were preserved) were seen only at the moment of their initial telecast and never again. In such cases, our only resources were our fallible memories.

Our book, then, is a presentation of those shows which we, in our perhaps presumptuous opinions, have deemed most important for such a book. Our choices were sometimes determined by the availability of reference material or by personal taste. If we have neglected to discuss your favorite show, please forgive us. We do not claim to have written a history of the medium but rather a nostalgic look back upon the greatest and most exciting years of television—its infancy.

For a while, then, forget the hostilities of the Bunker family and re-call when Lucy was talked into impersonating a Martian for a publicity stunt staged atop the Empire State Building. Ignore the Saturday morning kids' cartoon shows with their insipid formula plots and abysmal animation and remember when programs starring *live actors*, impersonating Superman and Captain Midnight, were made especially for the younger members of the audience. Erase from your minds some-one trying to teach you the number 3 or the letter R and recall a silly clown in a striped suit, honking a horn and squirting a seltzer bottle.

Remember when a television set was not regarded scornfully as an "idiot box" but was considered something special.

Yes, those were more innocent days in which we, also more innocent, lived and found entertainment in this phenomenal new instrument of information. Return with us, then, to the forties and fifties—the Golden Age of Television.

Donald F. Glut
Jim Harmon
Hollywood, 1974

Preface

My idea of a proper Preface is one which neither dissects the book nor exposes all the highlights. Here I intend merely to compliment, with a few laudatory remarks, the efforts of Don Glut and Jim Harmon, who have made a valuable contribution to the history and evolution of television.

Too often the fascinating details of the birth and growth of important innovations which change the mode of life for the whole world are overlooked and in due time forgotten. What these two gentlemen did in this book is to record, for your reading pleasure and historical knowledge, the intimate details of television's evolution into the most powerful of all media of communication. In the short span of a few years, television has changed the world politically, scientifically, economically and socially.

I hope you, the reader, will find this book the cornucopia of interesting facts and entertainment that I did.

Duncan Renaldo
The Cisco Kid
Santa Barbara, California, 1974

Acknowledgments

The authors of this book are indebted to the following people, who shared with us their memories of times spent either before the television cameras or on the other side of the small living-room screen:

Forrest J Ackerman (editor, *Famous Monsters of Filmland* magazine), Cleveland Amory (critic, *TV Guide*), Dick Andersen, the late Daniel Blum, author of the original *Pictorial History of Television*, Mel Brooks, Larry M. Byrd, Greg Chalfin, Bob and Sody Clampett, Alan Copeland, Ray Craig, Skip Craig, Christine Dittmeyer, Lindagray Glut, Julia Glut, Bob Greenberg, Valeria Harmon, Ron Haydock, Bernie Hoffman, Larry Ivie (editor, *Monsters and Heroes*), Marvin Jones, William and Jane Karstens, Edward Kean (writer of *Howdy Doody*), Allen G. Kracalik, Robert Q. Lewis, Shari Lewis, Ferris Mack, Frank Marth, Clayton Moore, Michael Nesmith, Joe Reddy of Walt Disney Productions, Duncan Renaldo, Zelma Richey, Joe Sarno, Jim Shoenberger, Arthur Shulman and Roger Youman, authors of the book *How Sweet It Was*, Jay Silverheels, Buffalo Bob Smith, Adam Spektor, the late Glenn Strange, Jeremy Tarcher, Frazier Thomas, Burr Tillstrom, John C. Walworth (designer of countless radio and TV premiums) and Bill Warren.

Finally, thanks to Stan Lee for letting us have time off from our jobs as associate editor and editor, respectively, of *Monsters of the Movies* magazine to do this book.

D.F.G. AND J.H.

Contents

List of Illustrations

Following page 174

Ray Guns,

Puppets

and Coonskin Caps

PART I

by Donald F. Glut

CHAPTER 1

Zap!

Captain of the Video Rangers!

ANNOUNCER (*Sounds of* MORSE CODE SIGNALS *over* Wagner's Flying Dutchman): P-O-S-T . . . P-O-S-T . . . The cereals you like the most! The cereals made by Post . . . take you to the secret mountain retreat of . . . *Captain Video! Master of Space! Hero of Science! Captain of the Video Rangers!* Operating from his secret mountain headquarters on the planet Earth, Captain Video rallies men of good will and leads them against the forces of evil everywhere! As he rockets from planet to planet, let us follow the champion of justice, truth and freedom throughout the universe! Stand by for . . . *Captain Video . . . and his Video Rangers!*

Captain Video was television's first interplanetary hero. Like another hero with the same rank, Captain Midnight, Captain Video was a private citizen who used his scientific genius (and solid fists) to battle crime and injustice everywhere, on this world or any other. And like Captain Midnight, Captain Video operated from a secret mountain headquarters and commanded a vast network of agents known as the Video Rangers.

The intrepid leader of the Video Rangers first donned his familiar uniform in June 1949, when *Captain Video* premiered from New York on the Dumont television network at 7 P.M. EST as a Monday-through-Friday serial. Wearing his military togs, laced combat boots and headgear fashioned by the wardrobe department to look like a football helmet with goggles, Captain Video mastered electricity, time and space in his eternal war against evildoers.

The Captain's name was well chosen. Not only was he the first such "video" hero (no, there wasn't a "Captain Audio" on the radio) but he also made use of that adolescent medium. Of course, since Captain Video's world was the twenty-second century and since the Hero of

Science was undoubtedly the greatest inventive genius of all time, by necessity he had to improve on television. Captain Video was the master of the video medium. The culmination of his genius in the field of advanced television was a wondrous device called the Remote Tele-Carrier.

Unlike most inventors, who were dreaming of innovations such as color or three-dimensional TV or video tape, Captain Video ignored these passing toys in developing the Remote Tele-Carrier. The world was plagued by terrible villains, the worst of which was a mad scientist named Dr. Pauli. The Remote Tele-Carrier enabled the Captain to spy on anyone anywhere in the world regardless of disguises or solid walls. No one, not even the head of the future FBI, had any privacy when the Captain of the Video Rangers switched on his electronic peeping tom.

In the early days of the series Captain Video hardly used the Remote Tele-Carrier to full advantage. For reasons known only to program director James L. Caddigan (who also budgeted the show as economically as possible for a hero utilizing the most sophisticated laboratory retreat of either 1949 or 2149), the Captain's agents were stationed at various points out West. It was amazing how much of the West still resembled the 1800s even during the twenty-second century, with cowboys riding horses and using six-guns while Video was the Master of Space. What was even more astounding was the fact that some of these agents, on whom Video would check once during each half-hour episode, looked suspiciously like such old-time cowboy stars as Ken Maynard. One might almost suspect that Captain Video (like Captain Midnight) was really running old Western movies to cut costs so that more money could go into maintaining his secret mountain headquarters.

The first actor to portray Captain Video was Richard Coogan, formerly of stage and radio, and one of the stars of television's *Californians* in later years. Coogan was tall and handsome, with the deep voice necessary for a hero like Video. The fan following he attained in 1949 was the first such phenomenon of television and presaged the hero-worship of Superman, Davy Crockett and other such champions of justice.

When Captain Video was not running old movies on his Remote Tele-Carrier, he was involved in adventures of espionage and scientific hokum, usually to combat some new villainy performed by Dr. Pauli (played by Hal Conklin in a gangster-style double-breasted suit and a cigarette with holder that suggested the typical Nazi bad guy). Dr. Pauli was almost as much of a genius as Video himself, inventing such remarkable devices as a cloak of invisibility which caused numerous headaches beneath the Captain's goggled helmet.

Pauli was one of those villains that viewers loved to hate. Even though he was officially killed four times in the series, script writer M. C. Brook (who also scripted the *Dick Tracy* television series starring Ralph Byrd) was deluged by fan mail for the scoundrel and was forced to bring him back to life. Each time Dr. Pauli was killed off his subsequent resuscitation became more difficult. When he was "finally" blown to bits in a terrific explosion, his fans again demanded his return. Brook knew that the only man to revive the doctor was an even greater scientist—Captain Video himself. And so he concocted a plot wherein Video needed Dr. Pauli to help avert some incredible catastrophe. With his usual speed, Captain Video invented a device which reassembled Pauli's atoms.

In battling menaces like Dr. Pauli, Captain Video needed a partner. He had his entire corps of adult Video Rangers from which to choose. But he selected instead a teen-ager with apparently no name other than the Ranger. (If he had a real name he didn't use it, possibly for security reasons.) Fifteen-year-old Don Hastings, who played the Ranger, was the idol of every young television fan in America. What other young man could travel with TV's foremost hero, zooming about the world in Captain Video's personal jet?

Captain Video and the Ranger used a number of impressive (despite their low-budget construction) gadgets in combating evildoers. There was the Opticon Scillometer, which, like the Remote Tele-Carrier, enabled the Captain to scan great distances and look through walls. Similarly the Mango-Radar screen could be beamed to any place on Earth and show what was taking place. The Astra-Viewer could focus on the most distant stars, while the Astra-View Camera was a miniature prototype of the Polaroid.

Like the Lone Ranger, Captain Video found taking human lives—even in the name of justice—distasteful. Only on rare occasions did the Captain kill anyone, usually with the Atomic Rifle, which he used when confronted with too many killers at one time. Most of the time he shook his opponents into submission with his Cosmic Vibrator.

The popularity of *Captain Video* was phenomenal, especially in those pre-Crockett days of television. Coogan remarked while doing the program: "The fathers in my neighborhood used to take their children to a nearby bar and grill to see *Captain Video,* whenever they had time. The owner would stop serving any drinks that half hour. And what happened then? A lot of families got television sets, just so Father wouldn't miss the Captain's latest adventure in Electronicland."

Acting on *Captain Video* was a strenuous job. The show was done live, as were all the early space shows, and there was little time for rehearsal. Lines had to be learned in a few hours, day by day. As a result, actors usually improvised as they went along, working from a flexible script. The pressures were great, especially on Coogan, who continued to act on the stage while starring as Captain Video. Finally Coogan announced to Dumont that he was leaving the role. Within a short time there was a new Captain.

Al Hodge was a perfect choice as the second Captain Video. His voice was certainly worthy of so dynamic a hero. Hodge played the Green Hornet on radio, where his voice alone identified him as a hero. But he also looked heroic and, even more than Coogan, played Video with total believability. The character of Captain Video had matured just before some major changes were made in the story line.

Gone were the old Western movies that had padded out Captain Video's earlier adventures. The adventures of the Captain and the Ranger occupied the full thirty minutes of each episode. With theatrical films like *Rocketship X-M* and *Destination Moon* making audiences conscious of space travel, Captain Video could hardly be restricted to Earth.

His space ship was called the *Galaxy*. The craft was a sleek, silvery rocket in the standard form of the 1950s. It was bullet-shaped and blasted off vertically in an extension of the V-2. When Video or some other live actor was shown inside the rocket the hull and interior were obviously cardboard, with many of the controls literally painted on. They were accepted, however, because until that time nothing like the *Galaxy* had been seen on television.

The full shots of the *Galaxy* were more believable. The special effects team of Russell and Haberstroh created numerous miniature space ships, atomic submarines, futuristic cities, and planet landscapes, all in minute detail. The *Galaxy* and other miniatures created for the show were filmed and later incorporated with the "live" action. Unfortunately there was considerably more story than special effects footage and the filmed sequences were eternally repeated. Even the youngest Video Rangers watching at home knew that so many of the Captain's enemies couldn't have owned the same rocket ship or launching pad.

Despite the impressive special effects sequences *Captain Video* was produced on an embarrassingly low budget. Twenty-five dollars went into props each week and when that was used up even the leader of the Video Rangers could not save the day. Once the budget was exhausted before two necessary props—a doctor's bag and stethoscope—

could be purchased. Minutes before the show went on the air, the crew realized that they didn't have the props. Two employees dashed to a department store, one returning with a toy stethoscope, the other with a full-size suitcase. Not only the performers but the entire crew exploded into laughter on camera as the actor playing the doctor opened the suitcase, which contained nothing but the tiny stethoscope, and tried in vain to make the instrument reach both ears.

Captain Video and the Ranger encountered more than three hundred villains in their television career, all of whom wanted to conquer the universe, destroy the universe, destroy Video or perform other heinous acts. There was Nargola with his weird rod by which he transformed the sun's energy into magnetic power; Mook the Moon Man, who captured Video and put him in prison; Kul of Eos, who used electronic inventions in his attempt to conquer Earth; Hing Foo Seeng, less ambitious, who only sought to conquer China; and other evildoers with such sometimes familiar names as Neptune of the underwater world, Hermes, Dr. Clysmok, and Dahoumie.

In one serial Captain Video and the Rangers met Spartak of the Black Planet. Spartak appeared to be a villain who was causing trouble among the Rangers until he proved to be only a misunderstood hero. In a later serial Video and the Ranger encountered what they thought to be a giant but later learned that he was a scientist who had shrunk down the *Galaxy* to the size of the miniature prop used in the filmed sequences. When the *Galaxy* was destroyed in its miniaturized state Captain Video had an excuse to design and build the new *Galaxy II*. In other adventures Video and the Ranger battled a crew of android ore miners on a distant world and the prehistoric monsters (filmed sequences of hand puppets and rubber models moved by wires) of a strange planet.

Captain Video's most dangerous foe outdid even Dr. Pauli in villainy. The leader of the Video Rangers could combat any human menace—but Tobor was not human.

Tobor was a giant robot constructed of indestructible metal (although it looked more like cardboard and cloth to the older and wiser viewers). His body was cylindrical with a great triangular piece of metal over the chest, featuring a circular lens which shot death rays. The back was equipped with rockets which transported the mechanical monster through space with the speed of the *Galaxy* itself. The hands terminated in great hooks (which became lobsterlike pincers when the slightly different miniature Tobor soared through space in the filmed inserts) which could rip a man to shreds. Radio antennae stood up from each shoulder while the head, with its gadget running up between the eyes and a foot above the head to give added height, was that of a monster.

The first story line to feature the monstrous robot was given the impressive title "I Tobor." The manlike machine was constructed as an experimental model by a manufacturing company hoping to create an army of tireless, indestructible workers and soldiers. Apparently all of the care went into the prototype robot's construction and not into the rubber stamp that placed his name, "Robot I," on his chest. The stamp somehow came out backward and "Robot I" appeared as a mythological deity pronouncing to his subjects, "I Tobor."

Controlling Tobor was beautifully simple. His master merely had to attune his voice to a pocket-size device and speak commands. Distance did not matter. Since Tobor had the power to destroy space ships and could not be destroyed, the person controlling him could conquer the solar system. The manufacturer should have known better than to give Tobor such power. At least he should have been more careful about hiring his personnel.

Despite the noble reasons for which Tobor was constructed, he was not to be used as his creator had intended. A conniving woman named Atar seized the voice controller from its inventor, set it for her voice, and escaped with the invincible robot. Tobor was free to destroy or conquer according to the whims of Atar.

Captain Video and the Ranger seemed to be up against a foe who could not be conquered. Even the guns of the *Galaxy* were useless against the monster, who retaliated with telling blasts of his own. More than once the *Galaxy* was crippled after Tobor released a destructive ray from his chest. And many episodes ended with either Video or the Ranger trapped as Tobor lumbered forward, each claw swinging like the scythe of the Grim Reaper.

Even though nothing worked against Tobor, Captain Video knew that if he concentrated long enough he could find a way to end the monster's career. At last he managed to construct a device which transformed his own voice to the wave length of Atar's. On a fateful Friday episode Tobor stood between Video and Atar. Every time Atar gave the robot an order the Captain commanded him to do exactly the opposite. Tobor's hulking body moved from side to side, from master to master. When his intricate mechanical insides were no longer able to cope with the conflicting orders, there was a puff of smoke and Tobor's mechanical life was gone.

Tobor was not only Captain Video's most powerful adversary, he was also the most popular. Fans of the robot demanded his return and so, months later on another Friday episode, viewers were warned to stand by their TV sets for an announcement of the gravest importance. When the announcement came it was indeed worth waiting for, since it showed the dormant Tobor abandoned on an asteroid. We were told that Tobor was returning. And he did, after what seemed to be months of subsequent announcements.

This time Captain Video himself was to control the robot, whose power was needed for some special mission. But another evildoer secured the blueprints for the robot and constructed his own, only slightly different in appearance. The high point of this serial was a battle between the two robots.

Tobor appeared occasionally on *Captain Video,* fulfilling the dream of his creator by working for the good of the universe—and the Video Rangers. The Captain eventually found a way to project his own mind into the head of Tobor and send the giant to planets whose atmospheres were too deadly even for a man wearing a space suit. The danger was that everything Tobor experienced was felt physically by Video, whose body was in a chair in his secret headquarters.

With such creatures as Tobor stomping about the TV screen and shooting through the black void of space, Captain Video's world was truly a world of the future. That feeling of a time yet to come was only rarely broken, as when an announcer was using an analogy to describe a new Post cereal during one of the commercials. Holding up a toy car of the future with incredible fins and rocket exhausts, he said, "I can remember when this antique model was all the rage here at Ranger Headquarters." It may indeed have been the rage. But then why, in that same episode, did Captain Video and the Ranger drive around the streets of New York in a 1953 Nash Rambler?

Captain Video was the most popular show of the genre it created, the television space opera. Manufacturers demanded products bearing the Captain's name. While the show was on the air the nation was deluged with Captain Video records, toy rocket sets, comic books, dolls, stationery, trading cards, bedspreads, wallets, clothes, dishes and other paraphernalia.

In 1951, Columbia Pictures in Hollywood also had designs on the property and adapted it to a fifteen-chapter movie serial titled simply *Captain Video.* As Al Hodge and Don Hastings were too busy saving the universe on TV, Judd Holdren and Larry Stewart were assigned the roles of Captain Video and the Ranger. But the serial, produced by Sam Katzman and directed by Spencer G. Bennet, was a disappointment. Although the budget of the television series was considerably less than that of the movie serial, its better scripts and more believable performances assured its fans that there was only *one* Captain Video. The "impostor" would soon be virtually forgotten.

During the later years of *Captain Video* television producers tended to move from live to filmed adventure shows. The hero who had so often saved the universe could not save his own program. For a while before going off the air, Captain Video acted as a host, showing old movie serials as he had when he began in 1949. No, he never ran the movie serial *Captain Video*.

The Space Cadets

In 1950 every young spaceman who watched television on ABC at six-thirty every Monday, Wednesday and Friday afternoon wanted to enroll in Space Academy. That was the school of the future where every budding rocket pilot received the best training in becoming a rocket jockey. Commander Arkwright, a veteran of many space flights and battles with space pirates and killers, was undoubtedly capable of heading the Academy and every would-be space cadet would be proud to learn under him.

But there was another advantage in enrolling at Space Academy. Among the student body was a young space hero who rivaled even Captain Video in popularity. He was teen-aged Tom Corbett, a curly-haired space cadet played by twenty-nine-year-old Frankie Thomas (star of such films as the serial *Tim Tyler's Luck* in 1937). Announcer Jackson Beck (most famous for his announcing chores on the *Superman* radio program) exclaimed over various shots of Space Academy, a V-2 rocket blasting off, and a trip through the starry void:

BECK: *Tom Corbett . . . Space Cadet!*
TOM: Stand by to raise ship! Blast-off minus five . . . four . . . three . . . two . . . one . . . ZERO!!!
BECK: As roaring rockets blast off to distant planets and far-flung stars, we take you to the age of the conquest of space . . . with *Tom Corbett . . . Space Cadet!!*

Tom Corbett, Space Cadet, suggested by the novel *Space Cadet* by Robert A. Heinlein, catered more to the young viewers than did *Captain Video*. While *Video* spotlighted the adventures of the adult Captain, *Tom Corbett* centered upon a teen-ager who, along with other space cadets, shared interplanetary adventures between classes. The teen-agers were the heroes and younger space fans found it easier to identify with the more youthful Corbett than with the head of the Video Rangers.

Viewers were first introduced to Tom Corbett at the Space Academy in the year 2352, the world beyond tomorrow:

TOM: I'm Tom Corbett. As a boy I dreamed of piloting space ships. When I was old enough I took all the exams and was admitted to the best school in the universe—Space Academy!

In the great assembly hall of Space Academy, Tom Corbett stood proudly as Captain Strong (Edward Brice), the father image who seemed hardly older than any of the cadets, led them in the space cadet oath: "I solemnly swear to safeguard the freedom of space, protect the liberties of the planets and defend the cause of peace throughout the universe."

Tom Corbett was officially a space cadet. As his mind began to contemplate future adventures as one of the Solar Guards, he snapped back to attention. The new cadets were all chorusing the Cadet Corps song:

> From the rocket fields of the Academy
> To the far-flung stars of outer space,
> We're Space Cadets training to be
> Ready for dangers we may face.

After weeks of physical and mental training, so rigorous it might have broken the toughest twentieth-century astronauts, Tom Corbett proved to be, naturally, the best in his class. In four years he would graduate and be a full-fledged rocketeer.

Tom was assigned to the rocket cruiser *Polaris*, of the general shape of a V-2, but with small fins along the hull and with a great circular port. Also assigned to the *Polaris* were the quiet Astro (Al Markham), the Venusian navigator with the crew cut, and blond, wise-cracking radar man Roger Manning (Jan Merlin), who usually believed he knew it all and let everyone know it.

ASTRO: Corbett, my name is Astro. I've come from Venus and I'm a former enlisted space sailor. Flew in commercial rockets.
TOM: Glad to know you, Astro. Hi, Manning.
ROGER: How did you guys get to this jail? Talk about discipline . . .
ASTRO: He's been complaining all morning. Nobody forced you to come here, Manning.
ROGER: Why, you Venusian hillbilly, I've got a good notion to . . .
TOM: Break it up, fellas! The intercom!

Captain Strong was on the intercom. It was usually the appropriately named Captain who kept Roger under control, although he never really knew just how much trouble he caused the other members of the *Polaris* crew. Captain Strong was the skipper and pilot of the *Polaris*. Seated next to him and allowed to pilot the great space craft on rare occasions or during emergencies when Strong was unavailable was Tom Corbett.

In one particular episode of *Tom Corbett, Space Cadet,* Roger Manning surprised everyone. All the cadets at Space Academy were anxious to learn who would receive a special award for being the cadet of the year. Naturally everyone (including Tom Corbett) believed that Tom would receive it. Tom was congratulated in advance by Astro, Dr. Joan Dale (Margaret Garland), Captain Strong's pretty girl friend, and Alphie Higgins, the intellectual cadet who was usually the recipient of Manning's practical jokes. Tom should have suspected something when Captain Strong failed to congratulate him prematurely. For some individual act which really impressed the Captain, the award was given not to Tom but to Roger Manning!

Although Tom Corbett was the star of Space Academy, Roger had most of the color. Frequently he would get the *Polaris* or the entire world into trouble with his jokes and sarcasm. One time it appeared that he had sold out to a band of space pirates but was actually working undercover for Captain Strong and Commander Arkwright. Script writer Stu Byrnes developed Roger's character most fully and gave him the most memorable dialogue, usually interspersed with phrases like (to Astro) "You Venusian swamp lizard," "Now you've done it, Junior," "So what happens now, space heroes?" or his never ending "Aww, go blow your jets!"

Before each flight Roger Manning climbed up the ladder to the radar bridge near the nose of the *Polaris* while Astro descended through the hatch in the control deck to the power deck where he tended to the rocket motors. With Tom seated next to Captain Strong the countdown proceeded from "five" to "zero." (Most viewers became familiar with the word "countdown" through *Tom Corbett.* But in later years, when a countdown culminated in astronauts rocketing into space, someone took the liberty of changing the dynamic "blast-off" to the less romantic "lift-off.") As the *Polaris* roared off the landing field of Space Academy, Tom and Captain Strong fell back in their movable chairs and strained as the accelerated force of gravity (or Gs, as every space cadet called it) pressed down on them.

The noted scientist and science fiction writer Willy Ley was technical assistant on *Tom Corbett, Space Cadet.* Because of Ley we knew that there existed particles of anti-matter that would cause annihilation if they came into contact with positive matter. We learned that an asteroid belt existed between Mars and Jupiter and that some of these floating chunks of rock were large enough to hide space villains. Meteors (which we'd previously called "shooting stars") could puncture a ship's hull. Ley familiarized viewers with terms like "intransmission," which was the official sign-off when ceasing radio transmission, and "space junk," which designated any man-made object drifting uselessly through space.

Most important of all, Ley informed us of the ultimate horror which might someday imperil any one of us. Nothing could be worse than to be clanking along the hull of your ship with magnetic boots and then to lose your footing or to be pushed off into the void. With no gravity in the vacuum, such a hapless person would float endlessly through space. Many of us went to bed and had nightmares of suffering such a fate.

Tom Corbett, Space Cadet had everything going in its favor. The portrayals of Tom, Astro and Roger were real enough to attract any adventure-loving viewers. The scripts were some of the best of their type ever written with even the wildest devices and phenomena (thanks to Willy Ley) working as they probably would work in real life. But *Tom Corbett* had better special visual effects than any of its contemporary competitors, including *Captain Video*.

Unlike *Video*, which used filmed special-effects sequences, everything on *Tom Corbett* was done live—and with hardly a mistake. There wasn't room for mistakes in a medium that could not be edited or corrected. The special-effects men behind *Tom Corbett* were not content with merely showing rockets blasting off and going through the starry void. Utilizing some primitive television mattes (with two separate pictures combined for a single effect), Tom and his pals floated about the control deck when the gravity devices of the *Polaris* failed and walked, clad in space suits and fishbowl-type space helmets, about the hull of the ship. The visual effects were imaginative, meticulous and, for the most part, convincing.

Tom Corbett, Captain Strong, Astro and Roger Manning rocketed to such adventures as the battle against the stickmen (literally stickmen moving over a black background) and excursions through the prehistoric swamps and jungles of Astro's native planet Venus.

In one particular adventure, Commander Arkwright sent the *Polaris* crew on a mission. While in space Tom Corbett and Captain Strong intercepted an urgent call for help from weather station number 5 on Mars. When the SOS was broken off, the space heroes knew that their help was needed.

Landing the *Polaris* on Mars, the earthmen put on their bulky space suits and hurried to the weather station. Cosmic disturbances had broken the airtight hut of the weather station operator, Captain Bex. The Captain lay unconscious on the floor, overcome by methane gas seeping from fissures in the ground. Acting with the efficiency with which they were trained, the space cadets got him into the *Polaris* and prepared to blast off.

Great upheavals rocked the planet and as the *Polaris* started to roar off the surface a Marsquake disrupted the delicate instruments and controls (most of which appeared to be enormous knife switches protruding from wall panels in the control deck). The gravitational control was the first device to be affected. Tom and the rest of the crew floated about the control deck. Working as a team, the crew members formed a human chain, with Captain Strong at one end and Tom at the other. Tom managed to reach the gravity control switch and got them all back to the floor. The rest of the trip back to Earth was rather uneventful.

The most spectacular adventure happened on one of the planets in the Alpha Centauri system. The *Polaris,* despite its being the greatest rocket cruiser in Commander Arkwright's fleet, had engine trouble and made a forced landing. Astro knew the ship's engines best and volunteered to stay on board and try to repair them, while Tom, Captain Strong and Roger went exploring.

The planet was a mass of jungle and jagged mountains, appearing to the earthmen like something out of their own world's prehistoric past. Suddenly there was a tremendous roar. The three heroes looked up to see an enormous dinosaur above them atop a cliff. (They had no real reason to worry. The dinosaur could not have moved even if it wanted to; it was merely a stationary model placed on a miniature cliff by the special-effects crew.)

In the succeeding episode, Tom, Captain Strong and Roger were attacked by a *moving* dinosaur (actually a spider which even the youngest fans knew wasn't a real dinosaur). Using the combined force of their non-lethal paralo-ray pistols, they froze the monster where it stood. Then they climbed about the hulk, careful to get off before the effects of the paralyzing ray wore off.

The rest of the adventure was a series of escapes from the prehistoric monsters of that uncharted planet. One giant reptile chased the earthmen into a cave where they promptly encountered another. Quickly Tom removed the radio transmitter from his belt and contacted Astro. "Astro, aye!" acknowledged the Venusian, who said that he'd try getting the *Polaris* repaired by the time his fellow crew members got there. That wasn't a long wait, for Tom, Captain Strong and Roger were already being pursued from the cave by a monstrous saurian. Astro miraculously finished repairing the rocket ship just as his friends entered and readied themselves for blast-off. The *Polaris* shot into the sky, leaving an angry dinosaur on its prehistoric world.

Tom Corbett, Space Cadet was also a radio program, running on Tuesdays and Thursdays in two-part serials and featuring the same cast as the television series. Both television and radio versions were so popular that soon all manner of merchandise bearing the name of Tom Corbett and the Space Academy emblem (a rocket ship in front of a lightning bolt) were appearing on the market. There were Tom Corbett comic books, newspaper strips, phonograph records, space helmets, toy spacemen, and a complete miniature Space Academy with buildings, rockets, cadets, villains and weapons that really fired.

But it was as a television series that *Tom Corbett* was most popular. There were many disappointed would-be space cadets when the program went off the air in the mid-1950s and the doors of Space Academy closed forever.

"Smokin' Rockets!"

ANNOUNCER: SPA-A-A-A-ACE PATROL! High adventure in the wild vast reaches of space . . . missions of daring in the name of interplanetary justice! Travel into the future with Buzz Corry . . . Commander-in-Chief of . . . the SPA-A-A-ACE PATROL!

Announcer Jack Narz exclaimed the opening narration of *Space Patrol* over an impressive display of thirtieth-century technology. Winged rockets blasted off launching pads into the black void of space. A strange aqua-rocket roared through a man-made river. The headquarters of the Space Patrol, an interplanetary agency of law and order situated on the artificial planet Terra, was the most spectacular sight of all with its futuristic design.

Since the Space Patrol was required to battle injustice not only all over the universe but in various time eras, a very special man was needed to be its Commander-in-Chief. Buzz Corry was as capable of commanding the Space Patrol as Captain Video was of leading the Video Rangers.

Buzz Corry had wanted to be a space pilot since his childhood. His family background proved advantageous to his future career. His father was a famous designer of rocket ships and made certain that his son learned everything there was to know about space travel. He enrolled the young Corry in Space Academy (probably not the same Space Academy attended by Tom Corbett). After graduating with top honors, Buzz went on with the experiments begun by his father. The most notable of these was the production of Endurium, an indestructible metal. Later Buzz Corry became the first man to rocket to Pluto and continued his exploration of space as the head of the Space Patrol.

It seemed reasonable that the Commander-in-Chief of the Space Patrol should be portrayed on television by a real-life hero. Ed Kemmer became a World War II flying hero while still a teen-ager. On his forty-eighth mission he crashed in Germany where he was promptly locked up in a Nazi prison. To help lessen the monotony Kemmer learned to act and began entertaining the other prisoners. When he was released and returned to the United States, he enrolled at the Pasadena Playhouse in California. Barely finishing his course, Ed Kemmer was signed to play Commander Corry on *Space Patrol*. A man who had flown in forty-eight missions over the Earth was the perfect hero to rocket away on missions in outer space.

The membership of the Space Patrol was as large as that of the Video Rangers or of Tom Corbett's Space Academy. But three members of that organization held prominence over all others. Corry's sidekick was Cadet Happy (played by Lynn Osborn), the comic equivalent of the Ranger on *Captain Video*. It was Cadet Happy who provided the laughs, gave the young Space Patrollers at home someone with whom to identify and usually exclaimed, "Smokin' rockets, Commander!" every time some danger arose. There were also Major Robbie Robertson (Ken Mayer) and brunette Tonga (Nina Bara), an interplanetary villainess who joined the Space Patrol after a dose of Corry's Brainograph device.

Comprising the upper echelon were the Secretary General of the United Planets (Norman Jolley, who wrote many of the *Space Patrol* scripts), the elected head of the solar system, who operated from his headquarters on Terra and usually entrusted the fate of the universe to Buzz; and his pretty blonde daughter Carol (Virginia Hewitt), who saw in Buzz still other qualities.

Both Carol and Tonga showed that the program was indeed futuristic by wearing thirtieth-century versions of the miniskirt. But neither of them ever managed to lure Buzz Corry away from his duties as Commander of the Space Patrol. He had more important things than romance on his mind. The universe, or at least the planet Terra, was usually in danger. It seemed as though Buzz and Happy were the only ones capable of saving it.

Space Patrol was, in a sense, created in space. Not outer space, but at least in the air. Mike Moser once claimed that he first conceived the idea of *Space Patrol* while soaring over the Pacific in a Navy plane. He envisioned a futuristic Western that would condition viewers— especially children, though many adults had been fans of space opera since the early days of *Buck Rogers* and *Flash Gordon*—to the marvels of the future age of science. Moser himself wrote many of the scripts (though the majority were written by Lou Huston) and did his home-work as far as scientific details were concerned, making sure that all navigation techniques, astronomy and explanations of atomic energy were accurate. His contention was that the wildest fantasy must be built upon hard fact.

Moser kept the show somewhat in the family. His wife Helen directed some of the episodes, leaving most of the others to Lew Spence and Dick Darley. They also directed the *Space Patrol* radio series, which featured the television cast.

Space Patrol began on television early in the 1950s as a local daily serial on West Coast station KECA. The show was so popular that within a short time it was featured on the ABC network on Saturday mornings, 11 A.M. EST. The Saturday episodes were complete stories in themselves but were actually linked with two succeeding episodes, comprising three-chapter serials without cliffhangers. Like *Captain Video* and *Tom Corbett, Space Cadet,* the show was done live, which meant that everyone had to be extra careful, especially when throwing punches or working the special visual effects. To get from set to set while the cameras were on, the actors allegedly zoomed about on roller skates!

The budget of *Space Patrol* was relatively high by comparison with other kids' shows such as *Captain Video.* Every episode of *Space Patrol* cost $2,500, which paid for the services of fifty people working behind the scenes. Much of the show's budget went into special effects, achieved by Franz, Oscar and Paul Dallons. The Dallons brothers went from the field of medical research to the more profitable motion picture industry, using their scientific knowledge to design the laboratories in such films as *The Devil Commands* and *Donovan's Brain,* and for the *Captain Midnight* television series. For *Space Patrol* the Dallons brought laboratories and control panels to dazzling electrical life and manipulated miniature space ships on usually unseen wires. A familiar Dallons shot was a space ship suspended before a rotating drum upon which the stars were painted. The effect was that of a space ship cruising through space. Unlike *Captain Video,* the special effects on *Space Patrol* were always done live.

Commander Corry and Cadet Happy rocketed about the universe clearing the space lanes, battling space outlaws and maintaining the peace, in the flagship of the Space Patrol, the *Terra I.* While Captain Video's *Galaxy* and Tom Corbett's *Polaris* were of the V-2 mold, blasting off vertically, the *Terra I* was a horizontally flying craft with long fins, side portholes and blinking lights, and shot off into the sky from an inclined launching platform. Apparently many space opera fans preferred the vertical ships and wrote complaint letters to the show. Eventually the Space Patrol ships were rigged to make an occasional vertical take-off or landing.

The *Terra I* was the greatest ship in the universe (notwithstanding the *Galaxy* and *Polaris*). But the ship was not indestructible. It was occasionally battered so badly that it was fit only for the Space Patrol junk heap. Such batterings usually took place when the Dallons had designed a newer model rocket. Buzz Corry piloted a number of *Terras* during the run of the show. When *Space Patrol* went off the air in 1955, Corry was flying his sleekest and most powerful ship, the *Terra V.*

In his Space Patrol uniform (with the lightning-bolt chest emblem designating him as Commander), Buzz Corry came up against an incredible set of space villains. The Space Spider entangled the Space Patrollers in his monstrous webbing. The Wild Men of Procyon emerged from hiding on their supposedly uninhabited world and almost killed Buzz and Happy. Raymo (Larry Dobkin, later to become a noted television director) created a band of androids on a planet of the star Algol which were assuming the identities of the members of the United Planets Security Council. The Space Pirate, Captain Dagger (played by Glenn Strange, later Sam the Bartender on *Gunsmoke*), tried to kill Buzz and Happy in the manner of a pirate of old. One of Corry's more frequent adversaries was Mr. Proteus (played by Marvin Miller, later Mr. Anthony on *The Millionaire*), a master of disguise. In one episode Mr. Proteus trapped Buzz in the twilight zone of Mercury, hoping that as the planet rotated toward the sun the intense heat would burn the Commander to a crisp.

A particular story line on *Space Patrol* makes one almost believe that the writers were having lunch with the writers of *Captain Video* (even though *Video* was telecast from New York). While Video was battling Tobor the robot, Commander Corry was troubled by a mechanical man called Five. Like Tobor, Five was controlled by an evil woman and was impervious even to the ray guns of the Space Patrol. But unlike Tobor, Five was more manlike, wearing fatigues and with a dark, artificial face. (When it came to robots *Captain Video* spared more of its budget.)

Tobor was destroyed on Friday. The very next morning Commander Corry devised a way to destroy Five. The robot stalked toward him like the Frankenstein Monster. There was nothing left for Buzz to do but test the device he'd been working on in his spare time. Buzz flashed out his pocket-size invention that changed his voice to the same wave length as that of Five's mistress and began shouting contradicting orders. Five exploded with a puff of smoke set off by the special-effects men. To viewers who had seen *Captain Video* the night before, the destruction of Five the robot was nothing new.

In one *Space Patrol* serial titled "Terra, the Doomed Planet," Buzz, Happy and Major Robertson tangled with a fanatic named Io, who tried to annihilate the solar system, before it collided with his own, with a terrible device called the Contraturene Generator. But Corry blew up the machine and left Io bound to a pillar in his giant, spherical space ship. Returning to the *Terra V,* which was hovering in free fall, Buzz discussed Io with Happy and Robbie.

ROBERTSON: Well, Commander, what are we gonna do with Io when we take him into custody?

BUZZ: Send him back to Andromeda, his own galaxy.

HAPPY: Smokin' rockets, Commander! He'll just come back again with more of those machines and start blowing up all the suns in this galaxy again.

BUZZ: I don't think so.

ROBERTSON: But how can you be sure?

BUZZ: Because of something Io himself said. He said that among the Galactic Dwellers there are no leaders. And even communications are unnecessary among them. All the beings on Andromeda . . . and all the Galactic Dwellers . . . are on the same intellectual plane. They're of one mind.

HAPPY: One mind?

BUZZ: Io said that the Galactic Dwellers developed beyond the plane of individual thinking. The minds work as one to determine the galaxy's destiny.

ROBERTSON: I still don't get it. How does that mean that Io won't try to destroy our galaxy again?

BUZZ: If he fails to accomplish his mission once, it simply means to the collective minds of Andromeda that the task was impossible.

Buzz should have known that a Galactic Dweller would find some way to free himself from ordinary Terran rope. Io switched on a miniature heat ray and burned his way free. Then, using his advanced knowledge of force fields, the man from Andromeda hit the *Terra V* with a force battering ram and drew it into his own ship.

Io trapped the three Space Patrollers behind a force beam, then laughed with delight as he prepared to destroy the planet Terra by remote-control force rams. On Terra, the Secretary General and Carol saw doomsday coming, with great quakes on the artificial world that sent them hurtling from one side of the room to the other. Carol tried to make contact with Buzz.

CAROL: Secretary General's office, Terra, calling Buzz Corry. Do you read me? Buzz . . . (*crying*) please answer. . . .
SECRETARY GENERAL: It's no use, Carol. If something unexpected hadn't happened to Buzz, this disaster would not be taking place now.
CAROL: We can't . . . give up.
SECRETARY GENERAL: We're not giving up, Carol. And you can count on this. Neither is Buzz Corry!

The Secretary General's optimism was, as usual, well founded. Corry managed to slip out from behind Io's force beam and grab the fiend, knock him away from his controls, and capture him. The damage had already been done, however. Terra's rotation had been slowed down and soon the artificial planet would be drawn into the sun. Buzz had to use his quick wits to save Terra and he switched on the force beams in the opposite direction. The Secretary General, Carol and some of the office furniture went soaring back to the other side of the room. There was no doubt in the minds of the Secretary General or his daughter that once again Buzz Corry had saved them.

Corry prepared to send Io back to Andromeda a failure, proving that his mission was impossible. In order to show that no hard feelings existed between the Galactic Dwellers and the Space Patrol, Buzz said:

BUZZ: Io, I'm sorry you have to go back to your galaxy with your mission still not complete . . . but it'll be two hundred thousand years—our years—before our stellar systems collide. I think that's enough time to work out a better solution. Good-by, Io.

The most popular villain ever to face Buzz Corry and the Space Patrol was the Black Falcon, alias Prince Baccarratti (played by Bela Kovacs, the associate producer of *Space Patrol*), the diabolical pretender to the Venusian throne. Baccarratti was evil incarnate and with his lieutenant Malengro (again Larry Dobkin), an evil genius, caused Buzz Corry more trouble than any of his other adversaries.

Prince Baccarratti took over the rule of Planet X, a runaway world which resembled Earth during prehistoric times. Buzz and Happy rocketed to Planet X and encountered a number of giant reptiles. A Tyrannosaurus (a non-moving model pushed along step by step by an off-screen stage hand holding onto its tail) prowled through the jungle, sniffing the Space Patrollers' scent. Its enormous head peered over the treetops and roared. (This time a moving hand puppet was used.) Luckily the Tyrannosaurus didn't find Buzz or Happy. But there were other horrors on Planet X with which to reckon.

First Commander Corry and Cadet Happy encountered a carnivorous plant. They escaped the thing only to be trapped by an enormous ice demon, a creature similar to Earth's prehistoric sea serpent, Plesiosaurus, but with two long fangs (a rubber model with a too often seen wire manipulating the elongated neck). Again the two heroes barely escaped being devoured.

Their objective was Baccarratti's castle. But upon entering the castle they learned that Baccarratti's atomic pile was about to blow them all to atoms. The only way to prevent the explosion was to use all their strength to push in the control rods of the atomic pile. Malengro made that nearly impossible by shrinking Buzz and Happy to six inches. But again the stalwarts triumphed and, by utilizing the fourth dimension, rescued Tonga, who had been tossed into a pit of prehistoric monsters.

Prince Baccarratti's moments of freedom were coming to an end. Space Patrol fleets were attacking his kingdom. He fled to the Valley of Illusion and there managed to conjure up a number of phantasms that baffled the Space Patrollers. When the good guys observed that the illusions had no shadows, they were able to discern what was real and, after a final battle, capture the Black Falcon and rocket him back to Terra.

Eventually Prince Baccarratti escaped the artificial planet and devoted his life to seeking revenge on Buzz Corry and Cadet Happy. His favorite trick was transporting them to Earth's past and leaving them to face death. Buzz and Happy were nearly killed by wild Indians on the American plains and blown up during the first atomic bomb test in New Mexico. Another time they were sent to Salem during the time of the famous witch trials in an adventure titled "Revenge of the Black Falcon."

HAPPY: Smokin' rockets, Commander! We're really in a spot! We'll never convince those colonists that we came here in a space ship.

BUZZ: Don't even mention it. Whatever you do, don't tell them who we really are. That would convict us as sorcerers for sure and you know what happened to those convicted of witchcraft.

HAPPY: Yeah! They were burned at the stake!

Space Patrol followed the usual merchandising procedures of the other space shows. There were *Space Patrol* comic books, pictures, trading cards and so forth. But the greatest single object ever made in connection with a kids' television show was given away in connection with Buzz Corry's adventure on Planet X.

The *Terra IV*, the "Ralston Rocket" built by one of the show's sponsors, was a thirty-foot working model of a Space Patrol battleship. It didn't fly, but its instrument panels lit up and blinked and did everything else you would expect. A small stamping on the side of the ship assured us that it was "built on Terra." The *Terra IV*, its hull white and fins a contrasting red, toured the United States, occasionally with Ed Kemmer in his Commander's uniform going along to answer questions about space travel and rocketry. Lucky fans got to enter the ship, see the realistic equipment (space helmets, ray guns, etc.) and even work the controls. For a while it was possible to actually exist in the thirtieth century of the Space Patrol.

One Saturday in 1954, Jack Narz announced that the greatest message in the world would be given for all Space Patrollers at home. The message had to be spectacular to top the announcement that the *Terra IV* would soon be pulled by truck into your very own neighborhood. When the program came to an end, Narz's announcement was the most incredible thing any of us had ever heard.

Space Patrol was having a contest. All viewers had to do was name Prince Baccarratti's Planet X. Certainly there had been "name-the-whatever" contests before, but none like this one. The grand prize was the *Terra IV*. The thought of having a "real" rocket in your back yard was almost too much to contemplate. The winner of the "Name Planet X" contest was envied by every normal kid who owned a television set.

The giving away of the *Terra IV* would have been a spectacular grand finale. But *Space Patrol* endured until late 1955. Lynn Osborn continued to act in motion pictures such as *Invasion of the Saucer Men* until his premature death about 1960 (a year after the death of Mike Moser). Ed Kemmer continued to act in such feature-length films as *Earth vs. the Spider,* television commercials and *Twilight Zone.* In the soap opera *Clear Horizon* he played a two-fisted astronaut at Cape Canaveral. To former *Space Patrol* fans, Buzz Corry was back in action.

While Captain Video, Tom Corbett and Buzz Corry were blasting off into space and zapping pirates and mad dictators with their officially issued ray guns, other heroes of minor space organizations were also helping to keep peace in the universe.

In 1953, *Rod Brown of the Rocket Rangers* premiered on CBS with somewhat the same format as *Tom Corbett, Space Cadet*. A youthful Cliff Robertson starred as Rod Brown, who with fellow Rocket Rangers played by Bruce Hall and Jack Weston solved the mystery of "Operation Dinosaur" and, the next week, fought a pet chimpanzee that was enlarged to the proportions of King Kong. Fans preferred the other space shows and *Rod Brown* went off the air the following year.

Besides *Rod Brown of the Rocket Rangers* there were many science fiction shows made for kids that had brief lives on television in the early and mid-1950s. *Commando Cody,* starring Judd Holdren, showed space fans what the old Republic serials were like in the theaters; *Rocky Jones, Space Ranger,* starring Richard Crane, was the first space show made exclusively for television entirely on film; and *Captain Z-RO* (written and produced by the star, Roy Steffens) kept the hero on Earth but sent him into different time periods where he helped make history happen. There were also shoddy television versions of *Buck Rogers* and *Flash Gordon,* neither of which had much appeal to former home Video Rangers, Space Cadets and Space Patrollers.

The younger viewers of early television knew what to expect in the world of the future. There would be silvery rocket ships controlled by fantastic arrays of gauges, dials and enormous knife switches. Paralysis weapons would replace the firearms carried by law enforcers. And the future universe would be populated by such fiends as Dr. Pauli and Prince Baccarratti. However, as long as such heroes as Captain Video, Tom Corbett and Buzz Corry were in that universe, the future safety of Earth was assured.

CHAPTER 2

"Look! Up in the Sky!"

Jimmy Olsen, an ambitious cub reporter working for the Metropolis *Daily Planet,* burst into the office of Perry White, the editor-in-chief. The boy was frantic but managed to blurt out the fact that a man was hanging by a rope from a doomed dirigible.

Also in White's office were Lois Lane, the career-minded star reporter of the *Daily Planet,* and an intruder, a mild-mannered young man with horn-rimmed glasses named Clark Kent.

Immediately White roared an order for Lois and Jimmy to hurry to the scene of the impending catastrophe for a story and pictures. Clark Kent, who had come to White's office seeking a job as a reporter on the *Planet,* took advantage of the excitement and got the editor to promise him the job if he wrote the story first.

Clark Kent rushed down the hall to a storeroom, yanking off his glasses and loosening his tie and shirt. Within moments Kent had ceased to exist. He had become an impressive hero that this world had never before seen. A blue costume clung to his powerful physique. He wore red boots and trunks (held up by a yellow belt with gold buckle). On his chest was a scarlet S emblazoned on a shield of yellow. A red cape draped his powerful shoulders; it hung to his calves and bore the red S insignia. He was no longer Clark Kent, the mild-mannered would-be reporter—but Superman, making his first television appearance that evening in 1951 when his syndicated series began. When Superman, the mighty Man of Steel, leaped out of the window to fly to the rescue of the man suspended from the dirigible, he simultaneously launched himself into a series that would last until 1958.

At the opening of this first half-hour episode, entitled "Superman on Earth," the announcer told us a little about the brightly outfitted crusader.

ANNOUNCER: Superman! Faster than a speeding bullet! More powerful than a locomotive! Able to leap tall buildings at a single bound! Look! Up in the sky!

MAN: It's a bird!

WOMAN: It's a plane!

MAN: It's SUPERMAN!!

ANNOUNCER: Yes, it's Superman . . . strange visitor from another planet who came to Earth with powers and abilities far beyond those of mortal men. Superman . . . who can change the course of mighty rivers, bend steel in his bare hands . . . and who, disguised as Clark Kent, mild-mannered reporter for a great metropolitan newspaper, fights a never ending battle for truth, justice and the American way!

The announcer didn't tell us of all of Superman's strange powers. He didn't inform us of his invulnerability, his X-ray and telescopic vision, his supersensitive hearing or his super-breath. But then there was little need to tell us. Every red-blooded American boy who read *Action Comics* or *Superman*, both published by National Periodical Publications, already knew just who the Man of Steel was and what he could do.

Superman was the creation of two teen-agers, writer Jerry Siegel and artist Joe Shuster. After unsuccessfully trying to sell their comic strip of a superhuman being for years, Siegel and Shuster finally sold the idea to publisher M. C. Gaines, who worked him into the first issue of *Action Comics* in 1938. The character was so popular that he was given a serialized radio program that same year. In 1939 the Man of Tomorrow (another phrase used to describe Superman) was given a newspaper comic strip and his own magazine, *Superman*, which is still one of the best-selling comic books. Other dramatic adaptations of the character were a series of seventeen animated cartoons made in color by Paramount Pictures in 1941 and two movie serials starring Kirk Alyn as the Man of Steel, *Superman* (1948) and *Atom Man vs. Superman* (1950).

The Superman movie serials were unrivaled in popularity. But the second of these was made just as television was becoming *the* popular form of visual entertainment. The same kids who loyally flocked to Saturday matinees to see weekly installments of *Atom Man vs. Superman* were now staying home watching *Captain Video* and *Howdy Doody* on the small circular or rectangular picture tube that held a place of honor atop that awesome god of the previous era, the expensive radio console. Whitney Ellsworth of National Comics had become a television producer and knew that the time had come for Superman to fly into living rooms.

The *Adventures of Superman* television series became a virtual extension of the radio series (which by that time had gone into a weekly half-hour format, each episode a complete story). The opening lines, the sponsor (Kellogg's), and many of the story lines were the same. When the writers of the television show could not adapt a radio theme or failed to come up with an original idea, they went to the source, *Action* and *Superman* comics (or even *Batman* with Jimmy Olsen adapted to the role played in the comics by Robin, the Boy Wonder).

Casting *Adventures of Superman* was another matter. Although the radio versions of Superman, Lois Lane, Jimmy Olsen and Perry White *sounded* right, they did not fit the physical requirements imposed by the Superman line of comic books. Besides, Bud Collyer, Superman's radio voice, had been busy as master of ceremonies on TV's *Beat the Clock* since 1950 and the Man of Steel could hardly be seen moonlighting on a game show.

Kirk Alyn had vowed never again to play the part of Superman. The two serials he did at Columbia had already hurt his acting career by typecasting him as the Man of Steel. Another actor who fit both the parts of mild-mannered Clark Kent and the dynamic Superman had to be found before the show went into production.

Producer Robert Maxwell knew that the part required an actor with the appeal of Alyn and found that man by accident. According to the press releases, Maxwell was on a vacation when he saw a man taking a sun bath on Southern California's Muscle Beach. In his sunglasses the man surprisingly resembled Clark Kent. Later he learned that the man was not only a friend of Kirk Alyn but also a veteran actor whose many credits included a featured part in *Gone With the Wind* and the starring role in the Columbia serial *Adventures of Sir Galahad* (1949). The fact that he could act was wonderful; that he had experience as a courageous hero was perfect. The actor was six feet, two and a half inches tall and weighed a hundred and ninety-five pounds. When he took off his glasses, to Maxwell's delight, George Reeves *did* look like Superman.

Superman's girl friend Lois Lane was first played by Phyllis Coates as a career girl who wasn't afraid to slap the worst criminals in the face. Miss Coates's Lois was one of the first women's liberationists on television. After the first season of *Adventures of Superman* Lois' character mellowed in the person of Noel Neill, who re-enacted her role from the two Columbia Superman serials. Unlike the comic book Lois, whose main reasons for living were to expose Superman's secret identity and to marry him, the television Lois was more concerned with her job as a crack reporter.

White-haired John Hamilton portrayed Perry White. His thunderous "Don't call me Chief!" became a standard line on the show. Although the editor-in-chief sounded like a roaring locomotive (that was not as powerful as Superman), he was probably the most lovable member of the *Daily Planet* staff. Jimmy Olsen, played by Jack Larson, was the young man who usually called White "Chief" and aroused the wrath of the tough old editor. It was Jimmy who rivaled Lois in the number of times each was rescued by Superman. The only other regular character was Inspector William Henderson (Robert Shayne), created on the *Superman* radio program. Henderson provided the necessary link between the *Daily Planet* and the Metropolis Police Department.

Before *Adventures of Superman* went into production, Ellsworth decided to make a feature-length pilot film to play in movie theaters and test the popularity of the new version. *Superman and the Mole Men,* directed by the reliable television director Lee Sholem, was about the world's deepest oil well breaking into the center of the earth. A group of midget radioactive creatures emerged from the well. The film was a story of racial prejudice for young people—the Mole Men were immediately persecuted and hunted like animals by the bigoted residents of a small town. Soon the creatures decided to fight back with a weird ray gun (cleverly disguised as a vacuum cleaner with a funnel at one end). But Superman, always the champion of the underdog, saved the creatures from the mob and returned them to the well, teaching the townspeople a much-deserved lesson. *Superman and the Mole Men* was well received, the new actors in the old roles were accepted, and the film was later split into two parts to be run as "Unknown People" on the television series.

The first episode, "Superman on Earth," depicted the origin of the strange being who streaked through the sky on his first rescue mission. On the planet Krypton, a world with a futuristic civilization (but which had not yet mastered space travel), there was much concern among the members of the Council. They sat at the great conference table and murmured among themselves, anticipating the insane ramblings of their foremost scientist. Jor-El (played by Robert Rockwell, best remembered as Mr. Boynten on *Our Miss Brooks*) had always been respected for his knowledge and wisdom. But now he sounded like a fanatical doomsayer.

Jor-El's studies convinced him that Krypton would soon be drawn into the sun. The only way to save his people was to fire them in rocket ships to Earth, a planet with an atmosphere almost like their own. As Jor-El tried to convince the stubborn Council of their approaching doom, an ominous rumbling sounded from outside the building.

JOR-EL: Do you hear that rumbling?
GO-GAN: I hear only thunder. (*Laughter.*)
JOR-EL: It is not thunder. It is an internal eruption . . . gas exploding in subterranean pockets. (*Laughter.*) The time will come. And that time is perhaps very near at hand when you'll wish you heeded the words of Jor-El . . . when Krypton is shattered into a hundred million stars . . . when the glorious civilization we have built is no more . . . when you and your families are swept from the face of the planet like dust! (*Laughter.*)

Jor-El returned to his laboratory where he had been working on a model rocket, the miniature prototype of the great fleet he envisioned would save his people. Lara (Aline Towne), his beautiful wife, sympathized with her husband. As the quakes became more violent, Jor-El pleaded with Lara to escape in the model rocket. But she convinced him that it was more important to save their infant son Kal-El.

JOR-EL: The model *might* carry both of you, Lara.
LARA: No. I'm not going.
JOR-EL: You must!
LARA: My place is here with you.
JOR-EL: Lara, please, there isn't time. The take-off pressure's building up and in a few seconds . . .
LARA: I'd be lost in a world without you, Jor-El. If anyone is to survive, let it be our son.

Jor-El placed his infant son in the silvery rocket and fired it out of the laboratory window and into the sky. "Our son is on his way to Earth," he said, embracing his wife. Canyonlike fissures split the surface of the planet, causing buildings to crumble and mountains to fall into rubble. While the planet Krypton died, the baby destined to be the greatest superhero of all rocketed toward Earth.[1]

[1] The first episode of *Superman* was economically produced but was nevertheless quite spectacular for those early days of television. The scenes on Krypton proved to be an excellent opportunity to cut production costs. Many of the costumes and scenes were taken from earlier movies and the predecessor of the television adventure series—the movie serials. Fans of Saturday movie matinees were surprised to see Superman's competitors from the comic books, Captain Marvel and

The model rocket bearing Jor-El's son crash-landed in the farmlands of Smallville, U.S.A. An elderly couple, Eben and Sarah Kent, saw the bullet-shaped object catch fire. Hearing a baby crying from inside the blazing ship, Eben rescued him seconds before it exploded.

The Kents were childless and took in the baby, whom they named Clark, as their own. As the boy grew older he discovered that he possessed abilities beyond those of ordinary men. He was stronger, could run faster, jump higher. On his twelfth birthday he realized that he could see through solid objects with his X-ray vision. Sarah Kent, believing that Clark was old enough to know, told him how Eben had saved him from the burning rocket ship.

On the twenty-fifth anniversary of Kal-El's arrival on Earth, tragedy struck the Kents. Eben suffered a fatal heart attack. Clark was now a man and destined for a life more significant than working on his mother's farm. As Clark waited for the bus that would take him to Metropolis where he would seek work on the country's greatest newspaper, Sarah handed him the red, blue and yellow costume she had made.

SARAH: The bus will be along any minute, Clark.

CLARK: I still hate to leave you, Mother.

SARAH: I'm gonna be just fine . . . your cousin Edith coming on to live with me and all. Besides, you've got a great responsibility to the world, Clark. You've gotta accept it. Make use of your great powers. You sure you packed that costume I made for you?

CLARK: It's in the suitcase.

SARAH: Nothing'll ever hurt it, Clark. Not acid, nor fire, nor nothin' else. It's made out of the red and blue blankets you was wrapped in the day your pa and me . . .

CLARK: I know, Mom. Here comes the bus. Good-by, Mom.

SARAH (*crying*): Good-by, son.

In Metropolis, Clark Kent put on a pair of glasses and adopted a mild-mannered secret identity. He went to the *Daily Planet* to get a

---

Captain America, sitting at the conference table (or at least actors wearing the costumes from the Republic movie serials *Adventures of Captain Marvel* and *Captain America*). Jor-El himself wore Buster Crabbe's shirt from the old Universal *Flash Gordon* chapter plays. All this made it seem likely that Kryptonians *had* been on Earth before, where they stopped to rent some clothes from Western Costume Company in Hollywood. Further costs were eliminated by the use of stock footage, such as the famous newsreel film of the V-2 rocket and the earthquake scenes from the movie *Lost Continent*. But despite the use of familiar costumes and scenes, "Superman on Earth" was a minor epic to those of us who were the right age in 1951.

job that would keep him informed of criminal activities and emergencies requiring the powers of Superman.

Superman rescued the man hanging from the dirigible and gave to history his first superfeat. The man passed into unconsciousness as he was flown to safety by the strangely garbed hero. When he awoke in a nearby airplane hangar, Clark Kent stood over him, waiting for an exclusive interview. So impressed was Perry White with the scoop brought in by Clark that he gave him a job as a reporter on the *Daily Planet*. Superman had begun his career on television.

George Reeves was padded with some supermuscles by the wardrobe department. Then he was given the famous Superman costume (actually brown and light gray, which photographed better in black and white).[2] The Man of Steel was ready to fly toward any emergency. Or almost ready.

The transformation of actor George Reeves into Superman required more than a padded costume. The writers and artists of the comic books had created a legendary character—a true American folk hero—whose powers were as familiar to most kids as were the heroics of Wild Bill Hickock and Daniel Boone. It was relatively simple to draw Superman performing his impossible feats on the comic book page. Duplicating those feats on a screen with live actors was another matter.

The prop department worked overtime producing balsa-wood furniture that would shatter upon impact with Superman's invulnerable body, iron bars that would bend and guns that could be squashed in his superhands, "invisible" wires that helped the Man of Steel lift people into the air with one hand, walls that shattered as he flew through them, and special jacks to lift up the rear of a car as Superman grabbed the bumper. These were all within the means of the prop department. However, the task given to the special-effects crew was to make Superman do the really impossible—*fly*.

The Man of Steel had flown to only a slight degree in *Superman and the Mole Men*. But the scenes of Superman airborne were so brief that the fans felt cheated. Wires had been attached to Reeves's

[2] In later years, in anticipation of color television, *Adventures of Superman* was shot in color but released in black and white. In these episodes Reeves wore a costume with the official blue and red colors. But on the black and white screen it was almost impossible to distinguish the blue from the red. After more and more American families bought color television sets, the series was re-released in color. In a way *Superman* (like *The Lone Ranger, The Cisco Kid, Science Fiction Theater* and others) was like a brand-new series with a new audience craving color. The vivid colors of the Superman costume made the program even more appealing.

body. As he sprang forward he seemingly took right off into the air, the wires being concealed by the darkness as he only flew at night. After various point-of-view shots looking down from the air, we saw the film's single shot of Superman in flight. That shot was done by the cartoon animators who were responsible for the flying scenes in the two Superman movie serials. For that brief shot of Superman swooping down over the dam to rescue the Mole Men, he had been reduced to an animated cartoon.

Flying scenes which had to be shot at night or animated could not sustain a long-running television series. Although the scenes of Reeves on wires were impressive, they were brief. Reeves himself eventually refused to do any more of these when, during the shooting of "The Mind Machine" (one of the best of the 104 episodes), Superman made a number of impressive flights on wires in bright daylight before they broke, sending him crashing to the ground. (During that same episode, says director Lee Sholem, Reeves knocked himself out while crashing through a breakaway door. The stage hands had forgotten to remove the two-by-four braces from the other side.) There had to be a simpler way.

The solution for making Superman fly was the use of a traveling matte, a process by which two separate pictures are combined to make a composite. Reeves put on a steel harness and took his place upon a steel bar, maintaining a horizontal position. Behind him was a stark white background and off screen was a wind machine to rustle his hair and make his cape stream in the wind. After the film was shot and taken to the laboratory, a moving background was substituted for the wall.

Reeves would leap out of a window (which was at a distorted angle so that he appeared to be shooting upward) or over the camera lens. Then we would see him streaking through the sky with the appropriate sound effect of a shrill wind (the same sound used on the *Superman* radio show). Half shots in medium close-up reassured us that it was indeed Reeves flying through the air. When he landed it was occasionally done in slow motion with the famous whooshing sound familiar to radio listeners.

During Superman's first year on television he encountered a number of menaces. A robot named Hero in "The Runaway Robot" was stolen by crooks and used to commit robberies until it struck Superman with its arm and was reduced to a pile of tin cans and scrap metal. In "The Stolen Costume" Superman's outfit was stolen from Kent's apartment by a burglar and turned over to a pair of criminals who tried to blackmail the Man of Steel. In "Ghost Wolf" a supposed werewolf haunted the north woods area while a forest fire nearly burned Superman's friends to death.

Perhaps the most spactacular of these early adventures was "Crime Wave," in which Superman waged a one-man war against the underworld. The show was crammed with action, most of which came from previous episodes. The Man of Steel confronted the leader of Metropolis' criminal empire, who then tried to destroy the red- and blue-clad hero in a specially constructed electrocution chamber. Superman fell to the floor as his body was struck by enormous jagged blasts of electricity. The master criminal revealed his true identity and rushed into the room to see the corpse of the supposedly indestructible Superman. Miraculously, Superman leaped to his feet, revealing that he had been faking all along in order to bring the criminal boss to justice.

If Lois Lane ever needed the help of Superman, it was in "The Human Bomb," one of the episodes from the first season of the program. But even the mighty Man of Steel seemed powerless to save her that time. In order to win a hundred-thousand-dollar wager that he could control Superman for thirty minutes (conveniently the length of the show), "Bet a Million" Butler visited Lois Lane at the *Daily Planet*. Wearing a vest rigged with sticks of dynamite and a detonator, Butler identified himself as the Human Bomb. He left one of the sticks with Jimmy Olsen, then forced Lois onto the ledge outside her office window, some twenty stories up. Minutes later Perry White, Jimmy Olsen, Police Inspector Hill (played by Marshal Reed) and Clark Kent were in Lois' office. Butler demanded the appearance of Superman and Kent's mind worked fast to invent an excuse to race to the storeroom.

CLARK: Chief, I never thought the *Daily Planet* would be guilty of a thing like this.
WHITE: What do you mean?
CLARK: The cheapest kind of publicity stunt. Manufacturing headlines.
JIMMY: But, Mr. Kent, this is for real, for sure!
CLARK: And risking the life, not only of some stunt man, but that of Lois too. Well, it she's crazy enough to let you talk her into it . . .
WHITE: Kent, you're crazy if you think . . .
CLARK: Sure, I'm crazy, if I let myself become a party to this kind of sensational journalism!
JIMMY: But look, Mr. Kent . . .
CLARK: I don't want any part of it. I'm leaving!

Superman appeared, exploded the dynamite sample left with Jimmy, and then flew to the ledge where the Human Bomb was holding Lois. There Butler told Superman that no harm would befall the girl reporter providing he allowed a minor robbery to take place without his inter- ference for thirty minutes. The Man of Steel agreed to his demands, then jumped back inside the building through an open window.

But Superman could not allow even a petty crime to take place. He leaned out the window and replied, "No comment until the time limit is up," to every remark made by Butler while Perry White took it down on a tape recorder. White stood with his back in the window as Super- man placed Inspector Hill in a chair (Reed's profile resembled that of Reeves), removed his cigarette and draped his coat over his shoulders like a cape. When White left the window Superman's shadow was seemingly on the wall. Even as Superman dashed off to thwart the robbery at the museum, Butler heard his voice from the tape recorder.

Unfortunately Jimmy Olsen's propensity for getting into trouble in- terfered with Superman's ruse. Somehow forgetting that the first stick of dynamite had exploded, he looked up the manufacturer's name in the telephone book. Not finding it, Jimmy was convinced that the dynamite was phony, rushed out to Lois' defense, and blurted out the fact that Superman had double-crossed Butler. Luckily the Man of Steel arrived in time to catch Jimmy as Butler knocked him off the ledge. Once safely inside the building, Lois gave the Human Bomb a well-earned slap in the face.

Lois and Superman hardly ever had any romantic entanglements, which were so prevalent in the comic books. Even with Superman con- stantly rescuing her, he had little time for romance and she seemed more concerned with getting scoops for the *Planet* than anything else. Throughout the duration of the series Superman always referred to Lois as "Miss Lane," scarcely the address expected of a super boy friend. In one adventure Lois snared the Man of Steel with her charms (beauty again triumphing over brawn) and told him that, since they would soon be married, he could call her "Lois." To younger fans this was surely the worst predicament Superman had ever gotten into. Luckily Superman's courtship of Lois was only a dream (a popular device of contemporary comic books) and he went back to calling her the less sentimental "Miss Lane."

To sustain suspense on a weekly program that lasted for seven years and featured an invulnerable hero, the writers had to devise new methods of endangering the Man of Steel. Kryptonite, a fragment of the planet Krypton which could weaken Superman, cause him pain or un- consciousness at certain distances from him, or even death from over-exposure, initially appeared during the first season of the series. (It had been created years before on the Superman radio series.) Superman disposed of the fragment (which had been placed in a lead pipe through which its radiations—and his X-ray vision—could not penetrate) by tossing it into the river. In later shows Superman collided with an asteroid containing Kryptonite which gave him amnesia; a criminal scientist learned to synthesize the alien mineral and hid it in a bust for which Superman was posing; and crooks fished the original chunk out of the river in an attempt to kill the Man of Steel.

But exposure to Kryptonite every episode would have been monotonous, as would the constant rescuing of Lois and Jimmy. The writers tried to subject the Man of Steel to new dangers unheard of in the comic books. In one episode Superman was trapped in a super-refrigeration chamber that froze him into a powerless weakling. Readers of the comic book were suspicious. Everyone knew that even the coldest temperatures had no effect on the Man of Steel. The comic book Superman could also move faster, break through the time barrier and perform greater feats of strength with less effort.

But even as the television writers invented new weaknesses for the Man of Steel, so did they devise new powers. He learned to cause Lois' body to levitate in the air. Once he found a way to split himself into two considerably weakened Supermen in order to be in two places at the same time. In one episode Superman gained the ability to will himself through solid matter. At least for that episode the prop department saved a breakaway wall.

As Superman continued to streak to the rescue year after year, age was beginning to show on him. Reeves was growing noticeably older, grayer, heavier, and performed fewer superstunts. Apparently, as Superman matured on the program his alter ego lost much of its original timidity. Clark Kent had become as bold as Phyllis Coates's Lois Lane. Instead of cowering before gangsters, he reprimanded them with a self-confidence worthy of Steve Wilson of *Big Town*'s top newspaper, The *Illustrated Press*.

There was another major difference between the early and late shows. While *Adventures of Superman* was originally played straight, the later episodes were mostly tongue-in-cheek or outright comedies. Usually these humorous episodes featured comic bad guy Ben Welden as a stout, bald crook with a growling Brooklyn accent.

A typical episode from the final season of *Superman*, featuring Welden as ex-convict Leftover Louie Lyman, was "Flight to the North." The episode also featured Chuck Connors (before his role as Lucas McCain on *The Rifleman*) as Sylvester J. Superman, "the strongest man in Skunk Hollow County." He was a country bumpkin, in red and blue coveralls, who could bend steel bars but had never heard of the Man of Steel. Leftover Louie bet his former partner Buckets half the "fifty grand" from a previous bank robbery that Margie Holloway, a girl he used to know, could bake better lemon meringue pies than his aunt Tillie. Coincidentally, Margie had baked a lemon meringue pie and placed an advertisement in the *Daily Planet* to elicit Superman's help in delivering it to her fiancé Steve, stationed at an Air Force radio shack in Alaska. To Louie's dismay Margie told him that she had promised her boy friend that she wouldn't bake the pies for anyone but him. After Louie made a grumbling exit, both Clark Kent and Sylvester J. Superman (who left his mule Lilybelle tied to a parking meter) arrived in answer to the ad. Sylvester agreed to take the pie via airplane to Steve in Alaska, but lurking outside the apartment was Leftover Louie.

LOUIE: Hey, you!

CLARK: Leftover Louie! What are you doing here?

LOUIE: My business is with Junior here, Kent, and it's strictly legal.

SYLVESTER: I'm in kind of a hurry, mister. I gotta fly this pie to Alaska.

LOUIE: Don't bother. I'll give ya fifty bucks for it.

SYLVESTER: That's right nice, mister, but I promised to dee-liver it to a soldier.

LOUIE: I'll make it a hundred.

CLARK: What do you want with a pie?

LOUIE: I wanna *eat* it, see?! What do ya *usually* do with a pie?

SYLVESTER: Ain't nobody gonna eat this 'cept the man it was whomped up fer. Now I gotta get goin'! Nice to make your acquaintance, Mr. Kent.

CLARK: Same here, Superman.

Steve was already talking to himself from loneliness and boredom when a hick and a mule delivered Margie's pie to his radio shack. A few minutes later Louie, wearing a muffler and aviator's cap and holding a gun, held up the radio shack and escaped with the pie. But the Man of Steel learned that Louie had rented a plane with skis and immediately took off after him in the direction of Alaska. Within seconds there was a third extraordinary visitor at the shack, Superman.

STEVE: Welcome, sir. It's a vast relief to realize that I actually have gone crazy. Now I can enjoy it.

SUPERMAN: Has he been here yet? The man who wanted the pie?

STEVE: Certainly. He left just a few minutes ago, but don't fret. I've got a nice can of plum pudding for you.

SUPERMAN: What kind of plane was he flying? I must've missed him.

STEVE: A yellow two-engine job . . . trimmed with lace with purple polka dots.

SUPERMAN: Well, I'm going after him . . . and get to the bottom of this once and for all (*Radio buzzes.*)

STEVE: That must be the general calling to tell me *he's* coming to lunch.

SYLVESTER: Who're you, mister?

SUPERMAN: Never mind about that now.

STEVE: Well, this sure is a realistic nightmare. That was the man who stole the pie.

SUPERMAN: I know. His plane was forced down by ice on its wings . . . and he's holed up with a portable transmitter in an ice cave . . . which fell in on him.

SYLVESTER: How could he hear that? I couldn't hear nothin'. (*Watches Superman fly off.*) Wahll, if that don't beat all! He just jumped in the air and kept on goin'!

STEVE: You mean that's unusual?

SYLVESTER: Wahll? . . . Ain't it?

The real Superman rescued the pie for Steve while Sylvester J. Superman and Lilybelle brought Leftover Louie back to Metropolis to reform with his feet in a bucket of hot water. As his teeth chattered away he learned that Buckets had been equally unsuccessful in getting a lemon meringue pie from his aunt Tillie.

Successful as *Adventures of Superman* was, it posed some problems for George Reeves. He managed to guest-star as the Man of Steel on programs like *I Love Lucy,* the appropriately titled *Super Circus,* and on *Masquerade Party,* to which he came disguised as a box of Kent cigarettes (which sponsored that quiz show). He acted in non-super films such as *From Here to Eternity* even while *Adventures of Superman* was being filmed. But by the end of the series Reeves was hopelessly typecast as the hero from Krypton. He shouldn't have minded too much, since television performers were finally being paid residuals when their shows went into reruns. Eventually he would have made more money than ever from *Adventures of Superman.*

George Reeves was forty-four in 1959 when, at a party, he retired to an upstairs bedroom. A short while later a gunshot sounded and Reeves was found dead from a bullet wound. The official story was that he was dismayed at being unable to find work because of his identification with Superman and committed suicide. The newspapers blew the story out of proportion with front-page photos of Reeves as the Man of Steel and lurid headlines like "Superman Kills Himself." Many children went to sleep crying that night.

In later years the superbeing from Krypton attempted to make comebacks on television, first in an unsold *Superboy* pilot starring Johnny Rockwell (who resembled Reeves) and later in a series of Superman and Superboy cartoons in limited animation and featuring the voices of Bud Collyer and other members of the radio cast. But the cartoons never had the appeal of the original *Superman* television series. In fact many local television stations across the country scheduled the old package of George Reeves *Superman* shows on Saturday mornings opposite the cartoons and drew away much of the new young audience.

Adventures of Superman is still being shown in various cities. In certain foreign countries feature films like *Superman Flies Again* have been made from three half-hour episodes. Except for *The Lone Ranger*, which began three years earlier, *Adventures of Superman* is the oldest adventure series still shown regularly on television, its unflagging popularity yet another facet of Superman's invulnerability.

CHAPTER 3

"Say, Kids . . . What Time Is It?"

There was no greater honor for a child whose parents had bought one of those new television sets in the late forties and early fifties than to be a member of Howdy Doody's Peanut Gallery. But most kids who resided in or were visiting New York City, the real "Hollywood" of TV in those days, could only dream of attending a live telecast of *Howdy Doody* and seeing in person the friendly host Buffalo Bob Smith, the mischievous yet lovable clown Clarabell, and myriad other characters with such colorful names as Dilly Dally, the Featherman and Mr. Bluster. Almost every child in the United States faced the same problem when it came to writing for tickets to be a part of the Peanut Gallery on *Howdy Doody*. The waiting list for tickets was several years long.

Howdy Doody's Peanut Gallery was the show's studio audience, composed of the luckiest kids in the world. Not only were they lucky because of the free balloons, loaf of Wonder Bread and tube of Colgate Dental Cream which was given to every one of them, but mostly because they were among the privileged minority who would actually see the juvenile world's number one television idol, Howdy Doody himself.

Those of us who couldn't sit in the Peanut Gallery would hurry home from school, our minds filled with such diverse images as Scopedoodles and Ooragnak Indians. If we switched on the NBC channel before the awaited 5:30 P.M. (EST) we had to sit before that network's test pattern, with its numerous geometric designs.

At last the test pattern would be exchanged for one bearing a familiar face: the face of a young boy with wavy red hair, high cheeks dotted with freckles, and the widest grin possible. There was no need to identify this most famous of television faces. It was the face of Howdy Doody.

Buffalo Bob Smith, dressed in his familiar yellow outfit with red fringe and buffalo insignia, would shout enthusiastically, "Say, kids, what time is it?!"

The Peanut Gallery, and the shut-in members watching the program at home, would shriek deafeningly the most quoted line of any children's television show:

"It's Howdy Doody time!!!"

Seated at his piano, handsome, dark-haired Buffalo Bob would play the *Howdy Doody* theme song (to the tune of "Ta-ra-ra Boom-der-é"), while the forty "peanuts" in the gallery and all the children at home roared:

> It's Howdy Doody time.
> It's Howdy Doody time.
> Bob Smith and Howdy, too,
> Say "howdy do" to you.
> Let's give a rousing cheer,
> 'Cause Howdy Doody's here.
> It's time to start the show,
> So, kids, let's go!

Never had there been, nor would there ever be, a television show as popular as *Howdy Doody*. There would be countless imitations in the following years, but none possessing the long-lasting appeal of the original. Surprisingly, Howdy Doody, the ideal that most kids of the early days of television aspired to, was not even human. Howdy was a marionette, twenty-seven inches tall, dressed in a cowboy outfit. There was no attempt to disguise the fact that Howdy was a puppet. His strings were certainly in plain sight at all times. But *Howdy Doody* represented everything that we wanted in a children's program.

Howdy Doody was unabashedly *our* show. As a type of primitive ancestor to today's *Sesame Street*, Howdy, Buffalo Bob and all the other characters who resided in the small circus town of Doodyville taught us lessons in manners and correct behavior. Unlike some pretentiously educational programs, *Howdy Doody* instructed its young audience to the tune of Buffalo Bob's piano. Buffalo Bob would teach us how to wash our hands and be good to our neighbors (Howdy Doody *do's* as opposed to Howdy Doody *don'ts*) and we believed him. But it was not just the educational aspects of the program that most appealed to us. It was the seemingly perpetual noise and mayhem, always involving such impossible supporting characters as Clarabell the clown, Chief

Thunderthud and Ugly Sam, among the live people on the show, and Phineas T. Bluster, Dilly Dally and the Flub-a-Dub, among those manipulated by strings.

The voice (and personality) behind Howdy Doody was Buffalo Bob Smith. Not a ventriloquist, Smith prerecorded Howdy's voice, higher but just as energetic as his own. In this way Howdy and Buffalo Bob could sing duets together before the live television cameras. (Smith also was the voice of Grandpa Doody, Howdy's kindly old relative.)

Bob Smith was not christened "Buffalo." In the early episodes of *Howdy Doody* he was known simply as "Mr. Smith," which was altogether too formal for his image as a "big brother." The Sycapoose Indians, a tribe friendly to the Doodyville community, found the solution when they made him their White Chief. Bob Smith had been born in Buffalo, New York. The Sycapoose renamed Smith in a very formal Indian ceremony. The "Buffalo" has stuck to Bob Smith's name ever since.

In the early 1930s, Bob Smith was a member of the Hi-Hatters, a vocal group that acquired quite a reputation on the radio. After leaving the group, Smith continued to perform on the radio as an announcer, singer and piano player. In 1945 he finally got his own radio show on WEAF, which was part of the NBC network in New York, and soon landed what he had been begging to do for years—a children's program.

Triple B Ranch (the three Bs standing for "Big Brother Bob") was the type of show Smith had desired. It was a Saturday morning quiz show for kids which also featured Bob Smith at the piano, leading his radio listeners in song. On *Triple B Ranch,* Smith changed his voice to simulate a character named Elmer, a country bumpkin who, in a voice like that of Edgar Bergen's Mortimer Snerd, would greet his mentor and his audience with "Well, uh, howdy doody!" Elmer's words had a powerful effect on the audience that would soon be huddled in front of a small television screen instead of a radio console. Children began to refer to him not as Elmer but as Howdy Doody. When they came down to the radio station to meet Big Brother Bob and Howdy they were disappointed. For Howdy Doody was not there. He existed only in Smith. When Smith saw the looks of displeasure on the faces of his fans, Howdy Doody was born in his imagination.

After two years of developing the Howdy Doody character and trying to convince NBC of the possibilities of doing a puppet show on television, Bob Smith was given an hour-long program, then called *Puppet Playhouse.* So enthusiastic were NBC executives over the new late afternoon children's show that when it premiered on December 27, 1947, the Howdy Doody puppet had not yet been completed. Smith would sit behind a desk, explaining that Howdy had never been on television before and was too shy to show his face. Opening the desk drawer, Smith would talk to Howdy, who was supposedly hiding inside. "Nope," Howdy would say, "I'm not comin' out there just yet." He didn't come out until puppeteer Frank Paris had completed the figure.

The original Howdy Doody puppet was hardly the character that became the idol of a nation of television-watching children. When Howdy first appeared on *Puppet Playhouse* he had an almost hideous face, with a lantern jaw, big ears and a head of bushy hair. The character, nevertheless, caught on with the youthful public and existed in that incarnation for the first month and a half of the show.

Paris had never signed a contract with NBC. When the network executives finally approached the puppeteer to sign with them, he protested, insisting that he owned the Howdy Doody character. The only solution to the problem seemed to be to create a new (and more appealing) Howdy Doody puppet that would be owned by NBC. There was no longer any reason to squabble with Paris. He filed a breach-of-contract suit against NBC.

The problem of explaining Howdy's new face fell to the writer of the show, Edward Kean.[1] Luckily 1948 was an election year. Immediately Kean saw the possibilities in staging an election in Doodyville and at the same time providing an excuse for Howdy to get a new face.

The election in Doodyville was for the coveted title of President of All the Boys and Girls. It seemed logical that Howdy Doody should be President. But for some mysterious reason Howdy's opponent, known only as Mr. X, was more popular.

No one in Doodyville had seen the elusive Mr. X. But reports were coming in to Buffalo Bob and the rest of the Doodyville residents that Howdy's opponent was a dashingly handsome young man whose looks meant more to the voting public than Howdy's personality. Both

[1] When he started his writing career at the age of twenty-three, Edward Kean wanted to be a song writer. He began working with Bob Smith in September 1947 when Smith was doing a radio disc jockey show opposite Arthur Godfrey. From 1947 until May 1955, Kean wrote 1,950 *Howdy Doody* shows. Counting records and books about the characters, Kean estimates his total wordage on Howdy Doody at approximately fourteen million words. Kean later wrote the Canadian radio version of *Howdy Doody,* consulted on the CBC television version (with a Canadian cast) and became coproducer of the American television series.

Howdy and Buffalo Bob agreed that something had to be done to make the little candidate more appealing to the voters. They both decided that Howdy would undergo plastic (or, better, *wooden*) surgery.

The entire presidential campaign lasted for nine months. Kean was prophetic in lowering the voting age, not to the current eighteen, but to anyone *under* the age of twenty-one. As the campaign got under way, no one gave much thought to the identity of the secretive Mr. X. What was of more concern to everyone involved with Howdy Doody was how his new face would appear.

A recording of Smith doing Howdy's voice was sent to the Walt Disney studios in California. There Disney's artists listened repeatedly to the voice and tried to sketch the face that the voice conjured in their minds. When the final drawings were completed, they were returned to NBC and the new Howdy Doody puppet was created.

After the Howdy Doody puppet was finished, NBC felt that it would be wise to make a duplicate in the event that something happened to the original. As in the case of twins, the second Howdy was subtly different from his "brother." The back-up puppet, which did resemble Howdy closely enough in long shots, was named Double Doody. In Double Doody, Kean realized the solution to the problem of Mr. X.

During the nine months of the presidential campaign Howdy Doody (or any of the show's puppets standing in for Howdy) appeared with his head all bandaged like the Invisible Man. At last the wrappings were removed and the face the world came to know and love as Howdy Doody was revealed for the first time. Naturally, Howdy won the election. When Mr. X finally strode onto the three-and-a-half-foot-long puppet stage, he revealed himself to be Howdy's twin, Double Doody.

Matters would have run smoothly in Doodyville were it not for the array of strange characters who populated the small circus town. As the format of *Howdy Doody* was basically that of a circus or rodeo, one of the main characters was a circus clown. Clarabell the clown was the cause of most of the little problems in Doodyville, as the perpetual instigator of pranks directed against Buffalo Bob and the other residents of the town. He was often the stooge of the many villains who appeared on the show.

Clarabell had a typical clown's face with sparse red hair and wore a green and white striped costume. He did not speak but wore a box over his stomach equipped with a Harpo Marx-type horn that served as a voice. Within the box was a loaded seltzer bottle which he squirted at whomever he chose, usually Buffalo Bob. In a typical *Howdy Doody* episode, Clarabell would sneak up behind Buffalo Bob while the latter spoke to the Peanut Gallery about something of interest. As Buffalo Bob talked, Clarabell crept behind him, seltzer bottle ready. The Peanut Gallery would shriek warnings as forty index fingers pointed toward Clarabell. Ignoring the kids, Buffalo Bob would continue speaking. The screaming and pointing continued until there was nothing Bob could do but turn around. Then it was too late, as a stream of seltzer water shot into his face.

Despite his feminine name, Clarabell was definitely not a woman. "We tried to think of Clarabell simply as a clown," Bob Smith told this writer. "A sexless clown. Clarabell sounded like a silly name and our clown was definitely silly."

The original Clarabell was portrayed by Bob Keeshan, who later had his own show as Captain Kangaroo. After Keeshan, Clarabell was played by Bobby Nicholson and, when Nicholson became the store-keeper J. Cornelius Cobb, by Lew Anderson.

Keeshan began his portrayal of Clarabell as an unnamed stage hand who walked before the live television cameras holding up various cue cards. When producer Robert Muir saw Keeshan wearing an ordinary pair of trousers and a T-shirt, he said an emphatic "No!" If Keeshan was to appear on the air he would have to be a character and look the part. There was only one costume in the wardrobe department that fit the husky Keeshan, a green and white clown costume. For a while Keeshan continued to hold up the cue cards wearing the outfit but still wearing no clown make-up. He never spoke while on camera because he had never acted before and, even more important, because it cost less to hire a non-speaking performer.

On a show based on the circus it was not surprising for such performers as Emmett Kelly and a fellow clown from the Ringling Brothers and Barnum and Bailey Circus to make an appearance. The famous clowns looked at Keeshan in his striped outfit and no make-up and said, "What's that?" To their disbelief, they were informed that Keeshan was the resident clown on the program. A clown with Kelly's reputation could not allow such a travesty to appear on television—it was a slight to his profession. Before the live cameras, Kelly made up Keeshan's face with clown white and colored greasepaint, gave him a bald skullcap with pieces of red hair and named him Clarabell.

The popularity of Clarabell was such that Edward Kean wrote the words for the clown's own song (sung to the tune of "Mademoiselle from Armentières"). The first chorus went as follows:

BUFFALO BOB: Oh, who's the funniest clown you know?
PEANUT GALLERY: *Clarabell!*

BUFFALO BOB: And who's the clown on Howdy's show?
PEANUT GALLERY: *Clarabell!*
BUFFALO BOB: Well, his feet are big, his tummy's stout, But we could never do without,
ALL: *Clara-Clara-Clar-a-bell!!!*

Clarabell was, in fact, so popular that he not only had his own song but was the only member of the *Howdy Doody* cast to be raffled off to some lucky fan. Buffalo Bob announced one day that Clarabell was leaving Doodyville temporarily. The clown would stay in the home of the fan who wrote the best letter, in the standard twenty-five words or less, saying why he or she wanted Clarabell, seltzer bottle and all. I entered the contest but was among the thousands of unlucky contestants. The contest was legitimate and Clarabell did spend a weekend in the home of one of his admirers.

Howdy Doody and Buffalo Bob had enough to do just keeping Clarabell under control. Since Howdy and Buffalo Bob seemed incapable of doing anything wrong, the shows would have become extremely boring unless there were some conflicts and other characters who could spread their madness over Doodyville. Howdy's Doodyville neighbors consisted of both puppet and flesh and blood characters. Some of them gave his wooden head colossal aches.

The biggest troublemaker was the man who would eventually become Mayor of Doodyville, the perpetually grumpy, stingy, crafty and all-around mean old man, Phineas T. Bluster. Mr. Bluster was a puppet with long white sideburns and an old-fashioned suit. The seventy-five-year-old Bluster was the ultimate capitalist, who would take the toys donated for the Doodyville Orphans' Fund and keep them for himself. When Clarabell was up to his mischievous tricks, it was not surprising to find Phineas behind them all. Mr. Bluster was not an evil man. In a sense he wanted to relive a childhood he had never had and preferred to deprive the young people of Doodyville as he had once been deprived.

Phineas T. Bluster was one of triplets. His brothers were kindly sorts and, except for physical resemblances, hardly seemed to be carved from the same block of wood as Phineas. Don Jose Bluster made his first appearance on *Howdy Doody* when his miserly brother was again infringing upon the rights of the residents of Doodyville. At first he was mistaken for Phineas. To everyone's surprise, he had just arrived from South America and was Phineas' complete opposite. The third of the brothers was Hector Hamhock Bluster, an Englishman.

Mr. Bluster's most permanent and reliable stooge was Dilly Dally, a big-eared, bespectacled carpenter who spoke in a whiny falsetto voice.

Since he was neither the bravest nor the smartest of the Doodyville residents, Dilly Dally usually let himself be talked into carrying out the schemes of the overbearing Mr. Bluster. Howdy and the rest of the group liked Dilly and made allowances for his fear-inspired loyalty to the cantankerous Mayor. Nor did they hate the man who caused them the most trouble, realizing that mean old Mr. Bluster was just a seventy-five-year-old man who had never had the childhood that Howdy Doody and his friends enjoyed.

The Inspector, Doodyville's own private detective, had a unique origin—in the beginning the Inspector was Howdy Doody himself! Or at least he was intended to be a duplicate Howdy Doody puppet when the original's head split open during an airplane flight (Howdy had been placed in an unpressurized part of the aircraft). The duplicate Howdy puppet made as a result of this catastrophe did not match the original. And so the new puppet was given a mustache and dark suit of clothes and baptized the Inspector.

During Dwight D. Eisenhower's first presidential campaign, Howdy again ran for the post of President of All the Boys and Girls. Once again, his opponent was called Mr. X. But while the first Mr. X had got so many votes because of his good looks, this new Mr. X kept his appearance a mystery to everyone. Mr. X wore a boxlike contraption with spinning wheels and flashing lights, giving him the appearance of a robot. When Howdy won the election and it was time for Mr. X to unmask, everyone was taken by surprise. Mr. X proved to be none other than the Inspector who, if for no other reason, ran against Howdy to make a spectacular announcement. He was no longer merely the Inspector. Now he had a name, which he pronounced with a blink of his eye—John J. Fadoozle, America's number one (*boing!*) private eye.

There were other puppet characters on *Howdy Doody*, including Heidi Doody (Howdy's sister) and Princess Summerfall Winterspring. But one of the most interesting was Howdy's pet, an impossible creature called the Flub-a-Dub.

One day in 1948, Buffalo Bob announced to Howdy Doody and his friends that he had just learned of a unique animal living in South America. There was only one example of the creature alive in the world and Buffalo Bob wanted to bring it to Doodyville. According to reports, this creature was made up of eight different animals, with a duck's bill, cocker spaniel's ears, cat's whiskers, giraffe's neck, dachshund's body, seal's flippers, pig's tail and the memory of an elephant.

Buffalo Bob's trip to South America to capture the Flub-Dub (as he was called at first) could not have been scheduled at a better time. Coincidentally, this was the time of Smith's first vacation from performing and he used the time off the air to good advantage, including seeking out the Flub-Dub. When he brought the bizarre animal back to Doodyville the Flub-Dub proved to be an easy pet to keep. Although it had an elephant's memory, the creature could recall only one kind of food that he liked to eat. He was usually hungry and would come onto the stage begging, "Meatballs! Meatballs!" When the name Flub-Dub proved awkward to pronounce, the animal was formally renamed Flub-a-Dub, by which he is remembered today.

Many of the characters on *Howdy Doody* were not controlled by strings. Among the flesh and blood characters, some of the most popular were American Indians with royal blood in their veins. Three Indian tribes were partial to Doodyville—the Sycapoose, the Ooragnak and the Tinka Tonka. Of the three, the Sycapoose and the Ooragnak Indians were constant opponents. These Indians were never actually at war, for such words as "war" were taboo on the *Howdy Doody* show. But they were constantly plotting against each other in a mild rivalry, never even thinking of attacking a Doodyville circus train or chipping the wooden scalp off any of the puppet characters.

Chief of the Sycapoose Indians was the Featherman, who made his first appearance on the show with all the pomp and ceremony worthy of one of his blood. All day long Clarabell was in a frenzy, worrying about the scheduled visit of the Featherman. (It was never explained that Clarabell was actually *afraid* of the Featherman, since that was another word on the list of Howdy Doody *don'ts*.) The speechless clown dashed about the Doodyville puppet stage, honking his horn, while Buffalo Bob and Howdy tried to calm him down. Nevertheless, Clarabell was not going to stay in the vicinity when the Featherman arrived in Doodyville.

There was good reason for Clarabell's consternation. Both he and the Featherman were played by Bob Keeshan.

When the Featherman did make his appearance, Clarabell was nowhere around. The noble chief stood before the gaping Peanut Gallery, his arms raised to display the spectacular array of feathers that gave him his name. If Clarabell could have stayed around he would have learned that there was no evil in the Featherman and that the chief proved to be a good friend to all the citizens of Doodyville.

Perhaps the Featherman's greatest gift to Doodyville was the introduction of the lovely Tinka Tonka maid, Princess Summerfall Winterspring. The Princess was one of the few female members of the *Howdy Doody* cast and gave the girls someone with whom to identify. Princess Summerfall Winterspring was a puppet until puppeteer Rhoda

Mann realized that Doodyville needed a real female face. The girls in the Peanut Gallery and those watching the program at home would probably identify even more with a living Summerfall Winterspring. She suggested that the Princess somehow be transformed from a puppet into a living girl. A beautiful young actress named Judy Tyler possessed the warm, vibrant personality needed for the part. One day, after much ceremony and an announcement by Buffalo Bob that something special was about to take place, the new Princess Summerfall Winterspring made her debut. She was so well received that the viewers soon forgot that there had ever been a puppet version of the same character. Judy Tyler played the Princess until 1957, when tragedy struck. The actress was offered a role in the Elvis Presley motion picture *Jailhouse Rock* and was given a three-month leave of absence from the television show. Judy Tyler never returned; she was killed with her husband in an automobile accident on July 4 of that year, shortly after the film had been completed. No other actress ever took her place as the Princess.

The Ooragnak ("kangaroo" spelled backward) Indians were more hostile than either the Sycapoose or the Tinka Tonka ever were. Their leader was the villainous Chief Thunderthud (played by Bill Le Cornec, who also portrayed Oil Well Willy and Dr. Singasong on the show and was the voice of Dilly Dally). Chief Thunderthud barely approached the noble image of his arch rival, the Featherman. He would skulk about Doodyville, seen only by the Peanut Gallery, whom he constantly *shsssshed!* Often he and Clarabell would join forces to work their mischief on the other characters. Whenever he was discovered in an embarrassing act, or whenever he saw something that surprised or startled him, Chief Thunderthud would exclaim, "Kowa Bonga!" In time Thunderthud mellowed and became capable of performing only Howdy Doody *do's*. "Kowa Bonga, Buffalo Bob!" he would say. "You-um right. Me-um do what you say-um." Eventually Bob Keeshan left *Howdy Doody* to go off on his own, leaving the part of the Featherman vacant and never to be filled by anyone else. Chief Thunderthud then became the foremost Indian in Doodyville.

Mr. Bluster's jealousy of the younger citizens of Doodyville became so outrageous that he decided to rob Howdy of his entire viewing audience. Using his money to start his own television program, Mr. Bluster soon became the star of *Howdy Bluster,* which was his attempt to repeat the success of the original. Naturally, Mr. Bluster needed an Indian character to rival those on Howdy's show. He managed to hire a bumbling Indian named Chief Thunder Chicken (played by Alan

Swift, who sometimes did the voice of Mr. Bluster and, when Bob Smith was unable to do the show, that of Howdy himself). But Chief Thunder Chicken and *Howdy Bluster* were short-lived.

Bob Keeshan also portrayed a character named Oscar, an absent-minded professor dressed in a graduation cap and gown, with a monocle in one eye and a thick mustache. Oscar would say little more than, "I'm Oscar! I'm Oscar!" raising his cap off his head every time he spoke his name. Oscar was a ready victim for Mr. Bluster's schemes and would often get himself into predicaments, totally unaware that he was inconveniencing anyone.

On one show in the early fifties, Oscar's blundering made him so many enemies that he felt unwanted. There was no alternative other than to flee Doodyville. Mr. Bluster, however, knew that it would be extremely advantageous to his own schemes to put in a double for Oscar. The perceptive Buffalo Bob soon learned that "Oscar" was an impostor and began an immediate search for the original.

Howdy, Buffalo Bob and Clarabell tuned in the Super Talkascope, a fabulous device that let them see and hear what was happening anywhere in the world. After considerable searching, the image of the real Oscar focused on the Super Talkascope screen. Oscar was in the African jungle, moping about how no one loved him and how he hadn't a single friend in the world.

Something had to be done to let Oscar know that no one hated him and that the Doodyville citizens wanted him back. But the jungle was so dense that not even a small plane could land. Then Buffalo Bob had an idea that might help Oscar realize that he still had friends in Doodyville.

Following Buffalo Bob's suggestion, Howdy loaded a television set into the Airo-Doodle, a fantastic craft made from the front end of a steam locomotive, the middle section of a ship, the back end and wings of an airplane and the propeller of a helicopter. Flying over the jungle in the Airo-Doodle, Howdy dropped the television set by parachute. Back in Doodyville, Buffalo Bob and Clarabell watched Oscar on the Super Talkascope.

Oscar received the television set but there was another problem: there were no electrical outlets in the jungle. But being the inventive wizard that he supposedly was, Oscar plugged the set into his flashlight, turned on *Howdy Doody* and received the plea for him to return to Doodyville.

Unfortunately, Oscar's popularity with the viewers was considerably less than his popularity with the Doodyville folk. He was not well received and, before too many appearances, was written out of the show.

Howdy Doody offended many adults because of the noise. There was scarcely a soft-spoken character on the show, and what noise was not made by the various residents of Doodyville was supplied by the squealing Peanut Gallery.

One of the loudest characters on *Howdy Doody* was Ugly Sam, a wrestler who wore an old-fashioned striped bathing suit and made outlandish facial expressions to conform with his name. Actually, Ugly Sam was no uglier than some of the other Doodyville people. Whenever he appeared on *Howdy Doody* mayhem usually followed. There was no reasoning with him as he grimaced and paraded around in his outdated swimsuit. Once he announced that he was no longer Ugly Sam but Salami Sam. To prove this, he carried an enormous salami with him and frequently bit off a hunk to give himself additional strength. Ugly Sam was portrayed by Dayton Allen, who also did the voices of Mr. Bluster, the Inspector and the Flub-a-Dub, and who would later make the saying "Why not!" famous on *The Steve Allen Show*. Besides being a talented comedian, Allen was also a fine puppeteer and worked with Rhoda Mann and chief puppeteer Rufus Rose in bringing Howdy and some of his friends to life.

Howdy Doody owned so many fantastic gadgets that one might easily suspect that he was a good friend of Captain Video. Besides the Airo-Doodle (which could travel on the ground, on railroad tracks, in the water and in the air), and the Super Talkascope, Howdy had at his disposal many other fabulous devices. One of these was the Scopedoodle, a device with a screen that could tune in old-time movies. Buffalo Bob would narrate as some ancient silent film comedies flashed upon the Scopedoodle screen, usually familiar characters like Ben Turpin or Fatty Arbuckle with new names, or a trio of rotund comics named the Three Tuns-a-Fun. Bob Smith frequently appears today on talk shows such as *Mike Douglas* and *Dick Cavett* with a story about what happened during one of the old-time movies.

Buffalo Bob was sitting on the Peanut Gallery ledge while an old-time movie about a character Smith called Rip Van Winkle was running during a Halloween show in the early fifties. A large hollowed-out jack-o'-lantern, illuminated from within by a burning candle, was set in front of the puppet stage. Suddenly Smith felt a tug on his pant leg. He looked down to see a small boy who whispered to him that he had to "tinkle." Since he was narrating the old-time movie, Buffalo Bob pointed to some of the other crew members and told the boy to go off in that direction. Inadvertently, Smith was also pointing in the direction of the pumpkin. The boy presently put out the candle.

Pandemonium immediately erupted on the *Howdy Doody* set. The camera crew exploded with laughter, inciting the Peanut Gallery and Buffalo Bob to lose complete control. The only person on the premises not laughing convulsively was Dayton Allen. Buffalo Bob hurried off the set in hysterics, while Allen completed the narration of the old-time movie and ended the show.

The people watching the show at home, naturally, had no idea what had happened to Buffalo Bob or the program that day, and the NBC offices were deluged with letters from thousands of parents. Buffalo Bob, in the record album *Buffalo Bob Smith at the Fillmore East* on the Project Three label, said that it was easier to send each correspondent the following printed poem rather than to make any serious explanation:

> So many of you asked what happened
> On the night of Halloween,
> When everyone was hysterical
> And Buffalo Bob had to leave the scene.
> It was during an old-time movie
> About a man named Rip Van Winkle,
> When a four-year-old boy from the Gallery
> Told Bob that he had to tinkle.
> Well, Buffalo Bob couldn't take him,
> So he pointed to someone who could.
> But the little kid didn't follow directions.
> He just walked to a pumpkin and stood.
> Well, the rest of the story is obvious
> And we didn't even need a mop,
> Because our little friend had great aim
> And he never spilled a drop!

Howdy Doody spawned a list of merchandise featuring the famous Doodyville characters that would not be approached until the Davy Crockett days, years later. There were Howdy Doody marionettes, hand puppets, lunchboxes, stereo viewer films, games, paints and crayons, dolls and every other conceivable item that might boast the images of Howdy, Clarabell, the Flub-a-Dub and other people of Doodyville. It was impossible to go into a toyshop and not find a plethora of Howdy Doody items.

Buffalo Bob Smith worked *Howdy Doody* every Saturday for an hour until 1948. Then the show went to Mondays, Wednesdays and

Fridays, every episode still sixty minutes long, and soon went to half-hour, five-day-per-week format. In the later days of the weekday show, Smith became ill and had to be temporarily replaced by such guest hosts as his good friend Gabby Hayes and Ted Brown, who took on the curious name of, not "Buffalo," but Bison Bill. In 1957, Smith suffered a heart attack, and, realizing that he had to cut down on his work load, NBC switched the program to a half-hour Saturday morning format.

The Saturday morning *Howdy Doody* episodes had an increased number of crew members and a budget of $9,000 per show in contrast to the $600 of the first telecasts. The serial-like continuity of the weekday show was abandoned. Each Saturday *Howdy Doody* program was a complete story in itself and was more in the realm of fairy tales than the madcap hilarity that had once been the show's trademark. Howdy, Buffalo Bob, Clarabell and the other characters were now concerned with helping King Yodstick, monarch of the kingdom of Urli Tibet, find his missing jewels, or with Splinters, a wooden stick man made by Howdy and brought to life by Sandra Witch. Mr. Bluster was still up to his usual villainy, however, such as trying to secure Grandpa Doody's Easter gift, intended for the Doodyville kids, for himself, or trying to stamp phony diplomas with his official Mayor's seal and selling them to the children in the Peanut Gallery.

The September 30, 1960, show was the 2,343rd episode of *Howdy Doody*. Clarabell darted about carrying a sign with the word "Surprise!" Howdy, Buffalo Bob and the other Doodyville characters spent most of the thirty minutes trying to learn what the surprise was but received only the honks of the clown's horn as an answer. The show was nearly at its close when Clarabell looked sadly into the camera, waved and spoke for the first time: "Good-by, kids."

That was the saddest, and final, day at Doodyville. Production costs had increased to such an extent that sponsors preferred to back shows with a more general appeal. *Howdy Doody* was replaced with reruns of a situation comedy starring Joan Davis and Jim Backus, *I Married Joan*.

Bob Smith left New York after the cancellation of *Howdy Doody* and moved to Fort Lauderdale, Florida. He bought three radio stations and did some broadcasting, but also became a member of a house-building firm. It seemed as if Bob Smith had settled down at last and that *Howdy Doody* was a part of his past.

Ten years after the show's demise the seemingly impossible happened. Students at the University of Pennsylvania, when asked what they would like to do most of all, commented that they would like to relive their carefree days before the Vietnam war, scares of atomic warfare and the threat of man's polluting himself into extinction. They wanted to relive their childhood days of Buffalo Bob Smith and Howdy Doody.

On Valentine's Day, 1970, Buffalo Bob Smith, slightly heavier but still fitting into his old Buffalo suit, stepped upon the stage of Irvine Auditorium and revived *Howdy Doody* for the University of Pennsylvania students. He ran a kinescope film of the hour-long, *This Is Your Life*-type *Howdy Doody* tenth-anniversary special, originally telecast on December 28, 1957. Howdy himself was not there in person, but Buffalo Bob filled almost every other desire of the audience of long-haired, "freaky" fans who were once devoted followers of his program. Leading these grown-up members of his Peanut Gallery in the old songs and answering the myriad questions about Howdy and the Flub-a-Dub and Princess Summerfall Winterspring, Buffalo Bob Smith proved that the loyalty of the *Howdy Doody* fans was a genuine feeling that is still a reality. This loyalty was no mere following of a fad but a way of life for anyone who knew that *Howdy Doody* was, and always would be, the greatest kids' show in the history of television. Buffalo Bob Smith continues to tour colleges with his nostalgic one-man show, appearing before screaming, weeping teen-agers and adults who once sang along with the Peanut Gallery on television, "It's Howdy Doody time!" Because of Buffalo Bob Smith, it is Howdy Doody time all over again.

CHAPTER 4

Friendly Dragons,
Sea Sick Sea Serpents
and Royal Geese

The Kuklapolitans

To many of us, *Kukla, Fran and Ollie* was the reason we ate our supper in the living room before a rounded television screen in the late 1940s and early 1950s. There was real magic, the kind that could bring figures of cotton and cloth to life, when we heard pianist Jack Fascinato play the show's theme song, composed by Fascinato with lyrics by Burr Tillstrom, and sung by Kukla, the little Everyman, blonde Fran Allison, and a friendly dragon named Ollie:

> Here we are,
> Back with you again.
> Yes, by gum, and yes, by golly,
> Kukla, Fran and dear old Ollie.
> Here we are again,
> Here we are again.

In many ways *Kukla, Fran and Ollie* was a television "first." The show, which began in 1947 as a local program on Chicago's WBKB, became the very first East-to-West network show in January 1949, when the NBC coaxial cable linking the big cities east of the Mississippi went into operation. The program was the first puppet show in the classic sense to feature a live person conversing with the puppets. By tradition puppet shows have not included real people in order to sustain a sense of reality in the miniature performers. But blonde and pretty Fran Allison hardly seemed out of place when she stepped before the scaled-down stage and became involved in the lives of Kukla, his best friend Oliver J. Dragon (affectionately known as Ollie) and the rest of their puppet friends. *Kukla, Fran and Ollie* was also television's first theatrical troupe.

Kukla, the first character to join the Kuklapolitans (and to give the troupe its name), was the real heart of the troupe. His origin dates back to a historic day in 1936 when a handsome young puppeteer named Burr Tillstrom fashioned a hand puppet for a friend. The little character had already been prepared for mailing and peered up at his creator from the shipping box.

Tillstrom had tried to create a miniature Everyman with which anyone could identify. He chose the most basic of theatrical costumes and make-ups for the fellow, that of the clown. The head was mostly hairless, with raised eyebrows and a tiny circular mouth that always seemed to register surprise, rosy cheeks, and a bulbous red nose. The outfit worn by the character was a clown's outfit with a ruffled collar.

There was something compelling in that painted face; the figure seemed to beckon his creator not to give him away. Tillstrom removed him from the box and said, "I can't send him away. He's too appealing." He made another puppet for his friend and kept the original.

A dance buff, Tillstrom was most enthusiastic when the Ballet Russe played in his home town, Chicago, later that year. He worshiped the ballet's star, the ballerina Tamara Toumanova, who symbolized the theater itself for Tillstrom. One day the puppet with the clown's face peeked up from behind a chair in Toumanova's dressing room and began to dance. Delighted with the antics of the little man, the ballerina exclaimed, "Ah, Kukla!" (*Kukla* is the Russian word for "doll.") The little actor had a name and one of television's most lovable and enduring stars had been born.

Among all the Kuklapolitan players, it was Kukla himself that kept everything stabilized. Kukla did most of the worrying and always felt responsible for the actions of the other characters. When one's best friend happens to be a dragon with a propensity for trouble, that responsibility can feel heavy indeed.

Ollie the dragon joined the Kuklapolitans long before their debut on local television. Dragons are traditional characters in puppet shows because of the up-and-down action of the mouth. Tillstrom, attempting to maintain a feel of the traditional, created Ollie in 1938. But while most dragons were fire-breathing monsters, Ollie was a softhearted creature with soulful eyes and a single tooth protruding from his grin-

1. The Ranger (Don Hastings) watches his superior officer Captain Video (Al Hodge) manipulate some pseudo-scientific apparatus on the rocket ship *Galaxy*, on the Dumont TV serial *Captain Video*. Hodge made the successful transfer to TV after playing another hero, the Green Hornet, on radio.

2. Standing at attention at a Space Academy rocket port, Space Cadets Roger Manning (Jan Merlin), Tom Corbett (Frankie Thomas) and the Venusian Astro (Al Markham) look off toward their waiting spaceship *Polaris* on the late afternoon adventure series *Tom Corbett, Space Cadet*. Thomas was a successful child star of the thirties and seemingly retained his youth for his Tom Corbett portrayal.

3. George Reeves shed the horn-rimmed glasses and drab business suit of newspaper reporter Clark Kent to become the dynamic Man of Steel in the highly successful *Superman*. Despite the show's age, *Superman* is still being shown in reruns across the country. Copyright National Periodical Publications, Inc.

4. *Kukla, Fran and Ollie* was more than just a puppet show. It was a veritable theatrical troupe in miniature, created by puppeteer Burr Tillstrom. Seen here with Burr are the show's three favorite performers, Kukla, Ollie the Dragon and lovely Fran Allison. The show was performed live and without scripts.

5. Perhaps no children's television program ever acquired as many loyal fans as *Howdy Doody*, a zany mélange of puppets, gadgets and live performers playing a variety of outrageous roles. Shown here is Buffalo Bob Smith, the human star of the show, along with the eternally smiling Howdy Doody himself. (Buffalo Bob also provided Howdy's voice.)

6. Hopalong Wong, Beany, Capt. Huffenpuff, Hunny Bear and, of course, Cecil the Sea Sick Sea Serpent originally appeared as puppets on Bob Clampett's award-winning series *Time for Beany*. Here Cecil greets his friends as they crowd about the deck of the captain's ship, *Leakin' Lena*. (Copyright Bob Clampett Productions.)

7. Shari Lewis and her puppets, Lamb Chop and Hush Puppy, joined Arthur Godfrey for a special. Both performers were video pioneers. Godfrey had all his little Godfreys—before he fired them all, one by one—and Shari Lewis still has her handy little fellows. Like Burr Tillstrom and Bob Clampett, her puppets appealed to both children and adults, but Shari added sex appeal.

8. (Above left) Hopalong Cassidy (William Boyd) brought his old theatrical movies to TV in 1948, some of them edited to half an hour, with new narration by him. Soon he was making completely new films for TV. Adult story values and good acting made Hoppy seem head and shoulders over the competition, the primitive talkies of Ken Maynard and Tom Tyler.

9. (Above right) Gene Autry had not bought rights to his old films (unlike Hoppy) and so made new half hours to sell to TV. The scripts followed the old B formula, but the action and general production were better than most contemporary television Westerns.

10. *The Lone Ranger* became the first Western series filmed especially for TV. The Masked Man (Clayton Moore) and his Indian companion Tonto (Jay Silverheels) here are searching a man (unidentified) carrying a watch belonging to the Lone Ranger's nephew, Dan Reid. Radio producer George W. Trendle supervised the television version to maintain his personal vision of an American legend.

11. Duncan Renaldo, astride Diablo, brought *The Cisco Kid* to home screens, with occasional help from his dog. Renaldo still owns two of the horses known as Diablo, pastured on his California rancho.

12. *Wild Bill Hickok* was one of the many made-for-TV Westerns of the early fifties. It had a high-powered cast (Guy Madison as Wild Bill, Andy Devine as Jingles) but was in the old Saturday matinee mold. (Two shows spliced together were released to theaters as features for those declining matinees.) Madison and Devine also made a simultaneous *Hickok* radio series, thus covering all the media.

13. Walt Disney produced a three-part *Davy Crockett, King of the Wild Frontier* for his *Disneyland* program. It was wildly successful, making a star of Fess Parker as Crockett and re-illuminating Buddy Ebsen. Davy could chop logs better, shoot straighter and tell taller tales than any other frontiersman. (Copyright Walt Disney Productions.)

14. Matt Dillon and Miss Kitty (James Arness and Amanda Blake) were younger in those early days of *Gunsmoke*. Recent promotional announcements for the series, now in its twentieth season, call it "an American classic" and they are correct.

15. June Collyer and Stu Erwin were the married couple, on screen and off, in *The Trouble with Father*, a pioneer situation comedy.

16. *Amos 'n' Andy* came to TV in 1951 with Tim Moore as the Kingfish (top), Spencer Williams as cigar-chomping Andy, and Alvin Childress as Amos. Controversial today, the broad stereotypes originated on radio by Freeman Gosden and Charles Correll reach a kind of high camp magnificence.

ning mouth. Not so much as a wisp of smoke ever came from that snapping mouth, and in the early days, neither did a single word. At first content merely to snap his mouth open and shut and move his long neck, Ollie gained a voice by necessity when the Kuklapolitans presented a pageant of *St. George and the Dragon* at the RCA exhibit of the New York World's Fair in 1939. Once Ollie could speak, he gained his distinct personality. He sang in a baritone which contrasted nicely with Kukla's higher-pitched voice. And he developed an impetuousness with which to voice his strong opinions and objections.

Just as Burr Tillstrom was the voices of Kukla and Ollie, so were they the voice of their creator. Kukla accompanied Tillstrom wherever he went in those days before *Kukla, Fran and Ollie* and entertained impromptu at parties, answering people's questions. "Kukla was really smart with people," says Tillstrom. "He could talk to everyone and anyone. When I was too young or too ignorant to have an answer, Kukla took over. What would have been naïve coming from me sounded funny coming from Kukla." Ollie mouthed Tillstrom's own objections. If his car got stuck in one of Chicago's heavy winter snows, Ollie had something to say about it on that evening's show.

To Ollie, nothing was more enjoyable than to dance in the park on a warm spring afternoon. Of course, the sight of a dragon cavorting among the flowers and birds would usually cause a small riot. Kukla would receive a telephone call from the police station asking him to bail out a dragon who had been arrested for disturbing the peace. When Kukla later reprimanded Ollie over the matter, the friendly dragon seemed hardly "reformed."[1]

[1] Since *Kukla, Fran and Ollie* was done live and without scripts, it was impossible to obtain vintage dialogue from the show for this book. Recalling the old episodes, Burr Tillstrom has written all the "script" pertaining to them especially for this chapter, based on the actual story lines of the vintage programs—a gesture for which the authors of this volume are forever grateful

Enclosed with the pages of dialogue was an additional script, with the handwritten message at the top, "Here's a show just for you, Don. Best from Kukla & Ollie & Burr." Since it would have been criminal to file away this special "show," it follows:

Fade up on Fletcher Rabbit on stage alone. He is carrying his mail sack, and wearing his mailman's hat.

FLETCHER: Hoo hoo! Mailman. Hoo hoo! Anybody home? (*Blows his mailman's whistle.*)

KUKLA: Hi, Fletch . . . any mail for me?

FLETCHER: As a matter of fact, Kukla, I do have one . . . well, actually it's for the three of you . . . Fran and Ollie and you, that is, but I suppose it's not against regulations to give it to you alone.

KUKLA: Well, I wouldn't want you to do anything against your mailman's code, Fletcher.

FLETCHER: No, it's all right. Here (*hands him letter*) . . . it's from that chap in California.

KUKLA: You mean the one who's writing a book on TV?

FLETCHER: Yes . . . I couldn't help noticing. I hope you won't think I've been snooping, Kukla.

KUKLA: Don't give it a second thought, Fletch.

FLETCHER: I'd like to hear what it says, but it's time for me to be up and about on my appointed rounds. See you, Kuk. (*Exits.*)

KUKLA: See you, Fletch. (*Opens letter and reads. Calling to stage left and backstage*) Fran! Ollie! I need you.

FRAN (*off stage*): I'm coming, Kukla. (*Enters.*) Hi, Kukla.

OLLIE (*off stage*): What's up, Kuk? (*Crash enters.*) Is it an emerggency or something? Tell me! Tell me, little buddy! (*Crowding him, pushing into his face.*) Is it an emerggency, hmmmmmm?

KUKLA: No, no, it's not an emergency, Ollie. Take it easy. (*Pushes him away.*)

OLLIE: Well, if it's not an emerggency, then I'll go back to the kitchen. I'm about to pop some corn. (*Starts to leave.*)

KUKLA: No . . . I need you. Now just stay.

FRAN: Yes, just stay, Ollie. You can pop your corn later.

OLLIE: Well, ok, but make it snappy. I can only give you three minutes. I'm very busy today.

KUKLA: I'm just not going to bother, if you're going to be like that. Forget it.

FRAN: Now, Ollie, calm down. Kukla called us because he needs us. Let's just hear what he has to say.

OLLIE: Okay (*impatiently*), but hurry!

FRAN (*warningly*): Ollie!

OLLIE (*on her shoulder, full of the old charm*): I was just teasing, cutie. Go ahead, little Kukla, I'm all ears.

KUKLA: We got a letter from our friend in California who is writing a book on TV. And he wants a sample of script from one of our shows.

OLLIE: But we don't use a script, Kuk. We ad-lib. You know, ipro . . . ivmo . . . impro . . .

FRAN: Make it up as we go along.

KUKLA: Well, that's why I need you. I thought we might make up a little dialogue . . . just a little sample . . .

FRAN: I'll get my pencil and pad and maybe I can put it down—if we don't go too fast.

KUKLA: I'll get my tape recorder.

OLLIE: I'll get my typewriter and type it all up nice and neat.

FRAN: How *is* your typing these days, Ollie? Did you ever take that speed course you were talking about?

OLLIE: No, Fran, I never got around to it. I still use my old hunt and tooth method. I'm up to three and half words a minute.

FRAN: It must be wonderful to have a prehensile tooth, Ollie.

OLLIE: Oh yes, very handy . . . for many things . . . like dialing the telephone. But I'll be glad when we get a touch phone.

FRAN: How come?

OLLIE: Dialing is very hard on the *enamanel.*

KUKLA: You mean enamel, Ollie.

OLLIE: That's what I said, *enamanel.* (*Brightly*) Well, shall we start?

KUKLA: Ollie, I don't know how you get yourself into these things.

OLLIE: It's easy—if you're a dragon.

KUKLA: But dancing on the green in Lincoln Park . . . whatever got into you?

OLLIE: Spring fever, Kukla, spring fever. Haven't you ever just felt so happy you wanted to go out and cavort with the birds and the daffodils?

KUKLA: Well, yes, I have, Ollie.

OLLIE: And did you ever obey your impulse?

KUKLA: Well . . .

OLLIE: Come on, now, tell the truth.

KUKLA: Well, yes, I did, once or twice.

OLLIE: There, see?

KUKLA: But I looked where I was dancing.

OLLIE: I couldn't help it if the lagoon was there. One minute I was dancing on solid turf, the next I was scuba-dancing on the bottom of the lagoon with a couple of frogs.

KUKLA: Wasn't it cold?

OLLIE: Terribly . . . ahhhhh chooooo! Oh, Kukla, I'm so miserable!

KUKLA: Oh, Ollie, come on. Dry yourself with this towel and then we'll go downstairs. Fran's made a big pot of hot chocolate. Does that sound good?

OLLIE: Oh, Kukla, you're a real friend. (*Bites nose tenderly.*)

When Ollie's excursions into trouble proved too much even for Kukla to handle, the little character turned to Fran for advice. Fran Allison was the only real person to appear with the puppets. Her background included several years teaching school. But when her talents as a singer became noticed she secured a job as a radio performer. Eventually Fran became "Aunt Fanny," a small-town gossip, on radio's Don McNeill's *Breakfast Club.*

Fran was the special sweetheart of Kukla, Ollie and all the other Kuklapolitans. Every member of the troupe loved and respected Fran and sought her advice and understanding. In return Fran treated all of them as real people. To Fran the Kuklapolitans *were* real and not just puppets manipulated by Burr Tillstrom. When Kukla felt depressed over Ollie's lack of self-control, Fran gave him counsel.

KUKLA (*suddenly worn out*): Fran, you know what?

FRAN: What, Kukla?

KUKLA: I've got a better idea. Let's go downstairs and pop some corn.

FRAN: I'm with you, Kukla. Meet you in a second. (*They leave.*)

OLLIE (*backstage to Kukla*): Wait for me! (*To camera*) Sorry, kid. I guess you'll have to make it up yourself. (*Goes down.*)

KUKLA: Frank, I don't know what we're going to do. Ollie used up the whole budget to buy that used steam table for Gommie's birthday.

FRAN: I know, Kukla. Sometimes it's awfully hard to live with a dragon.

KUKLA: I think I'll just pack my little things and run away.

FRAN: Oh, Kukla, you don't mean that.

KUKLA: Yes, I do, Fran. Yes, I do. I think I'll just go away.

FRAN: Kukla, I'd miss you terribly. I wouldn't want to be here if you weren't here. I'll tell you what. Let me talk to Ollie. I'll tell him he's just *got* to take that steam table right back and get his money and report to *us* before he does one more thing.

KUKLA: Oh, would you, could you, Fran?

FRAN: I'll be firm. He won't get around me with his big brown eyes and his sweet talk.

KUKLA: Wanna bet?

FRAN: You're right, Kukla. I can't resist him. Maybe Gommie needs a used steam table.

KUKLA (*laughing*): Fran, I love you!

FRAN: Then you won't run away?

KUKLA: Never. Come on, let's look for some BIG gift-wrapping paper.

Every effort was taken to make the Kuklapolitans living characters. As there was no script, all of the dialogue was spontaneous, reflecting the personality of each character. Tillstrom would come up with a basic story line, sometimes only minutes before the program was telecast *live*. Without a rehearsal, Fran and the Kuklapolitans (who were as real to Tillstrom as they were to Fran) would not act but react to one another. The effect of actual persons living real lives within their special world was marvelous. To maintain her acceptance of the Kuklapolitans as real, Fran made it her policy never to view them backstage. Only while they were moving and speaking did Fran ever see Kukla, Ollie and the rest of her miniature friends.

Fran was the perfect choice for bridging the fantasy world of the Kuklapolitans with the real world of the television audience. According to Burr Tillstrom, "Fran was just what we needed to turn our make-believe real. She's the Alice who wanders through Wonderland, the Dorothy who goes to Oz." Every episode of *Kukla, Fran and Ollie* ended with a resolution to a problem and it was primarily Fran who made certain that everything commenced on a note of warmth and love. After a sad Ollie failed to land the leading role in a Broadway musical, Fran managed to lift his spirits.

OLLIE: Fran, I don't know what happened. There I was waiting in line backstage while all those other actors were auditioning, absolutely sure that I'd get the part. Then . . . they called my name and I went out . . . stood on stage . . . nodded to my accompanist to begin the music . . . opened my mouth and . . . Oh, Fran (*sobbing*), it was horrible!

FRAN: Nothing came out??

OLLIE: Not a sound. OOOOOOH, I was so mortified! (*Breaks down.*)

FRAN: There, there, Ollie. (*He gets worse with sympathy. She comforts him on her shoulder.*) Here. (*Holds up her handkerchief.*) Blow.

OLLIE (*blowing his nose*): What do you suppose it was, Fran? Stage fright?

FRAN: Well, whatever it was, I think it was a blessing.

OLLIE: A blessing?

FRAN: Yes, because if you had been able to sing, there's no doubt that you would have been given the part and then you'd have to leave us and what would we do without you?

OLLIE: That's true, Fran. I never thought of it that way. I would hate to leave the Kuklapolitans in the lurch without a baritone. Oh, thank you, Fran. You've made me feel so much better. I belong here with my buddies . . . you, and little Kukla. (*Kisses her.*)

The real genius behind *Kukla, Fran and Ollie* was Burr Tillstrom, who created, worked and spoke for all of the Kuklapolitans. While most television puppeteers were strictly performers, Tillstrom was an artist. Because of Tillstrom, *Kukla, Fran and Ollie* maintained an integrity and stressed a quiet humor that made the program shine over all others. The Kuklapolitans were a real theatrical troupe in which we saw a true microcosm of our world.

Burr Tillstrom's childhood was rich in fantasy. He especially liked such stories as *Alice in Wonderland, Peter Rabbit* and the Oz books. While still in kindergarten he pretended to make two teddy bears come alive. During most of his later school days in Chicago, Tillstrom put on puppet shows on stages made from orange crates and curtains given him by his mother. Eventually he received his first professional booking, a garden party on Chicago's North Side. But Tillstrom couldn't survive in the work he so loved at ten cents a head admission.

When he was a freshman at the University of Chicago he landed the coveted job of manipulating marionettes for the WPA-Chicago Parks District Theater. It was during that summer that the young artist began to experiment with hand puppets. Within a short period of time Kukla was born.

Since Kukla was a puppet, not a marionette, he performed only small jobs at first. When Tillstrom turned the pages of script for the narrator of a WPA production of *Romeo and Juliet,* Kukla had his own minor job. During scene changes, he would peer out from behind the marionette theater, commenting on both the audience and the performance. But the little Everyman was created for bigger things. Tillstrom realized that if he and Kukla were to be successful some supporting characters were needed to make up the Kuklapolitan players.

The first "person" to join Kukla's dramatic group was Mme. Ooglepuss. Tillstrom developed a wavering voice for her that satirized an opera singer. Mme. Ooglepuss was a middle-aged woman of the opera, with a great hooked nose, make-up to regain a lost youth and the most expensive gowns and furs. She was thoroughly convinced that she was irresistible to all men and frequently told the other Kuklapolitans about that magnetism.

Ollie followed Mme. Ooglepuss. In 1942, when the Kuklapolitans were playing U.S. naval hospitals in Chicago, Burr realized that Mme. Ooglepuss actually should have a boy friend. But she needed a boyfriend who simply could not talk back to her. When Mme. Ooglepuss sang "My Bill" one day, she met her dream man, a sailor (made for the benefit of the sailors in the hospitals) named Bill, and later called Cecil Bill. His every word came out "Tooie," a language understood almost exclusively by Fran. But even we could sometimes know what Cecil Bill was talking about if we listened closely enough. When the television show started, Cecil Bill retired from the Navy and became the Kuklapolitans' stagehand. While Mme. Ooglepuss always had the final word, Cecil Bill eventually had the last "tooie."

Mercedes was a character who was not created especially for the Kuklapolitans. Kukla's troupe was appearing at Marshall Field's and a company official requested that Tillstrom invent a nasty little girl character for the benefit of the clerks. Through the Kuklapolitans' handling of Mercedes, the Marshall Field's clerks could learn how to cope with pesky brats.

In 1945 two more performers joined the Kuklapolitans. Buelah Witch (named after the show's producer Beulah Zachary) was as lovable as she was hideous, with her elongated chin and nose and white scraggly hair. She zoomed about on a jet-propelled broomstick. But even her United States Army pilot's license didn't stop her being arrested for buzzing a police station. Buelah was originally a mean old witch for a production of *Hansel and Gretel* for the Junior League.

But she was, after all, only portraying an evil witch and remained with the troupe as the lovable person she really was. *Hansel and Gretel* also featured a buck-toothed rabbit. He too remained with the troupe, gaining the name Fletcher Rabbit and eventually becoming the official mailman of the Kuklapolitans and perhaps the troupe's most practical member. Fletcher would often inspect Buelah's modern broomstick just before she took off on another buzzing spree.

BUELAH: Well, Fletcher, what do you think?
FLETCHER: She looks good to me, Buelah.
BUELAH: Straw look all right?
FLETCHER: Yep, just fine.
BUELAH: I'm glad the weather cleared up. I hate to fly the mop on a mission like this.
FLETCHER: Not as fast, eh?
BUELAH: Oh, heavens, no! Flies so sluggish. But what's a girl gonna do? Can't fly a broom in the rain. Straw won't respond when it's wet. Well, it's time to take off. Am I cleared for take-off, Fletcher?
FLETCHER: All clear, Buelah. Happy landing!!! (SSSSSWWWWWW-HHHHHOOOOOOOOSHHHHHHHH!)

Other characters joined the Kuklapolitans in the following years. Colonel Crackie, a courteous Southern gentleman, stepped into the niche vacated by Cecil Bill and became the escort of Mme. Ooglepuss. Miss Clara Coo Coo, the official timekeeper of the north Pole, flew in one day to pester poor Ollie. And Doloras Dragon, with all the problems of youth, arrived to give Cousin Ollie more of a sense of responsibility.

Burr Tillstrom and the Kuklapolitans were first exposed to television in 1939. RCA Victor was demonstrating the new marvel of television at Marshall Field's and Tillstrom pestered the unit into putting his characters on the closed circuit screen. Kukla and Ollie adapted to the new medium impressively and Tillstrom realized that his characters were born for television.

The Kuklapolitans did the first ship-to-shore telecast from mid-ocean to Bermuda in the spring of 1940. From there it was the New York World's Fair with RCA again televising the antics of Kukla and the group. During this period Tillstrom developed the personality of each Kuklapolitan to such a degree that they seemed to be real individuals.

In 1941 the Kuklapolitans appeared on WBKB. But it was not until six years later that Tillstrom knew he had proven himself to Captain William Crawford Eddy, the director of the station. Eddy offered the puppeteer a Monday-through-Friday hour-long series. At first the job seemed impossible. James Petrillo, head of the Chicago local of the American Federation of Musicians, had temporarily barred union musicians from television. The show was to be done live, leaving no room for serious mistakes. Nevertheless Tillstrom recognized his first real break and accepted. The program was given the name *Junior Jamboree* and the old reliable sponsor RCA Victor.

Tillstrom asked Lewis (Gommie) Gomavitz, the director of *Junior Jamboree*, and Eddy for a girl to work out in front of the puppet stage to lessen his burden. They suggested Fran Allison, with whom Tillstrom had worked a few times in the past. Tillstrom was forever delighted over the choice.

Fran knew little about the Kuklapolitans when she went out cold for that first telecast on October 13, 1947 (a fine present, as this was Tillstrom's birthday). Tillstrom and Fran reacted to one another like children playing "pretend." The more Fran became involved with the characters the more their distinct personalities emerged. Within months the inevitable happened. *Junior Jamboree* became *Kukla, Fran and Ollie*.

This first verson of *Kukla, Fran and Ollie* lasted for a year, with guests, movies and cartoons, the announcement of viewers' birthdays and elaborate pageants filling the hour. In the fall of 1948 the Midwestern cities were connected by coaxial cable and, on November 29, *Kukla, Fran and Ollie* went on that early version of the NBC network. The following January the Kuklapolitans went to the full network, this time sponsored by Sealtest ice cream on Tuesday and Thursdays and on other weekdays by RCA. Early in 1951, *Kukla, Fran and Ollie* had an impressive list of sponsors—Procter and Gamble, *Life* magazine, Ford and RCA Victor.

Besides their regular programs, the Kuklapolitans presented spectacular adaptations of *The Mikado*, a Thanksgiving story of the Pilgrims, a version of George Washington crossing the Delaware (starring Ollie as Washington) and *The Arabian Nights*.

On Valentine's Day, 1951, Buelah decided to bake a special cake, using her witch's wiles to add a few ingredients not called for in the recipe. She began to mix the frosting. Kukla was contributing to the festivities by making an enormous valentine for Fran. He began to mix the paste for the card when the two batters got interchanged. When Fran tried the frosting she found her jaws suddenly pasted shut.

KUKLA: Fran, Fran, what's the matter?
FRAN: *(mumble, mumble.)*

KUKLA: Speak to me, Fran!

FRAN: (*mumble, mumble.*)

KUKLA: Ollie, Ollie, come up quick! Something terrible has happened!

OLLIE (*entering in a rush*): What, what . . . what's happened?

KUKLA: It's Fran. She can't talk.

OLLIE: Fran, Fran, what's the matter? Tell me, tell me?

KUKLA: I told you she can't *talk*, Ollie.

OLLIE: Kukla, I don't believe she can talk!

KUKLA: That's what I've been trying to tell you. *Honestly*, Ollie! (*Furious.*)

OLLIE: Well, well, let's not lose our pretty ways, Kukla. Nothing is gained by panicking.

KUKLA: WHO'S PANICKING??

OLLIE: YOU ARE, THAT'S WHO! (*Bites his nose*)

FRAN: Ollie, Ollie, stop that!

OLLIE: I'm not going to take . . . hey, wait a minute. I thought you couldn't talk.

FRAN: Well, I couldn't. But I can, now.

KUKLA: Thank goodness! Oh, Fran, I was worried.

OLLIE: What happened, Fran?

FRAN: Well, Buelah was making a cake and . . .

OLLIE: You tasted the wrong batch! And your mouth stuck together.

FRAN: Right!! But it's all right now. Everything's fine.

OLLIE: Oh, I'm so glad! Say, how did it taste?

FRAN (*looks around, whispers*): Better than Buelah's cake, but if you say I said that, I'll deny it, I'll deny it!

KUKLA & OLLIE: We won't! We won't! (*Laughing.*)

Ollie's chomping mouth finished off the "paste" of the valentine. As always, the episode ended happily, with Fran assuring everyone that no real damage had been done.

Kukla, Fran and Ollie finished its run on NBC on June 13, 1954, where it had been going on Sundays for two years. On September 6 the show moved to ABC as a daily, fifteen-minute series, because NBC could not offer Tillstrom the time slot which he felt right for the Kuklapolitans. The show remained there until August 30, 1957.

During their stay on television as a regular series, Burr Tillstrom and *Kukla, Fran and Ollie* won two Emmys and one Peabody award. (Tillstrom later won an Emmy and a Peabody Award for his "Berlin Wall" hand ballet on the show *That Was the Week That Was*.)

In their many years on television, the Kuklapolitans have appeared on such programs as the *Perry Como Show, Jack Paar Show, Summer*

Chevy Show, Shari Lewis Show, NBC Children's Theatre, the *Today Show, Dick Cavett, Mike Douglas* and *Merv Griffin.* More recently the Kuklapolitans have hosted the *CBS Children's Film Festival* and created a new twenty-six-week series of *Kukla, Fran and Ollie* for the PBS network. And there are new series being planned for the famed theatrical troupe.

Because of Burr Tillstrom's skill and love for both his characters and his audience, Kukla, Fran and Ollie the Dragon are still on the air. That makes Kukla, Ollie and the other Kuklapolitan players most happy. They should be, for they are, after all, real people.

"I'm Comin', Beany Boy!"

At six-thirty every Monday through Friday evening in the early 1950s, those of us who were young enough in body or spirit knew what time it *really* was. We would get close to the small screen of our RCA or Zenith television set as an energetic announcer exclaimed, "And now, it's *Time for Beany!"* If we were enthusiastic enough, we would join in with a pudgy smiling and beared seafaring explorer named Captain Horatio K. Huffenpuff as he sang his own lyrics, which also happened to be the theme music for *Time for Beany,* while an organist played the tune of "Blow the Man Down."

> I've sailed, oh, so long that there's salt in my bones,
> Yo, ho, and a bubble of gum.
> My old second mate used to be Davy Jones,
> I'm Huff-en-puff and tough as they come.
>
> Ooooooh, I've brought my good ship through the roughest of gales,
> Yo, ho, and a bubble of gum.
> And with my bare hands I've licked serpents and whales,
> I'm Huff-en-puff and tough as they come.
>
> Ooohhhhh, I've sailed in the Arctic so cold you would freeze.
> With a yo, ho, and a bubble of gum.
> I've sailed through the tropics in my B.V.D.s.
> I'm Huff-en-puff and tough as they come.

Time for Beany, a fifteen-minute-per day puppet show originating from the Paramount Studios in Hollywood, was seen nationally for an extremely successful run of nearly a decade. During this time it won three well-deserved Emmy Awards for its creator, Bugs Bunny cartoonist Bob Clampett.

On the very first telecast of *Time for Beany*, Clampett's cast of puppet characters was lost at sea in a small one-sail ship called the *Leakin' Lena*. Prop waves tossed the little craft about as Captain Huffenpuff, wearing an explorer's outfit topped by a pith helmet, made his appearance. With the Captain was his nephew, a young boy with a turned-up nose and a wide grin that never changed regardless of the danger. The boy wore a striped shirt, dark blue pants with shoulder straps, and a beany cap with a propeller on the top. Appropriately, his name was Beany.

Captain Huffenpuff was a husky blowhard with a penchant for getting his ship into trouble. Even while the *Leakin' Lena* faced destruction from a violent storm, the Captain could not resist bragging about his supposed past triumphs. Beany never let his uncle know that he did not really believe all his wild yarns.

CAPTAIN: Steam the whistle! Mizzun the mast! And put some air in those sails. Thirty-two pounds all around.

BEANY: Nose, nose, sir. (*Salutes.*)

CAPTAIN: Yes, sir, there's nothing like a shipshape ship—what?

BEANY: Nose, nose, sir. (*Salutes.*)

CAPTAIN: Not nose, nose, Beany. You're supposed to say aye, aye.

BEANY: I can't reach my eye. I can only reach my nose. See? (*Salutes.*)

CAPTAIN: Well, never mind. You keep busy now, while I go below and box the compass. (*Shadowboxes*) Ahhhh, boxing! Beany, did I ever tell you about the time I fought Dempsey?

BEANY: You mean *you* fought Jack Dempsey?

CAPTAIN: If that's not the truth may lightning strike me. (*Lightning strikes.*) EEEeeeyyyyyyy! Ha ha ha! Come to think of it, Beany, this fellow's name wasn't *Jack* Dempsey. His first name was Algernon.

BEANY: And you fought him?

CAPTAIN: And what a fight! (*Shadowboxes.*) I knocked him out in the first round. (*Lightning strikes.*) EEEEeeeyyyyyyy! Ha ha ha! Come to think of it, I guess we didn't fight. We wrestled. (*Lightning threatens.*) No, no, it wasn't him. It was his sister. I danced with her at the Seamen's Ball. Ha ha ha heeeee! (*Clears throat.*) Well, I guess I better go below.

Beany had all the wide-eyed enthusiasm and belief in wondrous things that any typical young boy might possess. And so when an enormous green head with button eyes and suction cup nostrils lifted out of the turbulent waters, supported by a long serpentine neck adorned by a fantastic dorsal fin, Beany had no doubt that he was seeing an authentic sea serpent. The creature was Cecil, a slightly lisping and admittedly "Sea Sick Sea Serpent" who would moan and hiccup incessantly. His long neck swayed from side to side as the waves rocked him back and forth.

CECIL: I'm Cecil, the Sea Sick Sea Serpent (hiccup) and I'm seasick. (*Goes into seasick routine.*) Stop rocking the boat! Steady the frame!

BEANY: Oh, you poor boy, you.

CECIL: I gotta go now.

BEANY: You're not gonna go so soon, are you?

CECIL: I gotta. It's gonna storm. And storms make me (hic) seasick! (*Cecil goes under.*)

BEANY: Goodby, Cecil.

CECIL (*gargling sound*): Goodby!

Unfortunately the more practical and mature Uncle Captain (as Beany called him) did not, like most grownups, believe in sea serpents. He was below decks when Cecil looked at the young boy and gave out a friendly "Howdy!" When Beany told his uncle what he had seen, the chubby skipper merely scoffed.

CAPTAIN: You say you saw a singing Sea Sick Sea Serpent named Cecil? I can't even *say* it. How could I *see* it? Beany, you know there's no such thing as a sea serpent and I'm ashamed of you for telling an untruth.

BEANY: It's the truth, Uncle Captain Huffenpuff. (*Puts up hand.*) If I didn't see a Sea Serpent may lightning strike me. See?

CAPTAIN: And I say there was no Sea Serpent! (*Lightning strikes Captain.*) EEEÉEeeeyyyyyy!

BEANY: See?

CAPTAIN: Never mind the fairy tales about Sea Serpents, Beany. We gotta get this tub into high gear. They're waiting for us at K.T.L.A.—and you know how Landsberg is when you're late.

BEANY: Maybe we're lost. Are you sure you know where we are?

CAPTAIN: Beany boy, I know every wave in this ocean. (*Splash.*) Ha! *There*'s one of 'em now!

Uncle Captain Huffenpuff and Cecil the Sea Sick Sea Serpent finally met after several years (and several hundred Monday-through-Friday episodes) of *Time for Beany.* Until then, Beany tried in vain to convince his uncle that the friendly creature did in fact exist.

Time for Beany was more than the average children's show featuring puppets. The program was designed to appeal to a full-spectrum age group. The adventures of Beany, Cecil and Uncle Captain Huffen-puff were filled with all the necessary ingredients of danger, action and thrills, plus a generous helping of slapstick comedy. But the stories and characters also possessed an underlying sense of adult wit and satire which appealed to as many parents as to their offspring. Groucho Marx, who at the time was pulling in the television ratings with his comedy quiz show *You Bet Your Life,* once sent Bob Clampett a letter stating that *Time for Beany* was the only kids' show on the air adult enough for his young daughter to watch. The names of characters and places were invariably puns or play on words.

Besides Beany, Captain Horatio K. Huffenpuff and Cecil the Sea Sick Sea Serpent, all of whose names were descriptive of their appearance or personality, there were such characters as Hopalong Wong the Chinese cook, Clowny the clown, Crowy the Crow, the Fat Bat, Smarty Pants the Frog (also known as The Brain, a psychiatrist who let his patients solve their own problems, then inadvertently took the credit), Tearalong the Dotted Lion, Peeper Frijole, Mr. Nobody (an invisible man occasionally represented by a floating umbrella), the eccentric scientist Professor X, Flush Garden, Sir Cuttle Bone Jones, the Little Goose, Ping Pong the giant ape (played on different occasions by George Barris and Walker Edmiston), Mama Knock Knock Hawk, Oogle, the Hum Bugs, Peg Leg McYegg, Dizzy Lou and Dizzy II (a take-off on Desilu, the television production company formed by Desi Arnaz and Lucille Ball), the Staring Herring, a robot named Clank Clank McHank, Tick 'n' Tock the tick birds, the Durante-like Inca Dinca Doo Bird, Mouth Full o'Teeth Keith, and that lovable villain Dishonest John.

The gang's adventures would take them to such colorful places as the Fifth Corner of the World, Shangri-La-Di-Da, the Ruined Ruins, Vitamin Pill Hill, Tin Pan Valley, Nothing Atoll, Close Shave Cave, Widow's Peak and Horrors Heights. These places were always indicated on a large map which sometimes filled the television screen for as much as five minutes, letting everyone at home groan over the unending list of puns. Beany and his friends often shared adventures literally out of this world. Once they took off for the Schmoon, which (unknown to real-life astronauts) is actually the moon's moon. There was also an adventure on the Square Planet which had been responsible for all manners of "square" phenomena on the earth.

In one episode set in India, the announcer did his best impression of radio newscaster Gabriel Heatter, opening with "Ahhh, there's untouchable news tonight." These bits of satire provided most of the fun backstage and also appealed to those of us who were too old to believe in the antics of puppets in impossible adventures.

Dishonest John was the archetypal villain of the old school of melodrama—almost. He was oily, with slicked-back black hair, sinister-looking eyes, a large nose that hooked over his pencil-thin mustache and a perpetual toothy grin. His attire was as sinister in appearance as his face, with a black coat and inverness cape and a pulled-down green hat. But the appearance of D.J. (as he was affectionately known) was deceptive, for underneath that leering face was a person not nearly as dastardly as you might have suspected. Although he was a charter member of the Villains' Union, with the characteristic laugh that many of us imitated ("Nya ha ha!"), Dishonest John was a lovable character. He never meant to harm anyone, but delighted in leading Beany Boy (as Cecil called him) and his friends through one incredible scheme after another. D.J. was the show's "Kingfish" in that he was always attempting to put some fast-buck deal over on his three adversaries. But in attempting to foil Beany and company, it was the villain himself who was inevitably foiled. Even in his worst failures, D.J. relished every moment of his villainous life because there was great fun in being such a rat.

Cecil the Sea Sick Sea Serpent was the real star of *Time for Beany*. He was one of those characters who trusted everyone, believing that goodness existed even in such scoundrels as Dishonest John. Unsurprisingly, the Sea Serpent was usually the last to realize that old D.J. was profiting from schemes that took advantage of Beany and Captain Huffenpuff. When Cece (as Beany often called him) discovered that his little pal was in trouble as a result of D.J.'s plotting, he suddenly roared, "I'm comin', Beany Boy! I'm comin'!" Then Cecil proceeded to tear apart everything in sight until Dishonest John was defeated and Beany Boy had been saved from the villain's crooked machinations. After such a triumphant rescue, Cecil would noisily lick Beany's smiling face in an ardent "slurp kiss." The grateful boy would reply:

BEANY: Golly, Cece, you're the best friend a little kid like me ever had.
CECIL (*bashfully*): Aw, shucks, Beany Boy. Tweren't nothin' any red-blooded American Sea Serpent wouldn't have did for his best lil pal. (*Slurp! Slurp! Slurp!*)

The fact that Cecil was actually the most popular and well-developed character on *Time for Beany* was due to the show's creator. Bob Clampett polished the characterization of Cecil during his own adolescence. He had already designed his Sea Serpent puppet and had been experimenting with the proper voice for the character. Cecil's voice was born on the day that young Clampett's voice changed to its more mature and deeper tones. This was also about the time that Clampett's height increased. Like all adolescents, he was extremely self-conscious about his new image. A slight variation on his new voice provided the proper voice for Cecil.

". . . I crystallized Cecil's voice and personality at the very moment that I'd grown from a short, chubby youngster to a tall, skinny adolescent," Bob Clampett says. "I suddenly felt as if *my* neck was six feet tall . . . and when I spoke it sounded to me as if my voice was coming from somebody else. A Sea Serpent is a thing apart. And that's exactly how I felt. Clumsy, unwanted, a minority of one, but with high hopes and great surges of new-found power.

"All the pains and pleasures, intense feelings and emotions of my own adolescence are ingrained in Cecil. So much of what I put into Cecil in my puppet show was deep-rooted emotion, which I am able to convey to other people. When you look at a Cecil gag you might say, 'Oh, that's just funny.' But there's a tear to it, too."[2]

One of Cecil's recurring difficulties was his lack of the companionship of a female sea serpent, which had overtones of what we all go through in our teen-age years in trying to meet and then impress someone of the opposite sex. Clampett applied this and other problems of youth to his serpentine brain child until Cecil was actually his alter ego. "In my daily puppet show," adds Clampett, "I was able to develop Cecil's personality and changing moods much more slowly, and get the feeling of loneliness and sadness. And Cecil has great changes of pace."[3] Because of his close identification with the character and his practice as a teen-ager of letting the puppet speak the words that he was too shy or embarrassed to say, Clampett has almost always been the voice of Cecil. Today, many years after the final telecast of *Time for Beany*, he still carries his Cecil hand puppet with him when going anywhere that he might be called upon to speak. Cecil, needless to say, always makes his appearance and, as in the past, speaks with the voice of Bob Clampett. At a recent awards ceremony during which Bob was presented with a gold statuette, Cecil feigned jealousy, angrily shouting, "Now just a darn minute, what the heck! Makes a Sea Serpent sore! Doggone you, Bob Clampett, I do all the work and you get all the awards." To this, Bob replied, "Well, I had a hand in it."

Actually, Cecil the Sea Sick Sea Serpent originated nearly twenty-

[2] Mike Barrier, "Bob Clampett: An Interview," *Funnyworld*, No. 12 (Summer, 1970), p. 32.
[3] Ibid.

five years before the telecast of the first *Time for Beany* show. The character was inspired by an event that occurred during Bob's highly impressionable childhood. Bob was a creative youth who spent his free time drawing amateur comic strips and presenting puppet shows for the other kids in his neighborhood. In the summer of 1925, Clampett's mother had decided it would be best for her son not to view the silent motion picture which would be the direct influence for the creation of Cecil. The film was too fantastic for his already wild imagination, she contended. But Bob, excited by the coming-attraction publicity for the film, managed to get her to change her mind. The picture was *The Lost World*, released that year by First National.

Based on the novel by Sir Arthur Conan Doyle, *The Lost World* was the story in which boisterous Professor Challenger (played by husky and bearded Wallace Beery) took an expedition to an isolated plateau to find a world inhabited by living dinosaurs and an unexpected "missing link" (played by Bull Montana made up to resemble an ape man). Challenger brought a live Brontosaurus back to London, where it created havoc and eventually crossed London Bridge, which promptly collapsed under its thirty-ton weight. The final scene in the picture showed the long-necked dinosaur swimming out to sea, presumably on a return trip to its prehistoric homeland, with Challenger watching forlornly.

The young Bob Clampett was totally enthralled by the prehistoric creatures, especially the Brontosaurus, which came alive on the screen. He was totally perplexed by the manner in which the dinosaurs attained movement in the film. Obviously the monsters in *The Lost World* were not real. (Actually they were models animated a frame at a time by special effects wizard Willis O'Brien.) Yet Bob knew they were three-dimensional creatures and not the products of drawn animated cartoons like the "Aesop's Fables" that were popular at the time.

Almost immediately after returning home from the movie house, Bob Clampett began to make sketches of his own humorous epilogue to *The Lost World*. First he designed a comical sea serpent who would greet the passengers on passing ships with his friendly "Howdy!" and receive the expected double-takes. He also drew a comic version of Professor Challenger, who would be the basis for Captain Horatio Huffenpuff. But the movement of that splendid Brontosaurus still seemed miraculous to Bob. His own sea serpent was so real in his imagination that it necessitated more depth than the two-dimensional cartoon drawings could afford. When no one was able to supply him with a plausible explanation of how the movie animal moved and breathed, he set out on his own to make his creature come to life in the simplest way possible.

Bob had been given a "Jocko" hand puppet by his aunt. Jocko was a monkey that reminded Clampett of the apish "missing link" he had seen in *The Lost World*. His problem of how to bring the sea serpent to life had been solved. With the assistance of his mother, Clampett began to work on his first Cecil hand puppet.

To begin, they found an old sock. They cut and sewed the sock, then inserted a piece of cardboard to keep the newly formed mouth in place. Bob's mother found appropriate buttons for the puppet's eyes in her sewing basket. Then Bob used Crayolas to color this first version of Cecil.

Thrusting his hand into his newly born Cecil, Bob made him come to life. Already it had begun to assume its own (and Bob's) personality. Before long Bob had built a prop boat constructed of cardboard. He took a Raggedy Andy doll and made him up to resemble Professor Challenger. The railing of his front porch served as a puppet stage, behind which Bob manipulated the puppets. With this arrangement, the youthful Clampett entertained the local children, who delighted in watching the Cecil character take bites out of the miniature ship and chomp on the foliage that grew up alongside the porch.

About four years later Bob began to make Mickey Mouse dolls for Walt Disney, who gave them out at sales meetings and to all important studio visitors, as well as marketing them in the stores. During this time head doll designer Charlotte Clark taught Bob much about the construction of puppets, starting from extremely detailed paper patterns. Already Clampett was making improvements on his sea serpent. But Cecil still had to wait for his screen debut.

Bob Clampett's professional career, primarily in the field of animated cartoons, began when he was just sixteen years old. For many years Cecil was forced to remain in the background while Clampett devoted most of his working hours to Porky Pig, Bugs Bunny and other Warner Brothers cartoons. Nevertheless the Cecil character was always in his thoughts, just waiting to be given life.

Clampett began working as an animator for the Warner Brothers cartoon department early in 1931. He helped draw the very first in that studio's series of Merry Melodies sound cartoons, *Lady, Play Your Mandolin*, animated to music composed by Oscar Levant and Irving Caesar. Bob also helped make the early Harman-Ising Looney Tunes starring such characters as Bosko, the first black star of a series of cartoons. In his first weeks at Warner's, Bob presented his idea for a musical sequence in which the advertisements on a streetcar came to life. The idea was utilized and became a highly successful and oft-repeated formula. In 1936, Clampett was made a director at Warner Brothers and his sixteen years with that studio was one of the prime creative forces behind the births of Bugs Bunny, Porky Pig, Elmer Fudd, Daffy Duck, Yosemite Sam, Beaky Buzzard, Sylvester the cat and Tweety the canary. Bob first introduced the catch lines "I tawt I taw a putty tat!" and "Sufferin' succotash!" familiar to fans of Tweety and Sylvester.

All the while that Clampett was making cartoons for Warner Brothers, he was experimenting with Cecil. Two of his Warner cartoons were actually intimations of what was to come. In the first of these, a satire on Columbus' discovery of America made ten years before *Time for Beany* was launched on TV, Bob's story board showed the Captain sailing toward what was listed on the map as a "sea serpent area." "That's silly," said the Captain. "There's no such thing as a sea serpent!" (Captain Huffenpuff would continually say this line during the early years of *Time for Beany*.) An enormous head rose from the water and replied, "So what am I? A brook trout?" As the sea serpent swam away it sang, "I'm the biggest serpent in the C.C.C." A second Clampett cartoon from the same period satirizing the Hal Roach film *One Million B.C.* had a pet dinosaur lick its caveboy master's face in a gesture that later became Cecil's famous slurp kiss, which Beany always received at least once per episode of *Time for Beany*.

Bob Clampett's (and Cecil's) first contact with television was in 1935 while on summer vacation from the Porky Pig studio. He visited the International Exposition in San Diego and its Palace of Science where a demonstration of that experimental medium was in progress. Clampett was as awed by his first view of television as he had been ten years earlier when he saw the dinosaurs of *The Lost World* seemingly come alive on the screen. Imagine, he thought, having someone stand in one spot and instantaneously show up on a screen somewhere else. As always, Clampett had his Cecil hand puppet in the glove compartment of his car. Several minutes later he was performing his very first Cecil telecast on that closed-circuit hookup. When people began to crowd around the tiny screen to watch as he put his puppet through every conceivable action, he knew that television was Cecil's medium. The immediacy of a puppet also eliminated any need for the time-consuming drawing of sketch after sketch, which was required for animated cartoons.

There was no doubt in Clampett's mind that television would be *the* next medium of entertainment. Naturally his fellow animators at Warner Brothers thought that his preoccupation of "playing with dolls," as they called his puppets, and with something as unperfected as "television" was sheer folly. But Clampett ignored the derision, for he firmly believed that television would someday replace movies in popularity and that his "dolls" would be stars in that medium.

In 1938, while working at Warner Brothers, Bob Clampett set up his own puppet studio in a garage across the street from the studio and made a film of Charlie McCarthy using a new twist on the animated puppet technique utilized in *The Lost World*. It was here that Bob developed Cecil's distinctive facial expressions. He was discontented with the standard puppets of the day, whose actions were limited mainly to working mouths. Puppets of the Charlie McCarthy variety had faces carved into but a single expression. None of the facial movements of the cartoon characters was possible with such puppets, so Bob began to experiment, learning techniques which he would eventually incorporate into his Cecil puppet and which would permit his Sea Serpent myriad expressions. Cecil was the first puppet character that ever had "controlled multiple facial expressions." Bob learned that he had to use a certain type of cloth which would stretch and come back to its original position. The patterns for the puppet necessitated cutting to the fraction of an inch in order for Cecil to perform as Clampett had envisioned him. The Cecil puppet was completely handmade. The blueprint pattern for Cecil is still followed when Bob makes new puppets to replace those that wear out.

Also in 1938, Bob began to experiment with the actual format which would someday be adapted to *Time for Beany*. Since his background was in theatrical animated cartoons he strove to give his puppet show all the freedom of a motion picture and obviate the extreme limitations of the traditional puppet stage. His characters would enter and exit from the wings as they would in a film rather than popping up from below the floor line as in most customary puppet shows. Clampett had visions of adventures set in many colorful locales with spectacular storms, lightning and thunder, gale-proportion winds, underwater shots, shipwrecks, volcano eruptions, jungles, space travel and explorations to strange and wondrous lands. Working with one of his Warner Brothers artists, he developed a system of producing a large number of multiple scenic backgrounds which could be set up and dismantled with incredible speed. Numerous miniature props and special effects were required within the story lines of the show. Ten years before the television premiere of *Time for Beany* all the technical aspects of the show had been perfected.

The techniques Bob had devised in his garage studio were solely to be applied to film. His contract with Warner Brothers stipulated that the studio had first refusal rights on anything he created. After some test footage was filmed to showcase Clampett's methods of puppetry, it was screened for Leon Schlesinger, head of the animation department at Warner Brothers. Schlesinger laughed at the puppets' antics and admitted that the concept had great potential. Leon particularly liked Cecil. But Warner Brothers was equipped for cartoons and not puppets. "A shoemaker sticks to his last," Schlesinger told Clampett, which turned out to be the most welcome thing he could have said. Now Bob did not have to surrender his copyrights on the characters to Warner Brothers. Cecil would continue to be entirely his own.

After helping Bugs Bunny grow from a first rough sketch on a blank sheet of paper to box office champion over Disney in the shorts field, and after sixteen productive years, Bob Clampett left Warner Brothers to open his own studio. In 1948, with full copyright ownership of his puppets, he prepared for the official debut of Cecil. CBS and the Los Angeles *Times* set up an experimental television station on the top floor of the Pasadena Playhouse, a cultural theater, to train cameramen and performers for professional television. Clampett was given a weekly children's program called *Cartoon Party* on which he would draw sketches of cartoon characters and feature special guests. All the while he observed what was occurring on the set until he was thoroughly knowledgeable about the technical aspects of the new medium. About the same time Ron Oxford, the head of the new KFI television station, asked Clampett to do a half-hour program when that station first began telecasting in Los Angeles. KFI, an NBC radio network affiliate, offered him twenty-five dollars a week as opposed to CBS' ten dollars, so Clampett began showing Cecil to the selected few who owned television sets and to the many viewers who crowded in front of appliance stores with sets in their windows. Cecil was always the most popular feature of Clampett's new program. Others who appeared on the same small TV stage with him were Jackie Gleason, Cliff (Charlie Weaver) Arquette and All-American Tom Harmon, doing his sports news. Bob appeared on the station's opening night premiere with movie stars Billie Burke (Mrs. Florenz Ziegfeld) and Adolphe Menjou, and the creator of *Jiggs and Maggie,* George McManus.

Bob Clampett was now firmly implanted in the infant television medium. Later that same year he interested a CBS executive in his idea for a show starring Captain Huffenpuff, a young boy character and, of course, Cecil. The executive liked Bob's idea but suggested that the preliminary drawings he had made of the boy character appeared a bit too young to be the "identification figure" for the age group he thought would watch the program.

"Following the meeting with the CBS executive," Bob told me, "I went to lunch on Wilshire Boulevard. And while I was sitting there a very appealing little boy walked in with his mother. He had on a striped turtleneck sweater and dark overalls with straps over the shoulders . . . and a most winning smile. When I saw this little boy I immediately took a paper napkin and sketched him. He had a little yarmulke which I also sketched. And then, I don't quite know why, I added a propeller on top. I knew this was 'my boy' and immediately began to think of the right name for him. When I went home that night I wrote down a list of different names. It struck me that because of his cap the best one was 'Beany' and my mother agreed."

The little boy who would befriend a giant sea serpent had been named. Luckily, Clampett had added the propeller to the cap. Otherwise the program might have been called *Time for Yarmulke.*

Time for Beany was sold to Paramount Television. Overnight it became one of the most popular children's programs in the history of the medium. The *Saturday Evening Post* labeled it "the first successful Hollywood TV show."

Viewers of *Time for Beany* soon found that they could purchase a seemingly limitless array of merchandise bearing the images of Beany, Cecil, Captain Huffenpuff and their friends. There were Beany and Cecil coloring books, costumes, masks, hand puppets, dolls, bubble bath, cookie jars, decals, buttons, pencil and pen sets, slippers and moccasins, socks, aquatic toys, wall paper, dishes, clocks, cuff links, Cecil lamps, 3D film strips, Explorers' Club membership cards, animated night lights, comic books, balloons, games, jigsaw puzzles, soap, banks and even a chain of Beany drive-in restaurants. And for those of us who wanted to emulate Beany, there were caps with propellers on the top.

Clampett also found that the public clamored to see his characters in person, expecting to meet a larger-than-life-size Cecil and *Leakin' Lena* as they appeared on TV. They were disappointed to find everything in miniature. In order to carry out the illusion of reality, Bob built a life-size Beany and Cecil for personal appearances. The characters were also asked to appear in the prologue to Arch Oboler's 3D movie *Bwana Devil* in 1952, with Robert Stack. When Cecil inflated a balloon to the point of bursting and Beany threatened to pop it, the entire theater audience ducked their heads.

With the success of *Time for Beany*, Bob Clampett expanded his television enterprises. New characters, always with the Clampett style of personalities and names, soon began to emerge on the television screen. Some of these characters starred in their own programs, such as *Thunderbolt the Wonder Colt,* starring a horse with a split personality and a stage-struck lupine figure known as William Shakespeare Wolf, which critics called a delightful satire of all superheroes.

In one spectacular adventure on *Time for Beany* telecast in 1953, "J. Edgar You-Know-Who" commissioned Captain Huffenpuff to investigate such unnatural disturbances as freak electrical storms and the flying of the Egyptian Sphinx off into space. On a remote island Beany and Cecil discovered that the disturbances were caused by a fleet of flying saucers (which were recurring news items in the 1950s) that arose from the craters of three active volcanoes—Gotta Glow, Mona Glowa and Boil Heights. Descending into the bowels of the earth, the intrepid Beany and Cecil discovered that a race of alien monsters had been manufacturing the saucers by the hundreds and that they were planning to attack the earth. Fortunately Cecil knew of a secret weapon which he called his 30-Second Men (twice as fast as Minute Men), consisting of robots, the giant gorilla Ping Pong and Pong's baby (played by a live chimpanzee), the Terrible Two-Headed Freep (Eddie and Freddie), not to mention a fighting mad Cecil. For one scene Clampett had the following elements working for him simultaneously before the live television cameras in a most complicated and believable fashion—a large armada of airbone flying saucers attacking numerous puppet characters, two humans in giant robot and gorilla costumes and a live trained baby chimpanzee. The chimp was capable of doing *anything* before the live TV cameras and on one show—just as the picture was fading to black—*did.*

Such spectacle was indeed impressive (and seemingly impossible to stage), especially since it was accomplished *live* and without the benefit of film or tape, as extravaganzas of considerably lesser scope would be done on television today. But then, Bob Clampett had been dealing with the impossible since he first gaped with wonder over the movements of the dinosaurs in *The Lost World.*

Bob Clampett and his puppets also appeared on national television with Bob Hope, Dean Martin, Bing Crosby, and on *The Ed Sullivan Show* and Ralph Edwards' *This Is Your Life.* For a while virtually every television program, including Groucho Marx's *You Bet Your Life,* was making references to *Time for Beany.* Actor James Stewart spoke with Clampett on the telephone, pleading with him not to let Paramount change the show's air time so that he would not be forced to miss it. Lionel Barrymore was also a great fan of *Time for Beany.* When Louis B. Mayer decided that television was a threat to the motion picture industry and forbade sets on his Metro-Goldwyn-Mayer studio lot, Barrymore sent his chauffeur to a local bar to watch the show and report on the plot developments. Everyone loved *Time for Beany!*

Some of the well-known names who performed on the Clampett shows were Stan Freberg (responsible for some of today's most creative TV commercials), Jerry Colonna, Jerry Lewis, Liberace, Will Rogers, Jr., Mel Torme and Bob's close friend Spike Jones. Daws Butler was the original voice of Beany himself.

After nearly a decade on TV as puppets, the Clampett characters made a successful transition to animated color cartoons. The first in the series, "Beany and Cecil Meet Billy the Squid," was filmed in 1959 with original music by Bob and his wife Sody. The cartoons were distributed throughout the world by United Artists. This animated version, entitled *Beany and Cecil,* had all the characters, situations, puns and much of the adult satire that had gone into the original puppet series. The cartoon show debuted over the ABC television network as a weekly series in January 1962, running continuously for six years.

Nearly every child in America knew the words to the closing theme song:

> So come on, kids, wind up your lids,
> We'll flip again real soon
> With Beany Boy
> And Your Obedient Serpent in
> A Bob Clampett CartooOOOooon!

Today Bob Clampett is as busy as ever, making TV commercials for top sponsors, and his cartoons are distributed world-wide. (Cecil is a new folk hero in Israel.) He takes his Cecil puppet on speaking engagements at universities and conventions where his fans bombard him with questions about the Sea Sick Sea Serpent and his pals. But regardless of where he goes, Bob meets parents of the new Beany and Cecil fans who ask him to bring back his original puppet show. For many of us grownups can remember fondly the days when we put on our Beany caps and huddled before our television sets, anxious to hear the announcer say those magical words:

"And now, it's TIME FOR BEANY!"

King of the United States

Only in a medium like television could a goose be King. Garfield Goose not only pretended to have royal blood in his veins but, while

Ollie and Cecil were content with being good American citizens, he boldly declared himself King of the United States.

No one actually believed that the character with the white feathers, beak clacking out dialogue that was never heard and a golden crown atop his head, was *really* King of this Republic. Everyone knew that he, like the children who watched his television program every day, was playing "pretend." Perhaps the person who was most aware of Garfield's elaborate fantasy was his Prime Minister, Frazier Thomas, the husky creator of all the little characters who lived in the King's castle. The announcer of *Garfield Goose and Friends* would describe the King and his Prime Minister as "the goose who thinks he's King of the United States, and his friend Frazier Thomas, who wouldn't tell him any different for the world."

Garfield Goose and Friends holds the record as the longest-running puppet show in the history of television. In the summer of 1952, Frazier Thomas created *Garfield Goose and Friend* for WBKB, the local Chicago television station affiliate of the ABC network. Although the program may be dismissed by early television aficionados as simply a local show, it has outlived all of its peers and certainly deserves mention here. The show changed stations three times (moving to WBBM-TV for a year, back to WBKB for another year and eventually to WGN-TV, where it remained) and is still on the air, as popular as when it first began. In September 1972 the series celebrated its twentieth anniversary, totaling over 5,200 shows. It has never been off the air for a single weekday except for an occasional pre-empting by some special program or news report. No other children's program can claim such a record.

When Garfield Goose, or "Gar" as Thomas affectionately calls him, first decided to become King of the United States, he moved into a medieval castle. He would peer out of the castle, which also served as a puppet stage, his beak futilely trying to communicate a *snap, snap, snap* language that no one could understand. Gar wanted Thomas to be his Prime Minister and wear a suitable uniform. Not wishing to offend his "King," even if he was a goose, Thomas put on a uniform complete with medals and epaulets and assumed the role of Prime Minister. Thomas would sit before the balcony over which Gar appeared and perform his ministerial duties, which included announcing viewers' birthdays, running cartoons and Our Gang silent comedies on the Little Theater Screen and trying to decipher what his liege lord was snapping about.

When Thomas first prepared the format of the show, which he not only created but also produced and wrote, he took his conception of

Garfield Goose to a seamstress. She stuffed the head (the same one used today, over twenty years later), sewed on the eyes and attached the body, while Thomas himself designed the beak which he had specially made by a tinsmith. During the first few weeks of the show his own secretary manipulated the Garfield Goose puppet. But Thomas had other plans for a new puppeteer whom he could mold and train so that Gar and his friends would act as he, their creator, desired.

From the first live telecast of *Garfield Goose and Friend*, Roy Brown did all the art work for the show. He was not a puppeteer and had no preconceived notions as to what puppetry was all about. In Brown, Thomas saw the ideal protégé, with fresh ideas and a mind open to Thomas' suggestions as to how the puppets should react to each other and to the Prime Minister. Brown has remained in the capacity of puppeteer and, with the exception of Gar himself, designed all of the other puppet characters, including bloodhound Beauregard Burnside III, MacIntosh Mouse and Romberg Rabbit.

The first puppet character to join Gar at the castle was his young nephew Christmas. Since his mother felt the city would be a better place for him to grow up in than Goose Bay, Florida, where the family spent the winter, or Goose Jaw, Saskatchewan, Canada, their summer home, Chris stayed at the castle, enjoying the cultural advantages of the big city.

Naturally a king, especially one who commanded the entire United States, required a secret service, even though security was hardly required to protect the Little Theater Screen or Magic Drawing Board. Like most of his subjects, Gar received an allowance, but it was not enough to hire a secret service. One day an aged bloodhound named Beauregard Burnside III, toothless, too old to continue working for the Chicago Police Department and surviving only because of his Social Security benefits, came to the castle and offered to take the job without payment. Luckily Gar's was a peaceful castle and nobody minded much that Beauregard was asleep most of the time.

A secret service was not enough for Gar. He was the King and all kings had butlers. "So he hired a real, live monkey who worked for peanuts," Frazier Thomas told this writer. "The monkey was on the show for several years (living at my house all the time), and had many costumes which he wore as he sat on the castle window sill. Then he retired to Florida, with a family who bought him when I was ready to dispense with his services. He was on the show only three years and retired to Florida! I've been at it for twenty years and I haven't been able to do that, and probably never will!"

When Gar began to be troubled with a mouse who had the entire castle in turmoil, he decided to set a trap for the little pest. The mouse, named MacIntosh, finally appeared before Gar had time to use the trap, enchanted all of the other characters, and was asked to stay and take charge of the mailroom. When a magician found himself out of work, Romberg Rabbit, his faithful assistant, left his master's hat and also sought employment at Gar's castle. With the already growing population of geese, dogs and mice, the King graciously received the rabbit as one of the royal family. Romberg is the most intelligent of the little group and for that reason acts as the liaison between the puppets and the Prime Minister. It is Romberg in whom Thomas often confides, conferring with him on how to keep the impetuous Garfield under control.

Perhaps the most popular character on the show, except for Gar himself, is his aged, bespectacled mother. Patterned after Thomas' own grandmother, "who could bait a fishhook with a crawdad tail better than any man," the irascible goose's primary goal in life is outdoing the younger male chauvinists at the castle. Her superiority in physical activities is not mere boasting, for she really *can* (and did) win log-rolling contests in Canada, speedboat races in Florida, save the day for the castle football and baseball teams, and teach karate at the Gooseboys Gym at the YMCA. She is loved by both children and parents alike, as is indicated by the fan mail sorted out by MacIntosh, probably because she is, after all, just one of the boys, a real goose to admire.

With all of these additional characters, Thomas changed the title of the program to *Garfield Goose and Friends,* the name it has retained. And because the castle is inhabited by such fanciful characters, Thomas, as a present-day Dr. Doolittle, is the only ordinary person who can understand them. Unlike the Kuklapolitans or the crew members of the *Leakin' Lena,* Gar and his friends never speak aloud. Although their mouths open and close, all that comes out is silence, because Thomas feels the animals will be more believable if they speak only among themselves and not to an audience. Communicating with Gar, on the other hand, is a different matter altogether. "Gar frequently communicates with a typewriter," says Thomas. "It's *conceivable* that a goose could peck at typewriter keys. But even as he clacks with much feeling, I admit I can't understand a single thing he says. I can understand the dog [Beauregard] and the rabbit [Romberg] and the mouse [MacIntosh]—but the clacking of a goose not even *I* can understand."

Frazier Thomas' total dedication to his young audience is apparent in *Garfield Goose and Friends.* He has molded the format of the program to fit the needs and requests of his viewers, carefully screening the commercials and films for offensive material, and providing information through entertainment. Using his own money, he has produced films of special interest, such as *Legends of King Arthur, the Phantom King,* for which he spent six months of research plus a month of filming in the actual sites of the legends in England, Scotland and Wales.

In the more than twenty years the show has been on Chicago television, *Garfield Goose and Friends* has remained virtually unchanged. Some of the films shown on the Little Theater Screen are new, but many of them are old and scratched from use. Thanks to Frazier Thomas, the series provides both a constant source of nostalgia for Chicagoans who are young in spirit and an excellent weekday experience for children watching it for the first time.

CHAPTER 5

"Now—to Get Your Secret Decoder Ring . . ."

No small part of the appeal of the space shows were the special premiums which gave young viewers a chance to identify with and participate in the space adventures. For a box top or a label and a small sum, usually a quarter, fans were offered for their very own the same ingenious devices which enabled their heroes to triumph over the forces of evil in show after show.

Most premiums were given a prominent part in the adventures in order to impress their value upon the viewers at home. In the bizarre episode which made the Captain Video ring available to the Junior Rangers watching at home, Captain Video and the Ranger had been rocketing toward an unknown planet in their battleship *Galaxy* when a weird force overcame them. The next thing they knew they were crash-landing on the planet. Quickly Captain Video rushed to the view ports and saw an enormous giant lumbering toward the rocket ship with something in his hand. It was white and rectangular and about the size of the Captain himself. When the giant dropped the object into the cockpit of the *Galaxy*, Video and the Ranger gasped with horror. The object was a card upon which had been imprinted the raised letters "CV."

Those of us who had been watching *Captain Video* for the past few days also realized the terrible significance of those letters. We knew that Captain Video and the Ranger were not being menaced by an alien giant. The supposed giant was a normal-size man. Our two stalwart heroes had been reduced to the size of insects.

The "CV" had been pressed into the card with a special Captain

Video ring, available only to Video Rangers and those of us watching the adventures at home. The ring was constructed of metal and, when pressed, crumpled a piece of paper into Captain Video's initials. Actually, the ring didn't work as well as the samples shown on television. You were lucky if the wrinkled paper boasted some resemblance to the "CV" at all, never making the dark, apparently inked impression shown in the commercials and on the giant card. But the ring, like most rings offered to us on our favorite television shows, also had the unique (and obviously secret) property of turning the fingers of earth kids green, just like those of Captain Video's Martian pals.

Like most television premiums, the Captain Video "CV" ring cost only a quarter plus a box top (in this case from Post cereals, one of the sponsors of *Captain Video*). The practice of offering premiums for a box top, usually with a minimal payment to cover postage and handling, was an extension of the radio kids' shows. On the radio such items as secret decoder rings that glowed in the dark usually cost a dime. But costs were already rising when television edged its way into our living rooms to replace the once revered radio console. Considering what we got for our quarter, and since we could actually *see* in advance what we were sending for, the extra fifteen cents was still a bargain.

Television premiums were not as varied or numerous as those offered on the radio. Since radio was not a visual medium, listeners were required to use their imaginations and found premiums perhaps the best way to become actively involved in the adventures of their heroes. Television, on the other hand, showed us the adventures of Captain Video and his kind. We were more likely to sit on the floor watching our television screen while simultaneously doing our homework. Radio required more of our attention and, consequently, prompted our desire for more personal involvement with our heroes.

The Captain Video ring was only one of the premiums offered by that series. For only twenty-five cents plus the wrapper from a Power House candy bar (which alternated with Post cereals in sponsoring the program) we could acquire a Captain Video secret ray gun.

The secret ray gun was made from sturdy plastic, painted red, and small enough to conceal in your hand and hide from enemies of the Video Rangers. (The size also conformed with the mere quarter you sent in.) The secret ray gun was such an ingenious device that it could only have been invented by the top scientist of the Video Rangers, Captain Video himself. Surely the gun could not have been invented by Power House because it fulfilled virtually every need of every fan of the Captain.

First, the gun was a real flashlight that shot a beam out the barrel. That was the premium's *obvious* function. But the miniature ray pistol came with a special Luma-Glo card that let us perform that most wonderful of activities—sending secret messages. The flashlight beam served as our pencil as we wrote with light upon the Luma-Glo card in a dark room. The message could then be seen glowing in the dark.

Naturally anyone (including the Captain's enemies) could blunder into a dark room while we were reading a secret message. For that reason the Captain (or Power House, to non-believers) devised a special secret code readable only to Video Rangers and to those of us who had sent in our candy bar wrappers and quarters. We were warned not to let the following space code fall into strange hands:

Symbol	Planet	Message Decoded
☿	Mercury	Emergency! Summon all forces.
♀	Venus	All clear. Situation under control.
♂	Mars	Come to my aid.
⊕	Earth	I am on a secret mission. Make no attempt to contact me.
♃	Jupiter	Arrange for meeting and advise me of time and place.
♅	Uranus	Disregard previous message and wait for new instructions.
♆	Neptune	Make no move until I return.
♇	Pluto	Follow me to secret meeting place. . . . I have discovered the enemy's plans.

Of course the secret ray gun would not save our lives if we happened to be stranded on another planet or thrown from our ship into airless space. For that reason Captain Video made available his official space helmet.

The space helmet sold for a box top and an incredible dollar but it was absolutely worth it. Made from plastic, the helmet was almost an exact reproduction of the current model worn by Captain Video on television. It had a red crown with a raised bubble in the center. This was attached to a piece of white plastic that encircled the head with black receiving phones over the ears, then snapped shut under the chin. In the front was a clear plastic visor that could be raised if we wanted to breathe more air than allowed by the circular hole at the mouth.

We were always attempting to make our own space helmets like the ones worn by the futuristic heroes on television. But putting together a space helmet with rounded domes and curbed visors was practically impossible when working with cardboard and pieces of cellophane. The Captain Video space helmet was the dream of the future within our grasp. All that hindered our chances of owning one of them was talking our parents into giving us a dollar instead of the usual twenty-five cents. Many parents could not see the necessity of owning a space helmet in those days before Alan B. Shepard was launched into real space. As a result there remained a large stock of the helmets when the premium was no longer offered on television. These were promptly shipped to toy stores across the country where you could purchase one without the need of a box top or candy wrapper.

Even Captain Video came to realize that his enemies could go to the grocery store, purchase (or, more likely, *steal*) a box of cereal or a Power House candy bar and mail off the box top or wrapper with a stolen quarter or dollar, probably with a disguised handwriting. Sent to a post office box number, even Captain Video would not know that his top secret paraphernalia was falling into enemy hands. Probably for that reason the Captain inaugurated an official branch of the Rangers, open to all of us who were grounded at home. Even Captain Video's worst adversaries would not become official Video Rangers, because to do so one had to recite the oath on the back of the authorized identification card.

OATH OF THE RANGERS
We, as Official Video Rangers, hereby
promise to abide by the Ranger Code
and to support forever the cause of
Freedom, Truth and Justice
throughout the universe.

If the evildoers of space thought that the Video Rangers had a strict oath, they would have shrunk with horror at the pledge of the Junior Rocket Rangers. *Rod Brown of the Rocket Rangers* had a unique club for the kids at home. For a quarter (along with the customary box top) he would receive a Junior Rocket Rangers kit, including a certificate which made him the officer in his sector of space (or his block, at least), and a set of small identification cards to give out to his friends. Anyone reciting the oath of the Junior Rocket Rangers was subject to orders given by the holder of the certificate.

On my Honor as a Rocket Ranger, I pledge that:

1. I shall always chart my course according to the Constitution of the United States of America.
2. I shall never cross orbits with the Rights and Beliefs of others.
3. I shall blast at full space-speed to protect the Weak and Innocent.
4. I shall stay out of collision orbit with the laws of my State and Community.
5. I shall cruise in parallel orbit with my Parents and Teachers.
6. I shall not roar my rockets unwisely, and shall be Courteous at all times.
7. I shall keep my gyros steady and reactors burning by being Industrious and Thrifty.
8. I shall keep my scanner tuned to Learning and remain coupled to my Studies.
9. I shall keep my mind out of free-fall by being mentally alert.
10. I shall blast the meteors from the paths of other people by being Kind and Considerate.

Tom Corbett, Space Cadet offered the usual variety of premiums. By sending a few coins along with a box top from Kellogg's Pep, we could get such futuristic items as a pair of space goggles which even our parents could wear to cut down the glare from the sun. But when it came to clubs that we could join to become active members of the television space organizations, *Tom Corbett* undoubtedly had the best.

When a large brown envelope arrived addressed to us we knew that our many weeks of waiting had mercifully come to an end. (Most of us who wanted to be junior members of Tom Corbett's Space Academy knew what was in that envelope because the mail was ordinarily addressed to our parents.) The fact that the return address on the envelope was Battle Creek, Michigan, removed any doubts we might have had that this was not a parcel from the Kellogg's company.

The contents of the envelope were enough to make any child of the early fifties believe that he actually had been accepted as a Space Cadet. The membership kit contained not only the usual membership card but a number of other items that even junior Video and Rocket Rangers didn't have (unless, like most of us, they were members of all three organizations). There was a blue metal badge with the emblem of the Space Academy, a green rocket ship blasting off before a red bolt of lightning, with the words that made us so proud, "Space

Cadet." The kit contained a cloth arm patch, also bearing the Space Academy insignia, which our mothers sewed onto a shirt or jacket sleeve after we offered to dry the dishes. There were the usual wall certificate, identification card and autographed photograph. But best of all was the official Space Academy newspaper with its many photographs and stories of Tom Corbett, Roger Manning, Astro, Captain Strong and the Space Academy (and "rocket rations" recipes for Space Cadets' moms).

Space Patrol competed with the other space operas, offering such items as a cardboard Space Patrol city that could be assembled with little effort, hats like the ones worn by Buzz Corry and Cadet Happy, a rocket flashlight that projected film strips, binoculars and a periscope, all for for a few coins and a box top or two from Ralston Wheat Chex or Rice Chex.

During one story line of *Space Patrol*, Buzz and Happy were on the planet Mars investigating the underground ruins once inhabited by the Karnikans, the extinct aboriginal race. The Karnikans had been the possessors of a vast treasure desired by a gang of space villains. In order to scare away future looters of their ancient dwelling, the Karnikans had left behind stacks of totem heads bearing the faces of demons, along with a poem that gave clues as to the location of the treasure. Buzz and Happy discovered the individual clues (which had been hidden in such places as the ears of the totem heads) one by one. When the adventure had come to an end, Corry decided to take the hundreds of totem heads back to Terra, but pondered how to transport so many of the things. As usual, Happy provided a flippant answer. "Why not tote 'em?"

Any one of us who could not guess that these totem heads were to be the next premium wasn't worth his weight in space junk. The Martian totem head was also a helmet that we could wear, made of sturdy cardboard and printed in vivid yellows, oranges and reds. We assembled the heads ourselves, fastening the tops with rubber bands. There was a one-way lens so that we could see out but no one could look in. Not only was there a ghastly face on the front but there was also one on the back. To add to the fun, one totem head fit snugly atop another. This gave us the incentive to purchase more of the sponsor's product so that with the demonic faces we could build totem poles that reached to the ceiling. For a while the aboriginal Martians hardly seemed extinct, for neighborhoods on Earth were populated with little creatures wearing these heads. When the novelty of this fabulous item wore down and the television show ceased to offer it, the Karnikan totem heads began to appear for sale in dime stores.

A set of plastic space-o-phones was offered with fifty feet of string. Using the principle of the tin-can telephone, the space-o-phones really worked if we read the instructions and pulled the string taut. There was the "Jet-Glow" Code Belt which not only had a miniature rocket for a buckle but also glowed in the dark and contained a secret decoder. The Cosmic Smoke gun didn't glow in the dark or decode secret messages but fired clouds of smoke when loaded up with some atomic explosive like baking soda.

Nothing was more exciting than to see Buzz or Happy actually use the premiums for which we had mailed in our box tops. When Commander Corry and Cadet Happy were fleeing from the terrors created by Prince Baccarratti on his prehistoric world, they managed to escape a tunnel cave-in which nearly ended their careers.

HAPPY: Air! Air!

BUZZ: Breathe deeply, Happy boy. There's all the air you want.

HAPPY: I'll bet Baccarratti would flip if he knew we'd escaped.

BUZZ: Speaking of "flip," what have you been doing with that coin of yours?

HAPPY: Well, it's been "heads" we escape from the trap and "tails" we don't. So far it's come down tails every time—according to the coin, we've been blown up four times, burned once, buried alive and suffocated.

BUZZ: I suppose if it ever came up "heads" we'd really be in trouble.

HAPPY: Um, that's what I figure. For instance, what are we doing now? Chasing Baccarratti. And we know he'd do anything to stop us.

BUZZ: What does your coin say about that?

HAPPY: Smokin' rockets, Commander! It came up *"heads"!*

Even if they hadn't been advertised in a previous installment, we knew that space coins were the latest gimmick Ralston was using to get us to buy Wheat Chex and Rice Chex. There was too much emphasis on such an item in the story for the coins not to be a premium. In a way the space coins proved that Junior Space Patrollers preferred other tangibles over money. We were sending real coins to Ralston in St. Louis, Missouri, in return for a few fake coins that could not be spent on Earth or anywhere.

One of *Space Patrol*'s most elaborate premiums was the fabulous Rocket Cockpit from Nestlé. Made of rugged cardboard, the Space Patrol Rocket Cockpit was a miniature version of the control board of Corry's battle cruiser, the *Terra V*. An announcer dressed in a Space Patrol uniform and his young pal Tommy described the item.

TOMMY: Golly, Space Patrollers! You don't wanna miss out on this!

ANNOUNCER: Just imagine! You can sit at the controls of your own ship, and go up . . . up . . . *up* . . . five . . . fifty . . . one hundred thousand miles an hour. Past the moon. Above Mars. Through the starry rings of Saturn. Even through the barrier of time. Tommy, will you show the gang all the swell features of the Rocket Cockpit?

TOMMY: Okay! Here's the Rocket Regulator! The Secret Star Drive that lets you travel into the future! The Master Coder, to send and receive secret messages in the official Space Patrol code! And here's the sensational Atomic Cannon . . . that really works!

The Rocket Cockpit was more than a toy. By moving the cardboard dials and pressing the printed-on buttons we really did blast into space. Yes, the Atomic Cannon *did* work, thanks to a rubber band that fired small objects out the front end.

ANNOUNCER: Don't you miss out on the fun! Write for your Rocket Cockpit today! Send a lid from a can of Nestlé's Eveready . . . or a tracing from the front of the label . . . together with your name and address . . . and twenty-five cents to Nestlé, Box 54, St. Louis, Missouri.

Ovaltine had devised the ultimate in premiums for the *Little Orphan Annie* radio program. After purchasing a jar of the milk supplement Ovaltine, you snipped off the inner foil seal and sent it in with a dime for a Little Orphan Annie Shake-Up Mug. The Shake-Up Mug fit nicely in your hand, had a cover on top and a picture of Annie on the side. All you had to do when you got the Shake-Up Mug was to put in four teaspoons of Ovaltine, add milk and shake it up. Most of the fun was shaking up our Ovaltine. It certainly made the small Ovaltine particles dissolve that much better. As we drank down the chocolate-flavored (or natural malt flavor, if preferred) mixture we never considered the fact that we had bought a product in order to acquire a premium for drinking more of that product.

Television may have replaced radio in the 1950s but Ovaltine was not about to let its Shake-Up Mug slip into oblivion. *Howdy Doody* was the most sensational kids' show on the air and Ovaltine quickly became one of the program's many sponsors. There was a new audience of kids who had never listened to *Little Orphan Annie* and who would give anything, especially a foil seal, to shake up their favorite drink and see a picture of Howdy at the same time. The Howdy Doody Shake-Up Mug was red with a blue top. It did the job as well as

Annie's and was absolutely free except for the foil seal. Howdy proved to be an even better salesman for the product than Annie. More kids than ever before sent in for Shake-Up Mugs with his picture on the side. Consequently, more of us were drinking Ovaltine.

Captain Midnight also got into the act of virtually giving away Shake-up Mugs on television. But now they were Captain Midnight Shake-Up Mugs and boasted his picture instead of Howdy Doody's. Again the mugs were free except for the familiar foil seal. Perhaps Captain Midnight realized that some kids might like to drink Ovaltine hot for breakfast. Eventually he offered a Captain Midnight Drinking Cup, a handsome cup in customary red, with a handle and the usual picture of the Captain. The price was the same as always.

Somehow it was not enough simply to drink Ovaltine and watch *Captain Midnight* on television. Listeners to the *Captain Midnight* radio program were involved in all manner of activities by becoming members of the Captain's Secret Squadron. It was inevitable that the flying ace should make a similar offer available to his television audience for a mere Ovaltine seal and twenty-five cents.

Members of the Secret Squadron who participated with Captain Midnight on television were equipped with a number of gadgets, including a tiny radio with which they could always contact SQ-1 (the code name for Captain Midnight). Naturally Ovaltine could not send out such equipment for a foil seal and a quarter. But what you did receive was worth the price.

As a home member of the Secret Squadron you received an arm patch with the corps insignia (a vertical picture of Midnight's superjet, the *Silver Dart*), an identification card with the squadron's motto, "Justice through Strength and Courage," and your own personal code number, a Secret Squadron manual and the Secret Decoder Badge.

The Captain Midnight Secret Decoder Badge was made from a round piece of silvery plastic with a raised rendering of the *Silver Dart*. On the back of the badge was a pin so that it could be worn with pride and used to signal other members of the Secret Squadron. There was also a white dial with which you could match up a series of letters with a set of numerals, thus forming an almost endless number of code combinations.

Captain Midnight would speak to us from his headquarters after his week's adventure had come to a close and tell us to stay tuned for an important message pertaining to next week's show. But first we had to set our Secret Decoder Badge according to his. For reasons known only to Captain Midnight the code combination was usually B 6. With the Secret Decoder Badge set on B 6 the code was broken down as follows:

Q 1	Z 10	K 19
D 2	O 11	U 20
I 3	Y 12	J 21
C 4	N 13	T 22
H 5	X 14	S 23
B 6	M 15	F 24
G 7	W 16	R 25
A 8	L 17	E 26
P 9	V 18	

Captain Midnight would wait until we had our decoders set to B 6. Then he would give us a clue to next week's adventure, leaving it to us to decipher the message. The message was usually something simple but direct:

23-3-17-18-26-25   2-8-25-22   3-13   22-25-11-20-6-17-26.
23-20-23-9-26-4-22   23-8-6-11-22-8-7-26.

Premiums were an important part of early television. If we were believers the treasures sent to us were the only real link we had with the heroes who performed on the screen what we dreamed of doing in our mundane lives. What greater thrills could there be in those days when television was something new and almost futuristic than receiving in the mail a Superman T-shirt, a Howdy Doody mask or a whole set of miniature cowboys and horses from Roy Rogers' Triple R Bar Ranch? It hardly mattered that the time that elapsed between sending in your box top and receiving your personalized brown envelope seemed eternal. Nor did it matter that once you received your coveted decoder ring or flashing ray gun it never quite looked or worked the way it did in the television commercials. Could there be any real disappointment in becoming an actual member of the Video Rangers, Space Academy or the Secret Squadron?

The offering of premiums on television is part of that past world of Captain Videos and Captain Midnights, of Space Academies and Space Patrols. Premiums showed a personal interest on the part of a sponsor for its audience and could only exist in those days when each program had its own individual sponsor. Today commercials are packaged and run by computers, with a prescribed number of showings every television day. Any program may run any commercial. When commercials are so scheduled there can be little room for a Captain Midnight Shake-Up Mug or a Secret Decoder Badge.

CHAPTER 6

"And in the Center Ring . . .."

They say that everyone loves a circus. It was, therefore, understandable that one of the most popular television shows of the forties and fifties on Sunday afternoons was ABC-TV's *Super Circus.*

The great days of the live circus, with the thrills of anticipation that aroused the entire community when the circus train chugged into town, had gone. Almost none of us had actually seen the mammoth circus tents miraculously billow into shape at the hands of experienced men who had performed the task hundreds of times before. Few of us had seen the acrobats and animal trainers practicing under the open sky, or watched the elephants feeding. An entire town of young (and young-thinking) people could be electrified by the circus in those simpler times, but few people fanatically attended circuses by the time television became the nation's leading medium of entertainment. And so it was through television that many of us became acquainted with that ageless means of escape from the drudgery of life, the circus.

Super Circus, which debuted from Chicago in 1947, provided every one of us with a seasonal ticket to see the many acts under the big top. The only admission was to switch on a television set and, the sponsors hoped, buy the products advertised on the program.

For those viewers who were accustomed to the grand and classic traveling shows such as the Ringling Brothers and Barnum and Bailey Circus and the King Brothers Shows, *Super Circus* might have been disappointing. But it was mostly to their children and grandchildren that the television circus appealed. Most of the action between the standard trapeze and juggling acts centered around the show's regular cast of characters, all of whom were so appealing that we would have watched them even if the guest acts had been abandoned altogether.

Ringmaster of *Super Circus* was six-foot, five-inch-tall Claude Kirchner, whose lean body added to his impressive height. Kirchner had been in show business since he was sixteen years old. Even during those younger years he showed signs of becoming a successful showman by working as Sally Rand's barker at the world's fair. Finally he landed a position as a staff announcer at NBC radio. Kirchner's personality was thoroughly pleasing. Mothers and grandmothers of *Super Circus* fans often watched the show just to see the handsome ringmaster in his striking uniform. The producer of the show, Phil Patton, was also glad that Kirchner had been hired for the part. Kirchner exhibited a phenomenal knack for memorizing his scripts. After only a few readings of the script, he could remember the names, ages and specialties of all the guest artists on the show.

While female adults watched the program for Kirchner, their husbands and fathers had their own reason for switching on their ABC channel on Sunday afternoons. It might have been to see the acrobatic or magic acts but was more likely because of the show's bandleader, Mary Hartline.

Mary Hartline was an attractive blonde who pioneered the miniskirt and boots on television as far back as the dark ages of the forties. A former model, she had a good figure and long, curly golden hair. When she led the *Super Circus* band in a rousing march such as "Entry of the Gladiators" (the classic "circus song") every male viewer who had reached the age of puberty sat up and took notice.

As Claude Kirchner and Mary Hartline were keeping the parents occupied, the younger members of the viewing audience were mostly concerned with the *real* stars of the show, the three resident clowns: Cliffy, Scampy and Nicky.

"Cliffy" Sobier was the leader of the *Super Circus* clowns. He was a veteran actor in radio, television and motion pictures. Although he was responsible for almost as much mayhem as the other clowns, he seemed the most mature of the three and never resorted to the mischievous antics of *Howdy Doody's* Clarabell.

Bardy Patton, the son of the producer, was the first Scampy the clown. Scampy was a clown with whom younger folk could identify, for he was hardly older than most of us and played the part with a natural, wide-eyed zeal. He was more or less the protégé of the elder Cliffy and the two of them even wore similar make-up, with traditional clown white and bald heads, cherry noses, and outlandish costumes complete with oversize shoes. Sandy Dobritch, the son of the show's booking agent, played Scampy after Bardy grew too tall for the part.

Almost out of place alongside Cliffy and Scampy was Nicky Francis, known by everyone simply as Nicky. A professional working clown in every respect, Nicky was able to play a number of musical instruments, ride a unicycle and perform gymnastics. He worked in circuses before and would continue to do so even after *Super Circus* went off the air. Nicky's image was that of an Emmett Kelly type of clown. He looked like a tramp, he was unshaven, wore baggy pants and an old top hat, and was usually flat broke. But Nicky, along with Cliffy and Scampy, always had a generous helping of laughs to give away.

A favorite part of the show came about halfway through, after Claude Kirchner had introduced some of the circus acts. He would make an announcement that the time had arrived when three lucky kids from the audience could actually come up on the Chicago Civic Opera House stage before the live television cameras and participate in a weekly stunt that was not only fun but also profitable.

In the center of the stage were three glass jars, each filled nearly to capacity with pennies. The three clowns would walk up to the jars and add a bit of silver to the accumulation of copper coins. As usual, Nicky had the least money of the three. He would search through the pockets of his ragged trousers, then toss a coin into each of the jars.

NICKY: First, let me throw in a nickel . . . a nickel here . . . here . . . and a nickel here.

SCAMPY: And I'm gonna throw in a quarter . . . a quarter here . . . here . . . and a quarter here.

CLIFFY: And wait a second, because I'm going to throw in a *fifty-cent piece* here . . . and a fifty-cent piece here . . . and here.

Naturally, Cliffy's generosity drew the loudest screams and applause. The three youngsters would step up to the jars and ready their empty hands. Cliffy would blow a whistle and the kids would dip their hands into the sea of coins, hopefully encompassing the nickels, quarters and half dollars with all the pennies. Whatever coins they were able to hold onto as they brought their hands out of the jars now belonged to them.

On one particular *Super Circus* show, the three clowns were buzzing with the news of the arrival of a monkey named Gnik Gnok. When Mary Hartline asked what all the excitement was about, Cliffy showed her the large cage with the monkey's name. In between the acts, the clowns planned the great times they were going to have with the addition of a monkey. Toward the end of the show, Claude Kirchner revealed the startling truth that the label on the cage was printed backward. "That's not Gnik Gnok!" shouted Kirchner, as the cage burst open and a giant gorilla emerged, pounding its hairy chest, "it's *King Kong!!!*"

This King Kong was actually just an actor in an ape costume. But there were also real animals on the program.

The animals on *Super Circus* appeared in a regular part of the show called "Bernie Hoffman's Animal Kingdom," named after a large pet shop in Chicago specializing in unusual and interesting animals for use on television. Hoffman, who also supplied animals for such shows as *The Quiz Kids, The Wayne King Hour* and *The Dave Garroway Show,* would come onto *Super Circus,* in a flashy red and white uniform. He was the head animal trainer of the program's menagerie and traveled all over the world in search of interesting and sometimes (to many viewers) unheard of species of animal life.

Hoffman told this writer of an incident involving a particularly mischievous chimpanzee that he was exhibiting to Kirchner and Mary Hartline on the show one day. Many fans of the show were skeptical about Miss Hartline's beautiful hair and wrote in suggesting that she wore a blonde wig. The chimp never had to write a letter to the show. He found out in the obvious way, grabbing her hair in his hand and violently jerking her head down against the table. The many people watching the live show were convinced as to the authenticity of Miss Hartline's locks.

In 1955, *Super Circus* moved to New York. During the process the entire cast of regulars from the Chicago version was dropped. It was depressing to see them all go, even though they went on to other work in television. Kirchner also moved to New York, where he became the host of some new children's shows and also acted in commercials. Mary Hartline suddenly acquired royal blood and starred in a local Chicago kids' program called *Princess Mary's Castle.* Cliffy Sobier retired from show business. But Nicky Francis continued to work on television and in live circuses for a few years before succumbing to a heart attack.

The New York version of *Super Circus* starred comedian Jerry Colonna as the ringmaster. But the show, despite a higher budget and more glitter, lacked the appeal of the original. On June 3, 1956, the program went off the air. What it needed but did not have was the team of Claude Kirchner, Mary Hartline, Cliffy, Scampy and Nicky.

CBS-TV scheduled its own circus show on Saturday mornings. On July 1, 1950, a clown (Ed McMahon previous to becoming the announcer on Johnny Carson's *Tonight Show*) appeared on nationwide television, his red light bulb nose blinking the message, "CBS PRESENTS." Then he lowered his head to reveal the name of the show, which had been painted on his bald pate . . . *The Big Top.* Ringmaster of *The Big Top* was Jack Stirling, a veteran radio producer, director and master of ceremonies, who served as ringmaster in 1932 on the traveling *Circus Days* show. While Claude Kirchner maintained a friendly image, Stirling's was as smooth as the silk of his shiny top hat. When he told you that Sealtest ice cream, which sponsored *The Big Top*, was the best ice cream around, you believed him.

Besides the usual circus acts, *The Big Top* boasted a strongman named Dan Luri. Every Saturday morning Luri rippled muscles that would have made Superman jealous. During the week he moonlighted as "Rewop" ("Power" spelled backward) the strongman for commercials on *Captain Video,* showing how we'd look if we ate Power House candy bars. Both authors of this book ate Power House bars but would have hated to get caught between Luri's biceps and shoulders when he flexed his muscles.

The Big Top was still running after *Super Circus* was canceled. On September 21, 1957, the show left the air. The budget was considerably higher than that allotted to *Super Circus,* but *The Big Top* never quite conveyed the warmth of *Super Circus,* especially since it lacked the bits of comedy that Kirchner and the regular cast supplied between the acts.

There were other circus programs on television during the 1950s, such as *International Showtime* with host Don Ameche and a format geared more to older viewers. *The Magic Clown* ran from 1949 to 1954 and starred magician Zovella, who played the title character, performing magic tricks and cavorting with puppets. In 1956, *Circus Time* debuted, featuring Paul Winchell, one of the most talented ventriloquists on television, who had been discovered on *Ted Mack's Original Amateur Hour.* Winchell and his dummies, Jerry Mahoney and Knucklehead Smiff, introduced the circus acts. That was also the year of *Circus Boy,* about Corky, an orphaned boy taken in by a traveling circus owned by big Tim Champion (Robert Lowery). Mickey Braddock, who would use his real name of Mickey Dolenz in the 1960s as one of the rock music stars of *The Monkees* television series, portrayed Corky.

Many of us had never attended a circus, with three rings of simultaneous entertainment performing to the vibrant strains of "The Thunderer" march played by a circus band. Some of us had never watched the antics of a white-faced circus clown while the canvas of a circus tent rustled in the wind. The expansiveness of a real circus was lost when shrunken down to a seventeen-inch television screen. But for those who had never thrilled to the whistle and smoke of the circus

train when it stopped in town with its cargo of colorfully cos-
tumed high-wire walkers and trampoline artists and its menagerie of
jungle cats that obeyed the crack of an animal tamer's whip, there
was genuine excitement in programs like *Super Circus*.

CHAPTER 7

For Kids Only

Buster Brown's Gang

Saturdays were invented for kids. No other day of the week offered such a wide variety of television programs created especially for the younger audience. There were children's shows on television during the week, but most Monday-through-Friday television entries were made primarily for grownups. Saturday was kids' day. If you were a child in 1954 you knew what a thrill it was to sneak out of bed before your parents, switch on the television set, and see the programs that older folks did not appreciate, such as *Winky Dink and You, Ramar of the Jungle* and *The Lone Ranger*.

On one Saturday of 1954 a husky, jovial man with white hair and a Southern drawl said, "Hi, kids! You better come runnin.' It's ol' Smilin' Ed and his Buster Brown Gang!" Smilin' Ed McConnell was well named. His face was almost always sporting a wide grin. Dressed in a light-colored suit and, naturally, smiling, he would raise his hand and conduct his audience of happy kids in the theme song of his show, *Smilin' Ed's Gang,* sung to the tune of "Mademoiselle from Armentières" (which followers of *Howdy Doody* preferred to call the tune of the "Clarabell Song"):

> The happy gang of Buster Brown is on the air.
> The happy gang of Buster Brown is on the air.
> We'll laugh and frolic and sing and play,
> C'mon, you buddies, and shout "Hurray!"
> Buster Brown is on the air.

Actually, little of Buster Brown himself was on the air. Buster was originally a comic strip character who first appeared in 1902. He was a mischievous little boy with long blond hair and bangs in those pre-Beatle days and a Little Lord Fauntleroy outfit that *no* member of his later "gang" would have been caught dead wearing. Now Buster Brown had reformed and was associated with the shoe company of the same name. His only real appearance on *Smilin' Ed's Gang* was in a quick commercial. Buster would grin and hug his famous dog while telling Smilin' Ed's fans, "Hi, I'm Buster Brown. I live in a shoe. That's my dog Tige. He lives in there too."

The only requirement for being an official member of Smilin' Ed's Buster Brown Gang (unofficial members could still watch the show on television) was to purchase a pair of Buster Brown shoes. Luckily no one crushed poor Buster to death by stepping into those shoes in which he supposedly lived. Upon buying a pair of the shoes we found only a picture of Buster and Tige. Even in selling his young viewers on Buster Brown shoes, Smilin' Ed did it by leading his gang in a rousing song, which was sung to the familiar tune of "I Got Shoes."

> I got shoes.
> You got shoes.
> Everybody's gotta have shoes.
> But there's only one kinda shoes for me . . .
> *Good ol' Buster Brown shoes!*

If Buster Brown played such a small role in a show reportedly catering to his own gang, none of us really cared. Buster was an anachronism, a throwback to another era. He was, after all, a symbol of the past—a past in which our parents might have lived. We had enough lecturings and scoldings from our parents anyway without having their influence touch our very own program, *Smilin' Ed's Gang*. There were enough characters on the show so that Buster Brown's participation was hardly necessary.

Smilin' Ed's Gang was originally a radio program. McConnell's kids' show was so popular that it was inevitable that it should finally make the transition to television. The format was geared for a young audience, with Smilin' Ed not a father figure but more in the image of a big brother or a favorite uncle, who sang songs that let us get even with such ominous adults as doctors and teachers, told exciting stories of adventure, and had some incredible characters as friends. Despite his being overweight, almost all of his fans would have liked to grow up to be Smilin' Ed.

At one point in every one of the filmed episodes of the program Smilin' Ed would flop down into an easy chair and pick up a book about the size of an unabridged dictionary, entitled in bold lettering, *Smilin Ed's Stories*. "It's time for a story," he would say. "But first let's open the big ol' storybook." Smilin' Ed would open the book halfway, turn a few pages, and say, "Ah, here it is." There seemed to be no limit to the number of stories in Smilin' Ed's storybook. What was so astounding was that week after week the stories were always located in the same place in the book! It almost seemed as if Smilin' Ed wasn't reading that enormous volume at all but might really have been reciting words off a cue card.

Smilin' Ed's story was always a filmed adventure, with such characters as Little Fox (Nino Marcel), a young Sioux brave. In one story, entitled "The Bear Cub," Little Fox befriended the cub of a grizzly bear that had killed the horse belonging to another Indian in order to restore honor to his tribe. In "The War Bonnet," Little Fox found himself in a predicament. He had won in battle over Two Knives (Lou Krugman), a Crow chief. But his victory would be meaningless unless a golden eagle appeared. Even Little Fox was hampered with the meaningless old rules of adults.

But while Little Fox was popular, Gunga Ram and his "great bull elephant Teela" took up most of the pages in Smilin' Ed's storybook. Gunga Ram was a mahout also played by Nino Marcel, a handsome and personable youth obviously supposed to suggest the movies' number one elephant boy, Sabu. Sometimes Marcel would even appear on stage alongside Smilin' Ed.

Gunga was the personal favorite mahout of none other than the Maharaja (Lou Krugman), who would frequently summon the boy to his palace, either to offer advice or to ask it. Gunga always looked out of place when visiting the Maharaja. He wore only a cloth draped around his waist and a turban on his head. The Maharaja, on the other hand, was always clad in the most magnificent garments. If Gunga felt improperly dressed in the palace, so much the Maharaja out of the palace. For when Krugman doubled as a villain in the show he was stripped down to sheet and turban, just like Gunga. Even the heavy beard he wore in such roles didn't stop us from spotting the apparently moonlighting Maharaja.

In "The Monkey Temple," the Maharaja conferred with Gunga Ram and told him of an ancient, abandoned temple, now inhabited by hundreds of monkeys. A white hunter asked the Maharaja for permission to capture the monkeys. The Maharaja told Gunga his decision to allow the hunter to go to the temple. As usual, Gunga looked sternly at the Indian ruler, nodded his head and said profoundly, "Ah-eeeee! Such is so!" As far as Gunga was concerned in every story, such was always so.

Some of the other Gunga Ram stories included "Nagas and the Water Buffalo," in which he and his mahout pal Rama (Vito Scotti) were attacked by a water buffalo while attempting to save a young princess from headhunters. In "Capture of the Rhino" the two elephant boys captured a rhinoceros in a pit. And in "The Bee Goddess," Gunga and Rama scaled the ominous Death Mountain. Their quest was to secure some honey needed for a medicine to save the dying Maharaja. Needless to say, the mahouts succeeded.

The Gunga Ram stories were so popular that the mahout and Teela were given their own feature-length film, made in color in 1955. *Sabaka* had an impressive cast, including Boris Karloff, Reginald Denny and Victor Jory, with Marcel again as Gunga. The story, adapted from one of the television episodes, was about a religious cult that worshiped a gigantic idol.

Little Fox and Gunga Ram certainly provided us with enough adventure on *Smilin' Ed's Gang*. But adventure was only one ingredient in the program. There was also an ample serving of music and comedy. These were usually supplied by Smilin' Ed's three most improbable friends—Midnight the Cat, Squeekie the Mouse (actually a hamster) and, most popular of all, Froggy the Gremlin.

Midnight was a pitch-black cat with a big bow around her neck. On Smilin' Ed's radio program Midnight was equipped with a full vocabulary, her words blending with her "meeows." On television, Midnight was either tongue-tied or had somehow lost her knowledge of most of the English language. Her entire vocabulary was now reduced to a simple "Nice!" She couldn't "meeow" even if it suited her.

After closing his storybook, Smilin' Ed would bring out Midnight the Cat and Squeekie the Mouse. Midnight and Squeekie were known for their musical abilities. While Midnight was a minor virtuoso on such instruments as the violin, the bagpipes and the organ, Squeekie preferred something smaller, like a miniature xylophone or a tiny guitar. While they performed, the audience would howl with delight.[1] Smilin' Ed would make such comments as "Awww, isn't that cute?" or "Look at that little feller," and Midnight the Cat would flash out her tongue and give a quite disinterested "Nice."

After Midnight's and Squeekie's musical duet came the portion of the show which many of us preferred even to the adventure from *Smilin' Ed's Stories*. This was the appearance of that magical pest, Froggy the Gremlin.

---

[1] Although Smilin' Ed might have liked us to believe that his shows were filmed before a live audience, the shots of the gang in the audience were always the same. It is even questionable whether or not those scenes were filmed for *Smilin' Ed's Gang* or some earlier production.

Smilin' Ed would approach the grandfather's clock on the stage and speak the mystic invocation, "Plunk your Magic Twanger, Froggy!"

Suddenly there would be a burst of flash powder. *Boing!* would go the Magic Twanger and the rubber toy known on television as Froggy the Gremlin would appear from out of nowhere. "Hiya, kids! Hiyah, hiyah!" Froggy would say to the kids in the audience, sticking out his tongue and giving everyone the raspberry. The audience roared with approving laughter. It did not matter that Froggy was in a sense spitting on them. Everyone loved Froggy, mainly because he did what all of us members of Buster Brown's Gang wanted to do. He put the grownups in their lowly place.

SMILIN' ED: A very famous chef has come down to speak to us today, Froggy.

FROGGY: Hah! Hah! Hah!

SMILIN' ED: Now I want you to be good for a change. None of your tricks.

FROGGY: I'll be good, I will, I will. Hah! Hah! Hah!

We knew (as did McConnell, who did the gremlin's guttural voice) that Froggy was incapable of being good—at least in the sense that Smilin' Ed meant him to be good. Froggy was one of the only reasons for Smilin' Ed not to smile. Once Froggy appeared with his Magic Twanger, the laughs were just about to begin.

The recipient of Froggy's jokes was sometimes Smilin' Ed himself but was usually some well-known comedian like Billy Gilbert. Gilbert would appear as a professor, mailman or famous chef. But every time he was about to finish an important sentence Froggy would interject his own suggestions.

"Now once I finish mixing the cake batter," Gilbert would say in his chef's role, "I take the bowl and . . ."

" . . . And dump it on my head," Froggy would cut in.

"Yes," continued Gilbert, "and dump it on my head so that . . . mmpphhhffff! glubbb!"

The audience would erupt with laughter as Gilbert struggled to free himself of the sticky, oozing cake batter, raving insanely, and Froggy stuck out his tongue and gave his famous "Hah! Hah! Hah!" Gilbert would threaten to strangle the impish frog, then proceed with his demonstration. If he was able to get through two more succeeding lines without Froggy's interference, it was miraculous.

When Smilin' Ed passed away it seemed as if Midnight, Squeekie and Froggy would be without a gang leader. Then, at the end of

Ralph Edwards' *This Is Your Life* honoring gravel-voiced Andy Devine, the heavy-set comedy actor announced that he was going to star in a new series called *Andy's Gang*. Devine, who had finished his stint as Jingles on the *Wild Bill Hickok* television series, brought the syndicated *Andy's Gang* into living rooms in 1957. To everyone's surprise, the show was not another Western series but a new version of *Smilin' Ed's Gang* with Devine in the role left by McConnell. Devine fit the part almost as well as Smilin' Ed. But McConnell's perpetual smile had been replaced by Andy's giggling.

In one particular installment of *Andy's Gang*, Andy made the foolish mistake of asking Froggy to give him a new, more serious-sounding voice, like that of a famous person. With his usual deviltry, Froggy gave him a voice that would allow him to retain his name of Andy. To Andy's surprise (and displeasure) he had been given the voice of Andrew H. Brown of *Amos 'n' Andy*.

ANDY: Ah is, uh, Andy. Did dat come outa me? Listen here, Froggy da Gremlin (*Froggy laughs*), dis here ain't funny. Ya hear me? Ah is Andy! Heah me, man?

FROGGY: Of course you is Andy! Hah! Hah! Hah! Hah! Hah! Hah . . .

ANDY: Well, ah don't like bein' Andy. Ah mean, not *dis* Andy, leastwise.

FROGGY: Hah! Hah! Hah! Hah! Hah! Hah! You said a famous person, you did, you did.

ANDY: Yes, but ah wants a more *dignified* voice.

FROGGY: Then you wouldn't be Andy.

ANDY: Well, I don't care iffen ah'm not Andy no mo'! Ah want a voice dat's fetchin', even on de telephone.

FROGGY: Fetchin'? Even on the telephone? Okay!

Andy should have kept quiet. Perhaps he was paying for his comment about not wanting to be *dis* Andy. Froggy used his magic once more to change Andy's voice. Now he no longer sounded like *dis* or *any* Andy. The voice that came from his gaping mouth was that of a telephone operator sounding suspiciously like comedienne June Foray. Andy was glad to eventually regain his old gravel voice.

Both Smilin' Ed and Andy Devine would end the show in the same way. "Yes, sir, we're pals," either one would say with total sincerity, "and pals stick together. And now, gang, don't forget church or Sunday school." Apparently Smilin' Ed and Andy both forgot some members of the gang who were Jewish or, like Gunga Ram, of an Eastern religion. But the show was loved by all the members

of Smilin' Ed's or Andy's gang, regular "fellas and gals" who wore
Buster Brown shoes.

No Grownups Allowed

If Smilin' Ed was capable of making the impossible happen, he
paled alongside Mr. I. Magination in the magic department. *Mr. I.
Magination*, starring Paul Tripp, was one of television's pioneer
children's shows and second in popularity only to *Howdy Doody*.
The program debuted on April 24, 1949, on CBS and remained there
until June 28, 1952.

The premise of *Mr. I. Magination* was that anything could happen,
surely a dream we all had sometime during our formative years. Tripp,
a successful playwright, actor and director, created the format of the
show, set in a magical place called Imagination Town. Dressed in
striped coveralls, Tripp would lead us through the gates and into the
town itself, where any child's wish could be made to come true.

The first telecast of *Mr. I. Magination* made one young baseball
fan the happiest kid in the world. The boy had great hopes of someday pitching in the major leagues. On the program, his wish was more
than fulfilled when he was able to pitch to baseball star Sid Gordon.
The thrown baseball, however, also seemed to be affected by Mr. I.
Magination's magic. The ball shot across the studio, smashing panes
of glass and causing Tripp to blush.

Mr. I. Magination was not only an entertaining show, it was also
educational. But while most educators seemed to turn off children
with their boring delivery and too apparent condescension, Mr. I.
Magination spoke to us as though we were intelligent beings and not
just little kids. Many fans would write in requesting to see certain
inventions on the program. Obligingly, Mr. I. Magination would
answer those letters by taking viewers to Inventorsville, a haven for
the latest in automobiles, airplanes and whatever else interested children
back in 1949.

While Paul Tripp tried to educate us, Pinky Lee's purpose was
strictly to entertain. Pinky Lee had been a burlesque comic and
when he went over to television he continued doing virtually the
same act. Dressed in a suit with a checkered hat and coat, Lee
would dance and jump about, singing with his lisp and, like a minor
Al Jolson, from the heart.

On November 27, 1951, Pinky Lee starred with pretty, blonde
Martha Stewart (and later Vivian Blaine) on an NBC series
entitled *Those Two*. The show was more for adults than children,

with Lee eternally trying to win the love of his pretty costar. Lee was a very emotional performer and sometimes there were genuinely heartbreaking moments on *Those Two*. The show lasted until April 24, 1953.

Pinky Lee realized that younger viewers were watching the evening show. His next venture, therefore, was a children's program called *The Pinky Lee Show*, which raised him to the status of a full-fledged television star. Betty Jane Howarth costarred in the new Monday-through-Friday-afternoon series on NBC. The show featured songs and skits, all with the usual Pinky Lee humor and tears and performed before a live audience comprised of parents and their children sitting on bleachers. Sometimes Pinky would drag the youngsters' moms out before the cameras, leading them in the tango or some game. The performer always opened the show with his theme song:

PINKY: Yoo-hoo! It's me!
    My name is Pinky Lee.
    With my checkered hat and checkered coat,
    The funny giggle in my throat,
    My funny dance like a billy goat.
    Put them all together,
    Put them all together and it's
    Who-ooooooooooooooooooo?
ALL: P-I-I-I-I-I-N-K-Y-!!!!!!

One day, before the live television cameras and during one of his vigorous performances, Pinky Lee collapsed on stage. The studio audience burst into laughter and applause. But even after the laughter subsided Pinky did not get up. An audience whom he loved (and who loved him) had seen him fall, the victim of a system poisoned by bad sinuses. (The newspapers blamed what had happened on a heart attack.) He recovered in the more suitable climate of Tucson, Arizona. Pinky's eyesight was also affected after such constant exposure to the extremely bright lights of early television, to the extent that, when he eventually returned to the medium, he was forced to wear specially tinted glasses. Today, Pinky Lee still makes appearances on television, with his checkered hat and coat, his funny giggle, doing his billy goat dance and proving himself to be a first-rate performer.

Pinky Lee obviously loved his juvenile audience; and so did Jack Barry, a television announcer who would go on to be master of ceremonies of *Life Begins at Eighty* and such contest programs as *The $100,000 Surprise, Tic Tac Dough* and the notorious *Twenty-One*, a prime offender in the infamous quiz show scandals of 1958.

Barry's initial venture into children's programing was *Juvenile Jury*, which debuted on NBC on April 3, 1947. *Juvenile Jury* was more a show about and starring children than it was *for* children. Barry hosted a panel of juvenile experts on juvenile problems. The Juvenile Jury would advise other children who came onto the show seeking answers to problems like what to do when Mom and Dad made you eat your spinach. Unlike Art Linkletter, who elicited laughs from his audience in response to innocent remarks of the children he interviewed, Barry never condescended to treat his panel as anything but mature adults. *Juvenile Jury* moved to CBS on October 11, 1953, then back to NBC on January 2, 1955. The program left the air on March 27, 1955, but was revived in the 1970s with a panel who could be the children of the original Juvenile Jury members.

Television has often been criticized because it does not involve the viewer's imagination. Jack Barry, attempting to give children a show in which they could take an active part, created *Winky Dink and You*, which premiered on CBS on October 10, 1953, and continued through April 27, 1957, remaining dormant until its recent revival *sans* Barry.

Winky Dink and You was designed with sheer ingenuity. Winky Dink himself was a little fellow with a large head, buck teeth, enormous eyes and hair that resembled a star. He was animated into cartoon adventures and had a propensity for getting into the most hazardous predicaments. It was the viewer's job to get Winky Dink out of trouble. Saving Winky Dink required a special, and naturally authorized, Winky Dink kit. This kit consisted of a clear plastic sheet that fitted over the television screen and some special crayons that would make impressions on the sheet that could easily be wiped off. Winky Dink would be chased by savage Indians or stampeding elephants to the edge of a cliff overlooking a bottomless chasm. He would scream for help and the picture would momentarily stop. At that point Barry would intercede, directing the kids at home to draw on the plastic sheet stuck to the television screen a bridge to save Winky Dink. Parents who did not get their children a Winky Dink kit soon learned to be more generous. A bridge drawn with ordinary crayons directly onto a television screen was not so easily wiped away. But, after all, wasn't saving Winky Dink worth a little scrubbing on Mother's part?

My colleague Jim Harmon recalls his own personal favorite of children's shows:

> Shari Lewis came along in the last glimmerings of the Golden Age of Television (in the fifties), but certainly, by her talent and her chosen means of expressing it, she belongs to that era.

Like Burr Tillstrom or Buffalo Bob Smith, Shari Lewis was a puppeteer. Unlike the two just-named gentlemen, Shari is a ventriloquist, and probably the best one ever to achieve national success. Not best girl ventriloquist, just best ventriloquist. She doesn't move her lips when one of her creations talks—she can even smile broadly. Edgar Bergen can't do that when Charlie McCarthy speaks—but then, he doesn't really have to.

Of course, with the charm of herself and her characters, Shari *could* settle for being less than the best ventriloquist, but apparently she won't.

"Lamb Chop" is her chief assistant, more lovable, less of a brat than Bergen's Charlie—although he shows signs of growing into a frisky goat on recent *Tonight* appearances. His classic moments, however, are those of the very small child afraid of his first day of school, or of being scolded for doing something wrong. As Shari Lewis handles the situation, it is always genuine, never syrupy pap. "Hush Puppy" is the ignorant country cousin—if a lamb can have a pup for a cousin. Like Mortimer Snerd with Charlie McCarthy, Hush Puppy sometimes steals the laughs from Lamb Chop.

Although her puppets have become only one aspect of her talent as an entertainer, the boys of all ages who spent Saturday mornings with the lovely Shari Lewis will never forget them.

Today, animated cartoons made especially for television dominate Saturday mornings and afternoons. In 1948, however, children were treated to the very first series of cartoons made with limited animation for the new medium, *Crusader Rabbit*, by Jay Ward and Alexander Anderson. *Crusader Rabbit* was also one of the first television series filmed (though not shown) in color.

Crusader Rabbit was one of three animated series planned by Ward and Anderson in 1948.[2] Starring were a little rabbit and his relatively giant companion, Rags the Tiger. Of the two of them, Crusader had the intelligence, while Rags possessed the strength and the propensity for getting both of them into trouble. Together Crusader and Rags became involved in adventures with such characters as Arson and Sterno, a fire-breathing dragon with a bad case of heartburn and two heads that constantly bickered; the brutish and evil Blackguard Brothers, with a family that included the Frankensteinian Boris and the Dracula-like "Batman" Blackguard; and the oily villain Dudley

[2] One of the other two pilot films made along with *Crusader Rabbit* was *Dudley Do-Right,* about the misadventures of a Canadian Mountie. More than ten years later, *Dudley Do-Right* was sold to television and is still being shown.

Nightshade. In all their adventures, Crusader spoke with the voice of Lucile Bliss, Rags with that of Verne Loudin, and Dudley with that of Russ Coughlin.

Each episode of *Crusader Rabbit* was five minutes long, ending with a cliffhanger and one or two title puns. "We wanted to get the effect of an animated comic strip," Jay Ward told this writer. "The commercials would go in between these short episodes. The show was done in Berkeley, California, and we used actors living in San Francisco to do the voices."

The original *Crusader Rabbit* series continued into 1951. Ward then sold the rights to the characters and moved on to other projects, including *Rocky and His Friends* and *The Bullwinkle Show*. The formats of these shows were virtually the same, with the diminutive hero, Rocky the Flying Squirrel, and his much taller partner, Bullwinkle Moose. Rags, however, was considerably smarter than Bullwinkle. Another series of *Crusader Rabbit* cartoons done in 1956 and maintaining the flavor of the original is still popular on television.

Local television stations in the early fifties offered their own children's programs, many of them being scheduled around the noon hour. I recall racing home from grammar school to eat my lunch in front of the television set. Chicago television provided children's shows on several channels, the most popular being *Noontime Comics* on Channel 5 (WNBQ), starring former radio actor "Uncle" Johnny Coons, and *The Happy Pirates* on Channel 7 (WBKB), starring heavy-set Dick "Two Ton" Baker, "the Music Maker." The loyalties of the fans were about equally divided between the two programs. Mouths chomped on peanut butter sandwiches as Uncle Johnny projected an old-time movie starring Our Gang or while Two Ton Baker ran archaic theatrical cartoons and talked to Squawky the Parrot and the hideous porpoise named Bubbles. Many young Chicagoans were scolded by non-believing teachers for being tardy with no better excuse than wanting to hear Two Ton Baker bang his piano and sing the last chorus of such classic songs as "One Meat Ball" and "I'm a Lonely Little Petunia in an Onion Patch."

Today's children's programming is just not the same as it was in the early days of television. Undeniably, the slick kids' shows that flood the Saturday mornings of the seventies, most of which are animated cartoons, are produced with greater budgets and proficiency. But these new programs have an assembly-line aspect that betray their producers' lack of genuine concern for their youthful audience. There was an apparent honesty about Smilin' Ed when he called his gang to assemble, about Pinky Lee when he sang to us with tears almost visible in his expressive eyes, and about Mr. I. Magina-tion when he explained the workings of the latest government sub-marine. We believed these grown-up stars of our very own shows. And there was no denying that it was wonderful to be a kid in those pioneer days of television.

CHAPTER 8

"Killed Him a B'ar
When He Was Only Three"

Born on a mountaintop in Tennessee,
Greenest state in the land of the free,
Raised in the woods so he knew every tree,
Killed him a b'ar when he was only three.
Davy . . . Davy Crockett,
King of the Wild Frontier.[1]

In 1955 every kid in the United States who had reached the age of talking could sing "The Ballad of Davy Crockett." Their parents also knew the song by heart since it occupied the number one spot on *Your Hit Parade* for weeks.

It was impossible to escape exposure to Davy Crockett in the mid-1950s. The Davy Crockett craze was the most incredible fad to seize the television audience, throwing most of its juvenile population back to the time of the American frontier and replacing Hopalong Cassidy and Superman merchandise with such paraphernalia as coonskin caps, powder horns and fringe jackets. I was thoroughly enraptured by the Davy Crockett craze and could virtually see the gray buildings of 1955 Chicago transform into the verdant backwoods of eighteenth-century Tennessee with the donning of a homemade costume similar to the one Davy wore on television.

Until 1955 *the* American frontiersman had been Daniel Boone. His was the name that came to mind when one thought of caps made from raccoon fur and tails. But Boone, with his reputation for

[1] "The Ballad of Davy Crockett" © 1954 Wonderland Music Company, Inc., and Walt Disney Productions.

killing a "b'ar" ("bear" to greenhorns), could not hope to compete with a frontiersman who had vanquished the same kind of beast while only three years old. Surely such heroics were not applicable to the real-life Davy Crockett, who was reputed to be of questionable courage, had deserted his wife and was a rowdy, to name some of his qualities. The historical Crockett had little chance of winning over Boone in a popularity contest. Perhaps he would have if Walt Disney had been there during his lifetime.

Disney created his own television series, the hour-long *Disneyland* (the name he had given his park in Anaheim, California, which was then under construction), which premiered on ABC on October 27, 1954. The program (just like the park) was divided into four individual "lands": Fantasyland, populated by anthropomorphic, four-fingered mice and ducks; Adventureland, which usually starred real animals trained to act in "true life adventures"; Tomorrowland, which predicted what the space program might be like decades in the future; and Frontierland, with stories about the heroes of the American frontier and Old West whose legendary exploits were usually more filmworthy than their actual and sometimes very unheroic lives.

The first story on Frontierland was broken down into three parts with the titles "Davy Crockett, Indian Fighter," "Davy Crockett Goes to Congress," and "Davy Crockett at the Alamo." When preview scenes of "Indian Fighter" were shown at the end of the show aired the week before, no one (except, perhaps, Disney himself and his executive board) had any idea that Davy Crockett would become the most popular television hero of all time.

Though Disney himself preferred the types of films he was making to any of those made by other studios, he did go to see a movie called *Them!*, a 1954 Warner Brothers science fiction film about giant ants. In a brief scene in the film was a six-feet, five-inch-tall actor with a pleasant Texas accent and a face that appeared both likable and heroic. Coincidentally, Disney was looking for an actor who could put on the buckskin outfit and coonskin cap, act well and be received by millions of children as their greatest idol since Hopalong Cassidy and Superman. The actor who was describing the giant ants with an easy backwoodsy way of talking was Fess Parker. To Disney, he was the exact Crockett image for which he had been searching.

Fess Parker had appeared in small roles in eight feature-length movies and had also acted on such television shows as *Dragnet, Death Valley Days, Outlaws of the Century, City Detective* and *My Little Margie* before testing for the part of Davy Crockett. His career was not going any place in particular. It was hardly any gamble to accept the part of the so-called King of the Wild Frontier; no one really knew who Parker was. But with Disney behind him, he might even become as famous as Mickey Mouse or Donald Duck. Fess Parker was the first human adult to sign a long-term contract with Disney (which he did in August 1954). With the premiere of "Davy Crockett, Indian Fighter," Parker became even more popular than the Mouse who had made Disney a multimillionaire.

Wearing his buckskin outfit, his famous cap, and clutching a rifle capable of making the truest shots on the frontier, Davy and his lifelong friend George Russel (played by former dancing star Buddy Ebsen, better known today for his portrayal of Jed Clampett on *The Beverly Hillbillies*) made their first television appearance during the Creek Indian War. General Andrew Jackson (Basil Ruysdael), realizing that he and his cavalry needed some superheroics to defeat the Creeks, who wanted to keep their land, sent for the even then legendary Davy Crockett. When the soldiers, led by Major Tobias Norton (William Bakewell), found Davy, he was busy with more important matters—like "grinnin' down a b'ar." Interrupted by Norton and his men, the bear snapped out of the trance caused by Davy's powerful grin. Davy was forced to finish off the critter with a more conventional weapon, his knife. That was certainly an impressive introduction to the King of the Wild Frontier. Major Norton may have had his doubts but we knew that Davy would really have grinned down that bear if given just another minute.

The leader of the Creeks was a bloodthirsty chief named Red Stick (Pat Hogan). Red Stick could almost make the "white eyes" drop dead with his terrible scowl. But Red Stick had never encountered a frontier hero like Davy Crockett, whose grin could counteract that scowl.

When Norton and his men blundered into a Creek ambush, Davy and Russel came to their rescue, making enough commotion to simulate an entire regiment. Later Davy showed that he didn't need an army or even his trusty rifle to show Red Stick the error of his ways. With "The Ballad of Davy Crockett" making all of us younger viewers want to ride off with our buckskin hero, Davy went after Red Stick alone. Russel had been captured and tied to a stake. But Davy arrived and boldly went up to Red Stick, squinted, and spoke with the mouth that could grin down a b'ar.

RED STICK: Speak, white man. Red Stick listen.

DAVY: I've come a long ways to tell you you all are fools. Your wise chiefs have given up and made peace. They know war is no good.

RED STICK: White man talk. War no good because soldiers all die. Because Red Stick take many scalps. Because soon I burn your friend.

DAVY: You could all go home in peace if you'd listen to reason, Red Stick. But since you won't, you're a bad chief. And I reckon' I gotta challenge you accordin' to Injun law.

RED STICK: You make challenge. Red Stick chooses weapons. Tomahawks!

Davy might have been the best shot on the frontier but when it came to tomahawks he was an amateur. Nevertheless, that did not mean that Davy couldn't learn, even in a matter of seconds. Red Stick, who was to the tomahawk what Davy was to the rifle, charged his adversary. But Crockett was quick to catch on and soon had the Indian chief at his mercy. Unlike the usual winners in Creek tomahawk fights, Davy would not kill his opponent. Life to him was too precious to destroy unless there was no other way. Risking his own scalp, Davy let Red Stick live, once again proving his old motto, "Be sure you're right—then go ahead."

DAVY: Now maybe you'll listen to reason, Red Stick. Turn my friend loose and go home. Sign the treaty. Do that . . . and I promise the government will let you keep your land.

RED STICK: Government lies.

DAVY: Davy Crockett don't lie. Here's my hand on it.

RED STICK: I believe. We go home. We make peace.

If a cutthroat savage like Red Stick could be so transformed by a bit of Davy's backwoods philosophy, we knew our hero had to be the King of the Wild Frontier. Disney and the merchandisers across the country also realized it. Instantly Fess Parker was a star. The next morning every child with a television set was singing what he could remember of the Davy Crockett ballad. And every one of them counted the minutes until the first shipment of Davy Crockett coonskin caps and related merchandise arrived at the stores.

The world never saw such a craze started by a television hero and most likely never would again. Even the phenomenal fad generated a decade later by television's *Batman* could not equal the Davy Crockett craze. Perhaps it was because the "Batmania" that hit the world in the 1960s was a camp phenomenon. There was a certain "in" status to being a Batman aficionado. The followers of Davy Crockett, on the other hand, were sincere with a genuine love for their hero. I can attest to that, having been exactly the right age at the time; I would rather have faced the entire Creek nation than give up my coonskin cap. Perhaps the currently popular leather goods and fringe jackets are the result of that former mass worship of Davy Crockett.

Within a short while toy and department stores were spilling over with Davy Crockett items. Besides the expected coonskin caps and costumes, there were Davy Crockett bows and arrows, powder horns, bedspreads, wallpaper, flintlock sets, comic books and magazines, and virtually every conceivable item that could possibly be tied in with the television hero. The price of raccoon skins skyrocketed and soon a hundred million dollars' worth of Davy Crockett merchandise was finding its way into American homes. "The Ballad of Davy Crockett" had quadrupled the coveted million-seller position on the popular music surveys. The real Davy may have lived from 1786 to 1836. But 1955 was *the year* of Crockett.

"Davy Crockett Goes to Congress," though extremely popular, was a bit disappointing to those of us who wanted to see our hero tangling with b'ars and Indians. Congress was hardly the place for action, at least the type that made us want to wear buckskin. After defeating a local bully named Bigfoot (Mike Mazurki), and after learning of the death of his wife Polly (Helene Stanley), Davy took Georgie and rode off for Congress. He was elected and received his famed rifle, "Old Betsy." But when Davy learned that "Old Hickory," Andrew Jackson, wanted to use him to force through a bill that would deprive the Indians of even more land and privileges, he walked out in favor of the frontier life. It seemed for the better. Davy just wasn't Davy wearing fancy clothes and sitting among the politicians.

Davy and Georgie were on the trail to action again in "Davy Crockett at the Alamo." After learning that Texas was fighting Mexico for her independence, Davy and his partner teamed up with a confidence artist nicknamed Thimblerig (Hans Conried) and an outcast Comanche rechristened Bustedluck (Nick Cravat) and rode for the Alamo, an old mission serving as a fortress against Santa Ana and his army. The Alamo was under the command of invalid Colonel Jim Bowie (Kenneth Tobey), "the feller who invented the knife," as Davy put it. Second in command was Colonel William Travis (Don Megowan). Neither of them had much confidence in their survival if reinforcements did not soon arrive. But neither would surrender to the Mexicans.

Those of us too young to have heard the historical accounts of the battle of the Alamo were confident that the group of heroes would somehow be victorious. Even when Russel rode through the enemy lines and came back with the bad news that no help was coming we believed that Davy wouldn't let us down. During the final battle for the fortress, Thimblerig and Bustedluck were killed. But those were only minor heroes. Then Georgie Russel received a Mexican bullet and, to our horror, *died*. None of us, even those of us who knew Davy Crockett died at the Alamo, wanted to *see* our hero die. Knowing that a hero died over a hundred years ago was one thing but seeing that death on the television screen was another, especially when that hero happened to be the most important person in our lives.

Disney was an artist who cared for his audience. Perhaps history itself provided a convenient alternative to showing Davy's life end on television. The historians remain uncertain as to the exact manner of Crockett's death. Disney simply did not *show* Davy dying. His final scene showed him heroically swinging Old Betsy at the onrushing horde of Mexicans, knocking them aside as the scene dissolved to a shot of the flag of Texas and the chorus sang that the spirits of all the heroes of the Alamo would live forever.

The three Frontierland episodes were bunched together and released as a feature-length motion picture called *Davy Crockett, King of the Wild Frontier*. But there was still a furor among Davy's fans with which Disney had to reckon. Those of us who were unsatisfied with Davy's ambiguous end began to look up his name in the encyclopedias and history books and were soon totally depressed with the knowledge that he did indeed perish at the Alamo. There was little Disney could do other than revive both Davy and Russel in adventures purported to be based on the *legend* rather than the life of Davy Crockett.

Two more hour-long Crockett stories were shown on *Disneyland*. The first of these, "Davy Crockett's Keelboat Race," pitted Davy and Georgie against the boastful riverboat captain Mike Fink (Jeff York). Davy barely won the keelboat race to New Orleans thanks to Mike's sabotage. But Mike eventually found himself the loser and eating his hat. The second story, "Davy Crockett and the River Pirates," had Davy and Mike the best of friends, mutual enemies of a gang of water-bound thieves. These two films were combined and released to theaters as a full-length movie, *Davy Crockett and the River Pirates*, but hardly with the popularity of its predecessor.

The Davy Crockett fad was mysteriously disintegrating almost as fast as it had come. Fess Parker felt somewhat relieved that Davy was no longer the national hero he once was. He was already terribly typecast as the King of the Wild Frontier. If he didn't get different parts soon he might find his career at a premature end. The actor presently starred in non-Crockett Disney films, *The Great Locomotive Chase, The Light in the Forest,* and *Westward Ho the Wagons!* but soon learned that the typecasting had already done its damage. For years no one seemed to hear of Fess Parker, except in reruns of the Davy Crockett episodes on Disney's subsequent television shows, *Walt Disney Presents* and *Walt Disney's Wonderful World of Color.* In the 1960s, when *Batman* was attempting to capture its own mass audience on television, Parker decided it was more profitable to capitalize on his old image by starring in a Davy Crockett television series. But Disney still owned the television rights to the character. Changing the format of the series to *Daniel Boone,* Parker put on his buckskins and coonskin cap and re-created his Crockett characterization. Only the name was different. Again there was frontier merchandise and again Fess Parker was a star.

Walt Disney tried to recapture the audience that had accepted and finally turned away from Davy Crockett. He introduced "Texas John Slaughter" (starring Tom Tryon) and other heroes on *Disneyland,* none of which ever attained fad status.

On October 4, 1955, the Monday-through-Friday *Mickey Mouse Club* premiered on ABC. The show featured the talented Mouseketeers and their adult leader Jimmy Dodd in a variety show for children. But the songs and cartoons never achieved the popularity of one of the programs many serials, "The Adventures of Spin and Marty," about life on a boy's ranch. Still, only a minor fad arose with the *Mickey Mouse Club,* the most significant aspect being the sale of Mouseketeer ears, worn like a cap, and sold to this day even though the program has been off the air for a number of years.

Disney's final attempt at creating another full-fledged craze was in his television series *Zorro,* which debuted on ABC in 1957. Guy Williams played the swashbuckling masked avenger and once again Disney enjoyed another fad. Zorro merchandise began to sell and sell, but still in no way approaching the success of Davy Crockett. *Zorro* lasted only through 1958, when it had long been obvious that a new type of hero had taken the place of Davy Crockett. He was a young man, also from Tennessee, with long sideburns, swivel hips and a guitar.

As for Walt Disney, he realized that there would never be another King of the Wild Frontier.

CHAPTER 9

Wacky Wives, Bumbling Hubbies and Con Men

Lucy and Ricky

Monday nights in the early fifties belonged to Lucy. Nearly every owner of a television set in those formative days of the medium watched her on the CBS network at 9 P.M. EST. Lucy was really the attractive red-haired actress and comedienne Lucille Ball, whose weekly situation comedy was the most popular and best-loved show in the history of television. The name of the show was *I Love Lucy*. And although the "I" of the title specifically referred to Lucy's husband Ricky Ricardo, a handsome Cuban band leader and singer played by Ms. Ball's real-life husband Desi Arnaz, it most certainly could have applied to a veritable nation of television set owners. Everyone loved Lucy.

I Love Lucy was the original television situation comedy as we know it today. Most of those that followed owed much of their format and style to this progenitor series. Ricky was a successful Latin night club entertainer and his life would hardly have been complicated if it had not been for his zany wife Lucy. Her schemes, some of which got her into the most impossible of situations, were always well intentioned. Yet their often disastrous and always hilarious results would send Ricky into hysterics, firing off Cuban dialogue perhaps best left untranslated.

The Ricardos lived in a modest apartment in New York City. Their landlords and closest friends were Fred and Ethel Mertz, played respectively by bald and pudgy William Frawley and by Vivian Vance. Ethel was always cajoled by Lucy into becoming an accomplice in her often bizarre machinations, while Fred would side with Ricky to turn the tables and teach the scatterbrained redhead a well-deserved lesson.

The *I Love Lucy* pilot film was shot in 1951 under the auspices of the Desilu Corporation, the new company formed by the husband-and-wife team. There was little difficulty in getting the series sold to a sponsor, a cigarette manufacturer. Desi handled most of the production aspects of the new series.

The filming of *I Love Lucy* was unlike that of most subsequent situation comedies. Each episode was shot, not in the myriad segments so typical of feature-length motion pictures and most television films, but in long continuous "acts" in the fashion of a stage play. Three cameras recorded the action while a live studio audience watching the performers from bleachers on the set provided the laughter. Most likely the action, when seen in the living room, aroused as much laughter from the viewers at home.

The premiere of *I Love Lucy* was on the Monday evening of October 15, 1951. The first installment set the format for the rest of the series, showing Ricky at work with his band and singing his hit song "Babalu" and with Lucy attempting to perform in her husband's show. Both characters were firmly established right from the beginning, with Lucy receiving a flat refusal from her husband, who always thought he knew what was best. Naturally Lucy would not accept so ignoble a defeat. Disguising herself as an Emmett Kelly-style clown, she surreptitiously entered Ricky's night club, the Tropicana, and successfully performed her entire act, proving her talents as a mime and a comic. Most episodes, however, would not culminate with such victory.

On Tuesday, October 16, it seemed everyone who had watched the premiere episode was talking about the Ricardos. Almost instantaneously *I Love Lucy* had become the most watched program on the video waves. Lucy and Ricky were not merely characters in a domestic comedy. They were real, they were loved. During the early months of the series they would become an American institution. *I Love Lucy* was to television what *Amos 'n' Andy* was to radio. During the 1930s motion picture theater managers were forced to stop the film during the half hour that *Amos 'n' Andy* came on the air, piping the radio program through the loudspeaker system. So it was with *I Love Lucy*. Public reaction to the show was astounding, as chronicled by Tedd Thomey in his book *The Glorious Decade*, which was published in 1971 by Ace Books:

> . . . The Lucy Mania was so widespread that it created such phenomena as the following:

PTA leaders in Lynn, Massachusetts, demanded that the town's TV outlet broadcast the program earlier so school children could get to bed. The huge Marshall Field department store in Chicago issued a bulletin declaring closing time would occur an hour earlier on Mondays so customers and employees could get home in time to watch the show. Members of a Lions Club in Santa Barbara, California, bought a TV set and installed it in their meeting room, declaring a half-hour recess so everybody could watch. Doctors and dentists in many cities changed their evening hours to prevent cancellation of appointments by Lucy fans.

How does one account for the overnight success of a situation comedy? We might state simply that *I Love Lucy* was a *quality* show, with many elements adding to the over-all magnificence of the series which were never duplicated in the same combination in any situation comedy that followed.

First of all, the writing is proof that television does not have to be the generally mediocre medium it is today. The *I Love Lucy* scripts were written to be quite visual, affording Lucille Ball the opportunity to demonstrate her great talents for comedy. Unlike some of the more "relevant" situation comedies of today, the conflicts between Ricky and his wacky spouse were written with love. Ricky would fume with anger and puff out his cheeks over Lucy's outrageous actions but the anger always subsided to be replaced by a warm smile and a firm hug. The scripts were also designed so that the pacing of each episode would increase as each story progressed. By the end of an *I Love Lucy* installment, the well-meaning yet unfortunate redhead was usually totally engrossed in some fast-paced action routine from which she seemed doomed never to emerge unscathed.

When considering the merits of *I Love Lucy* we should also note that Ms. Ball's comic antics were enhanced by the performances of the other regulars on the program. Desi Arnaz proved that he could be more than a straight man for Lucy's gags and emerged as quite a capable comedian himself. Lucy's zaniness and Desi's Latin temperament played well alongside the American humor of William Frawley and Vivian Vance. The teaming of these four performers worked with unquestionable harmony. As later years have proven, all four of them were somehow necessary for the magic generated by *I Love Lucy*.

Much of the humor of *I Love Lucy* evolved from Lucy's managing innocently to make some drastic mistake. In order to correct her original error, the redhead would make another . . . and then another, apparently ad infinitum, until she found herself in some outrageous situation from which there seemed to be no escape. Reminiscing in the March 31, 1973, issue of *TV Guide,* Lucille Ball said that three of her favorite *I Love Lucy* episodes involved her battles with objects. In one episode Lucy attempted to stomp grapes in a large barrel and nearly drowned in the process. Another episode, in which the Ricardos and the Mertzes pooled their money to purchase a walk-in freezer, climaxed with the hapless Lucy being frozen solid. The third episode utilized a routine also employed on numerous occasions by Jackie Gleason on his weekly variety program.

The show was entitled "Job Switchers," written by Madlyn Pugh, Robert Carroll, Jr., and producer Jess Oppenheimer. In desperate need of money, Lucy pawned Ricky's drums. To get back the drums she wrote a rubber check. One problem followed another until the inevitable war of Ricky and Fred against Lucy and Ethel got under way. The final solution seemed to be the girls' acquiring jobs in a candy factory. Lucy's task was similar to that shared by other comics in early television, including Jackie Gleason's Poor Soul. She was confronted with that veritable mechanical monster of early television comedy, the conveyor belt. Lucy was to remove the candy cream centers from the efficiently moving conveyor belt and then, in a series of operations using her hands, produce a finished piece of candy. It was woman vs. machine with the latter having the advantage. An interfering fly buzzing into the room augmented Lucy's problems as she continued trying to cope with the never slowing conveyor belt. The program climaxed with an eruption of chocolate and Lucy's dismissal from the job.

Lucille Ball's favorite comedy routine was in an *I Love Lucy* episode in which the star-struck Mrs. Ricardo happened to meet motion picture actor William Holden. The meeting was by chance in a restaurant where she somehow managed to spill a plate of spaghetti over his head. Later Ricky told her that Holden would soon be coming over to their apartment to discuss business. When Holden arrived, Lucy was there alone, awaiting him. Naturally Lucy could not let Holden know that Ricky's wife was the same clumsy person whom he had encountered in the restaurant. Lucy's mind worked in its usual unpredictable fashion. Disguising herself with a phony nose, she invited Holden into the apartment. The scene went according to the script until Lucy casually lit her cigarette. The following action was *not* in the script. The flames from Lucy's cigarette lighter accidentally set fire to the fake nose. Another performer would probably have yelled "Cut!" But the resourceful Lucille Ball nonchalantly removed the nose, extinguished it in her coffee cup, then replaced the burned proboscis.

In one historic *I Love Lucy* episode of 1952, Lucy discussed her bewilderment with Ethel.

ETHEL: Good morning, Lucy.

LUCY: Oh, hi, Ethel.

ETHEL: Where are you goin' so early?

LUCY: Oh, I thought I'd go down see the doctor.

ETHEL: What's the matter, honey? Are you sick?

LUCY: No, I just want to get a checkup. I need a tonic or something. I've been feeling real dauncey.

ETHEL: Dauncey?

LUCY: Yeah, that's a word my grandmother made up for when you're not really sick but you just feel lousy.

ETHEL: Oh.

LUCY: I don't know what's the matter with me. I've been getting a lot of rest and then I wake up feeling all dragged out in the morning. I don't have much energy and yet I've been putting on a lot of weight. I just feel blah!

ETHEL: Well, maybe you need some vitamin pills or a liver shot or somethin'.

Lucy then told Ethel not to tell Ricky. There was no need of his worrying over what might prove to be nothing. But then Lucy said something that made Ethel's eyes widen with awareness.

LUCY: Gee, I'm gonna have to go on a diet. You know I could hardly get into my dress this morning?

ETHEL: Hey, Lucy, wait a minute. You don't suppose . . . ?

LUCY: I don't suppose what?

ETHEL: You don't suppose you're gonna have a baby?

LUCY: Oh, of course not. (*Long pause.*) A *baby?!*

ETHEL: Yeah, baby. That's the word my grandmother made up for tiny little people.

When Lucy came back from her doctor's examination she was dreamy-eyed and speechless. Finally Ethel managed to get her to reveal the truth. Yes, Lucy and Ricky Ricardo were going to be parents. But Lucy Ricardo's pregnancy had particular significance to the television couple's fans. For in real life Lucille Ball was going to have a baby.

When Desi Arnaz first learned that his wife was pregnant he immediately considered taking her out of the show for the season. Then his mind began to consider the possibilities. A virtual nation of television viewers loved the Ricardos and religiously followed their adventures every week. Why not keep Lucy on the show, he thought, letting Mrs. Ricardo also become pregnant? This opened the show to all new subjects for comedy. And the fans could empathize with her until the moment that her child was born. A priest, a minister and a rabbi were called down to the Desilu studios and agreed with Desi's decision. In those days of television, pregnant women simply were not put before the cameras. Lucy was to establish a precedent. Yet the medium was not yet mature enough to allow the word "pregnant" to be used.

On that classic episode in which Lucy learned of her pregnancy, she attempted to give Ricky the blessed information as romantically as possible. But Ricky came home from the Tropicana in a bad mood. Nothing had gone right for the Cuban band leader at rehearsal. To further complicate the delicate situation, Lucy's every attempt to speak to her husband was interrupted by the ring of the telephone.

RICKY: Oh, what a business. Sometimes I think I go back to Cuba and work in a sugar plantation. Just the two of us.
LUCY: Just the two of us?
RICKY: Yeah. I don' mind to get you all involved in my affairs, but you should be happy you're a woman.
LUCY: Oh, I am, I am!
RICKY: You think you know how tough my job is, but believe me, if you traded places with me . . . you'd be surprised.
LUCY: Believe me, if I traded places with you, *you'd* be surprised.
RICKY: Now, honey, what's this all about? What's the matter?
LUCY: Nothing, dear. I just love you, that's all.
RICKY: Oh, oh. . . . How much are you overdrawn?
LUCY: I am not overdrawn. I want to tell you something.
RICKY: Lucy, what did you buy?
LUCY: Nothing! Ricky darling . . .
    (*Doorbell rings.*) Oh, I'll get it!

There was no getting through to Ricky, and so the Lucy Ricardo mind began to click in its own unusual manner. Lucy's only recourse was to surprise Ricky with the information that night during his performance at the Tropicana.

During Ricky's performance, a page handed him a message written by someone in the audience who wanted to tell her husband that she was pregnant through Ricky's singing "We're Having a Baby, My Baby and Me." Ricky went about the various tables, first singing "Rock-a-bye Baby." When he came to Lucy's table, the importance of her being there did not register at first. When the realization finally struck him he exploded with joy and eventually broke into the requested song. Desi Arnaz was so moved by the significance of the scene that he began to shed real tears before the cameras.

The Arnazes predetermined the sex of the Ricardos' child. He would be a boy whose fictional name would be Ricky Ricardo, Jr., or more affectionately, "Little Ricky." Such predetermination was not possible, however, in real life.

Lucille Ball was taken to the hospital for her delivery on January 19, 1953. The television episode in which Lucy gave birth to her child was scheduled to be broadcast that same day. That single installment of a situation comedy was watched by more hopeful viewers than any other program up until then.

The Ricardos and the Mertzes had planned well for the moment when Lucy would emerge from the bedroom and say, as Ricky spoke it with his Cuban accent, "Da time has come." It was then Ethel's task to telephone the hospital, Fred's job to hail a cab, while Ricky casually escorted his wife out the door. Everything was rehearsed with the precision of an army drill. Yet when Lucy finally staggered into the living room and said that she was ready, chaos broke loose. Remarkably, the insanely nervous trio managed to get Lucy to the hospital.

Ricky was performing a voodoo number at the Tropicana when he received the news that his baby had been born. Still wearing the hideous make-up and garb of a voodoo high priest, including fangs and a wild fright wig, Ricky rushed to the hospital, nearly getting arrested for disturbing the peace. At last his infant son was revealed to him through the glass. The mighty voodoo priest's eyes glowed. Then he fell backward into unconsciousness.

The front page of almost every American newspaper carried the real story of Lucille Ball's baby the next morning. Just like her television counterpart, she had given birth to a boy, Desiderio Alberto Arnaz IV. The baby's photograph graced the cover of the very first issue of *TV Guide*. Other major magazines also contested for pictures of the eight-pound, nine-ounce celebrity. The real-life Desi Arnaz, Jr., never appeared on a *Lucy* program until he was a grown man.

In the comic-book medium there is the situation of the "crossover," or the appearance of one character in another character's strip. Such was the case in one of Lucy's more offbeat adventures, in which Lucy meets Superman. As was often the case after his arrival, Little Ricky provided the springboard for Lucy's antics.

The appearance of television's Superman, as played by George

Reeves, was handled with delicacy on *I Love Lucy*. The episode was written so that the adults would know that this was actually Reeves on a personal-appearance tour. But the name of the actor was never mentioned and Superman was portrayed *as* Superman so as not to disappoint the younger viewers and to maintain the credibility of the superhuman character.

The episode began with the friendly rivalry between the Ricardos and their friends the Applegates over their young sons. When both mothers scheduled birthday parties for their sons on the same day, and when Carolyn also invited a clown, a magician and a puppeteer, Lucy retaliated by saying that Superman, who was in New York making an appearance at Macy's department store, would fly into Little Ricky's party. Ricky, Sr., promised to try to secure the Man of Steel for his son's party. But when other commitments prevented Superman from remaining in New York, Lucy, not wanting to disappoint her little boy, donned a Superman costume and football helmet (to hide her red hair) and climbed out on the window ledge overlooking the city. At the proper moment she was to leap into the room, run about and make a quick exit before anyone realized the chicanery. With the usual twists of events, Superman was able to make a last-minute appearance at Little Ricky's party, performing his famous landing into the living room. Lucy, meanwhile, became stuck on the ledge, her cape caught in a gutter, and the window locked from the inside. To top it off, rain began to pour upon her. After the party Ethel finally remembered that Lucy was out on the ledge.

RICKY (*excitedly*): Oh, my goodness! Lucy, are you all right?
LUCY: I'm caught!!
RICKY: Wait! Don't move, honey! I'll come and get you right away! Wait a minute!
LITTLE RICKY: No, Daddy! Let Superman do it.
RICKY: All right.
SUPERMAN: Allow me.

Superman grasped the piano, rolling it aside with ease. Then he sprang out onto the window ledge and into the drenching rain, working his way over to the soaked woman in similar costume. Seeing the Man of Steel, Lucy reacted with shock.

LUCY: Oh!!
SUPERMAN: How do you do? My name is Superman.
LUCY: Oh, am I glad to see you. Tell me, when you're flying around do you have cape trouble?
SUPERMAN: No, but then I've had a lot more flying time than you have.

The Man of Steel took Lucy by the hand as Ricky shouted that this was the craziest stunt she had performed in all their fifteen years of marriage. "You mean to say that you've been married to her for fifteen years?" asked Superman incredulously. "And they call *me* Superman!"

I Love Lucy held the top ratings for five years, during which time it won a number of awards, including a few Emmies. The series remained on the air until June 24, 1957. The Arnazes wanted to experiment with an hour-long format and on November 16 of that year premiered their new series, *The Lucille Ball-Desi Arnaz Show.* This was the expanded version of *I Love Lucy* with an impressive roll call of guest stars. On October 6, 1958, the husband-and-wife team began *The Westinghouse Desilu Playhouse.* This was essentially a dramatic anthology show hosted by Desi with the Ricardos appearing about once every month.

The loving image of Lucy and Ricky Ricardo was so much a part of the American people that no one suspected that beneath the happy exterior of their public image the Arnazes' marriage was disintegrating. Ever growing conflicts between Lucille and Desi eventually culminated in the one action which their adoring fans could barely accept. Lucille Ball and Desi Arnaz, long regarded as the perfect American couple, finalized their divorce. Desilu, the multimillion-dollar corporation which eventually had produced myriad series for television, became the property of Lucille Ball. Six years after her divorce Ms. Ball, disenchanted with her role of tycoon, sold the company to Paramount for $17,000,000.

Lucille Ball returned to television in a number of series which were basically in the style of *I Love Lucy.* Yet despite her talents and energies and appearances by veteran Vivian Vance, these new programs, popular though they all were, never completely recaptured the magic of the original. *I Love Lucy* is still rerun in numerous cities, and each episode is still as funny as it was in the 1950s. An entire new generation along with those of us with fond memories of Lucy and Ricky Ricardo can experience the warm humor of the greatest of all television situation comedies.

The Other Families

While many of the situation comedies of the fifties, sixties and seventies would owe much of their humor to *I Love Lucy,* the adventures of the Ricardos was not the very first domestic comedy to be made for the small living-room screen. *Mama* debuted on CBS-TV on July 1, 1949, and established the style of the gentle comedy show centering upon a family. This series about the Hansens, a family of Norwegian immigrants living in San Francisco during the early 1900s, was based on the book *Mama's Bank Account,* which eventually became a stage play and later a motion picture, both entitled *I Remember Mama.* The television family consisted of "Papa" Lars Hansen, a stern carpenter portrayed by Judson Laire, his son Nels played by Dick Van Patten, the older sister Katrin played by Rosemary Rice and the impish little sister Dagmar, portrayed by Robin Morgan. In the role of Mama herself was blonde and maturely beautiful Peggy Wood.

Unlike *I Love Lucy,* which was filmed, *Mama* was telecast live every Friday evening. Each episode opened with Katrin's hand opening up the old family picture album. We heard her voice as she paused over the photographs of the various members of her immediate family. "I remember my brother Nels," she would say, following with a few words describing him. Then she would proceed with, "And my little sister Dagmar. And, of course, Papa. But most of all, I remember Mama." The introduction established the mood for the rest of the program. The stories were anything but controversial, with the Americanized Hansen children sometimes confounding Mama and Papa, still accustomed to the ways of the Old Country.

In one particular episode Dagmar was faced wth the problem of wearing braces on her teeth. The situation naturally made the young girl quite self-conscious. Nels hardly helped matters when he burst into laughter and teased, "You look like you swallowed a mousetrap and it didn't go all the way down!" Dagmar cried and decided to become a hermit until her teeth had straightened out. But, as always, Mama's warm advice gave her the confidence she needed to ignore Nels's derision.

The Hansen children were the only members of the family who learned to pronounce their Js correctly. The older-generation Hansens were the stereotyped Scandinavians. Thus the children's busybody Aunt Jenny (Ruth Gates) became "Yenny" to Mama and Papa. Mama's and Papa's inability to pronounce their Js, however, was not used as a comic device, as in the cliché figure of the "Yumpin' Yiminy Yanitor" which has been so prevalent in television and other media. They merely spoke that way and nothing more was made of the fact. When Aunt Jenny offered some bit of advice instructing Lars about how he should discipline his children, he would almost invariably reply, "Ya, Yenny," and let her continue talking.

One episode of *Mama* had Papa in his workshop, banging away at a secret invention that he had been developing for months. Mama and the children waited breathlessly for him to emerge from the room and unveil some marvelous device. How disappointed they were when Papa's invention proved to be a two-headed nail which would allow a carpenter to remove it easily from a section of wood if he had somehow made a mistake. Papa himself was even more disappointed than his family when he took his prized invention to the patent office and discovered that the two-headed nail had already been invented and on the market for years.

One particular episode of *Mama* became a classic in its own time and was performed once every year. "The Night the Animals Talked" was the program's special Christmas fantasy. The story revolved around Papa's telling Dagmar that every Christmas night animals were given the ability to speak as a reward for the all-night vigil of the beasts that witnessed the birth of the Christ child in Bethlehem two thousand years ago. Dagmar would then go out to the barn and await the conversations of the Hansens' animals. But the longer Dagmar waited the more tired she became. Eventually she fell asleep. When she awoke again she heard the animals talking. No one really believed her, of course, except the people watching the program on their home sets.

On July 27, 1956, *Mama* was canceled. But Mama and her family had so endeared themselves to the television audience that CBS was soon deluged with letters and telephone calls protesting the cancellation of the show. Newspapers and magazines carried editorials requesting that the program be reinstated. For once a major network succumbed to the demands of its public. A new filmed version of *Mama,* with Toni Campbell replacing the maturing Robin Morgan as Dagmar, debuted December 16, 1956, and remained on the air until March 17, 1957.

Lucy may have proved that wives can be wacky. But the majority of situation comedies that followed would have appeased the women's liberationists of today. In the early fifties it was usually the bumbling husband who caused all the trouble and who required rescuing by his intelligent and tolerant wife.

The Trouble with Father premiered in 1951, the same year as *I Love Lucy,* and starred another real-life married couple, June (Collyer) and Stu Erwin. Stu (both he and his wife retained their real names on the show) was the principal of a high school.

The Erwins had two daughters, typical teen-ager Joyce and the younger Jackie. Joyce attended her father's high school. But most of her attention was centered not on her studies but upon her romance with letter man Drexel Potter (Martin Milner), the not too bright star athlete of the high school.

Jackie, on the other hand, was an organizer. With the aid of the Erwin handy man Willie (played by black comedian Willie Best in the type of character he had enacted for years in motion pictures) Jackie concocted all manner of schemes, most of which involved her lovable yet bumbling father. It was Stu who became the brunt of Jackie's inventive endeavors, as when she decided to write a revealing novel in which her family, neighbors Harry and Adelle Johnson, and Stu's boss, the blowhard Mr. Selkirk, were all characters. Jackie had portrayed all of them as animals in a fantasy world called "Lamina Land" ("animal" spelled backward). When Stu blundered into problem situations on his own (or with the help of Willie) it was often Jackie who attempted to rescue her hapless dad. Yet it was still June who most often provided the comforting for Stu in his time of need, as when he and Willie decided to surprise her by cooking a roast and nearly set fire to the kitchen.

Willie's role was not reduced to the shiftless image established on the screen by black comedian Stepin Fetchit, yet he still retained the stereotyped characterization so detested by today's black community. When Willie became frightened his eyes would bulge large and his lower jaw would hang open. Negro performers were still new to early television and if they appeared at all in any capacity other than that of a music or sports celebrity it was in this image.

Less bumbling than Stu Erwin was Ozzie Nelson on *The Adventures of Ozzie and Harriet,* which began on October 10, 1952, on ABC-TV. Ozzie and his wife Harriet (Hilliard) had enjoyed a successful radio series which presented perhaps the most domestic of all the situation comedies. On television the husband-and-wife team, always playing themselves, brought humor to everyday living. But most of the comedy centered upon their sons, David and the younger and ubiquitous Ricky. No member of the Nelson family was a professional actor and therefore the dialogue was kept simple. A typical early episode of the show found Ozzie and Harriet overestimating the seriousness of David's dinner engagement with a young girl.

HARRIET: He's eating dinner at her house tonight.

OZZIE: I know—you said so. That doesn't mean he's going to marry her. After all, I ate dinner at your house lots of times . . .

HARRIET: Well?

OZZIE: Well, it was just that your mother was such a good cook.

HARRIET: You didn't marry her.

OZZIE: Well, no—she wasn't available at the time. . . . I was engaged to you. . . . Well, I don't think there's anything to worry about. David's too young to get married.

HARRIET: We were pretty young when we got married. In fact, we get younger every time you tell about it.

When Ricky entered the room with the usual blank look on his lean face, he failed to ease the minds of his parents over the matter.

RICKY: Is this all right?

OZZIE: What's that supposed to be?

RICKY: Mom told me to put on a tie.

OZZIE: Yeah, I know—but she told you to put on a shirt, too.

RICKY: This is a shirt—a sweat shirt.

HARRIET: Where are you eating dinner—at the gym?

RICKY: I thought that was too clever for David to think up.

OZZIE: You see, Harriet, you're worried about the boys getting married and they can't even dress themselves.

RICKY: Who's getting married?

OZZIE: David . . . that is, your mother is worried about his getting married.

RICKY: What's the matter, Mom? Don't you like Susan?

HARRIET: Who told you about Susan?

RICKY: David.

HARRIET: Oh? (*She looks at Ozzie O.S.*)

RICKY: I wouldn't mind having her for a sister-in-law. Sure—then if they had any children, they'd be my nephews and nieces. I think Uncle Ricky'll put on a shirt after all.

Simple situations such as these, which could befall any of us, and the very natural acting of the Nelsons helped make the show one of the most popular and long-running of all situation comedies. Viewers frequently wondered just what Ozzie did to maintain the attractive home in which his family lived. Ozzie was always home, puttering around the house or engaging in uninspired conversation. Apparently he was unemployed. What the television program failed to bring to light was the fact that on radio Ozzie's profession was the same as in real life: a band leader, now retired.

As the series continued year after year the boys, especially Ricky, became the real stars. The lanky and now seventeen-year-old Ricky, whose full name was Eric Hilliard Nelson, was prominently featured in the episode of April 10, 1957, entitled "Ricky the Drummer." Ricky appeared as a rock 'n' roll singer and performed an emotionless rendition of Fats Domino's million-selling hit "I'm Walkin'." The morning after the telecast of this episode Ricky was a teen-age idol, maintaining the same style of singing through an impressive list of rock 'n' roll hits. The television show began to introduce Ricky's latest records, while the record-buying teen-agers boosted the ratings of the TV series. Certainly this was an ideal publicity situation.

The Adventures of Ozzie and Harriet, mainly following the adventures of the married David and Ricky and their wives, continued into the early 1960s, when it left the air. In 1973, Ozzie and Harriet returned, *sans* their two sons, in a new series which continued from the old. It was entitled *Ozzie's Girls* and concerned two coeds who rented David's and Ricky's old room, proving that the Nelsons are always welcome in our living rooms.

My Little Margie premiered on June 16 of the same year that brought Ozzie and Harriet to television. Perky Gale Storm was approached by sponsor Philip Morris to star in this summer replacement for *I Love Lucy.* A pilot film was never made. Little Johnny, attired in his bellhop's uniform, merely exclaimed his famous, "Call . . . for . . . Philip . . . Mooorrrraaaaiiisss!" and the first episode went on the air.

Margie Albright was almost as zany as Lucy Ricardo in the weird schemes hatched in her clever mind. These ploys nearly always got her father Vern Albright (played by former matinee idol Charles Farrell) into trouble with his boss, Mr. Honeywell, one of the top executives of the advertising firm of Honeywell and Todd. Margie's antics would often get the hapless Vern into such pitfalls that the pompous Mr. Honeywell would puff, "Albright, this is the last straw! You're *fired!*"

Margie occasionally hatched her schemes with the aid of Mrs. Odetts, the alert old lady who lived down the hall from the Albrights.

MRS. ODETTS: Yoo-hoo! Margie!

MARGIE: Come on in, Mrs. Odetts.

MRS. ODETTS (*entering*): Hi, honey.

MARGIE: Hi, Mrs. Odetts.

MRS. ODETTS: I thought I'd just drop over and see what you were doing that your father says you shouldn't.

MARGIE: Mrs. Odetts, I told you I'm not disobeying my father any more.

MRS. ODETTS: You're not really serious? If you're going to be obedient, what are we going to do for *kicks* around here?

No, Margie could not keep her promise. And before the half-hour episode had ended Vern was in as much trouble as always with Honeywell and Todd. When Margie realized that she had overblown the situation beyond the point of credibility and there was little chance that the problems would right themselves, she would turn directly to the camera and trill, "G-g-g-r-r-r-r-r. . . ." Yet despite Vern's infuriation with his daughter, every episode would end happily with both of them appearing as a photograph in a frame. Their images would come to life, Margie would explain the reasons for her strange behavior and Vern would conclude with a smile, "Well, that's my little Margie!"

My Little Margie was castigated by the critics right from the initial telecast. The show was branded as being inane and not funny and an insult to the intelligence of the viewers. The fact that the show was virtually slapped together after two weeks' notice that it was going on the air did not matter. The viewers, on the other hand, whose intelligence had supposedly been insulted, loved the show and supported it. Before many episodes were telecast *My Little Margie* had taken third place in the national ratings. In a kind of reverse situation the series later became a radio program. On radio *My Little Margie* reached the top ten, bypassing in the ratings game *Fibber McGee and Molly, Bob Hope* and *Jack Benny*. To this day *My Little Margie* is snubbed as one of early television's poorer efforts, and that criticism is not entirely unjust. But it was watched regularly in reruns for years after it officially ended on July 30, 1953.

The most lovable bumbling father of early television was Chester A. Riley on the NBC series *The Life of Riley*. Originally, when the series debuted on October 4, 1949, Jackie Gleason portrayed Riley while Rosemary DeCamp played his wife Peg. But Gleason's and DeCamp's version of the series was not well received and is almost forgotten. The second attempt at *The Life of Riley* was an immediate success after its premiere on January 2, 1953. William Bendix, the original Riley on radio, long predating the Gleason TV version, was now Chester A. Riley on television as well. He was also familiar to motion picture audiences for a number of impressive roles, usually as a tough all-American sort of guy. Bendix was accepted by the public from the start and seemed to have been born for the role. In fact, so busy was Bendix in his new television position that he proceeded to cancel his motion picture contract in order to devote all his energies to *The Life of Riley*.

Chester A. Riley was an employee of a large aircraft company. His fellow employee and best pal Gillis, played by Tom D'Andrea, was a bit smarter than "Rile" (as Gillis called him). Riley's gullibility often set him at odds with his wife Peg (Marjorie Reynolds) and his son Junior (Wesley Morgan) before the usual happy ending in which everything returned to normal.

In one episode Riley eavesdropped on his neighbors, Gillis and his wife Honeybee (Joan Blondell). The Gillises were in the midst of a searing battle of the sexes. When Riley peered over the fence for a better look, he received in his face a wad of wet clothes which Honeybee had intended for her husband.

RILEY: What an arm on that Honeybee. She ought to be pitchin' for the Dodgers!
PEG: It serves you right for being so nosy.
RILEY: You want to know what they were fighting about?
PEG: Definitely not. What goes on between the Gillises is none of our business whatsoever.
RILEY (can't stand it any longer): Y'sure you don't want to know what they were fightin' about.
PEG: Absolutely not.
RILEY: Okay—then I won't tell you.
PEG (after pause): Riley—what were they fighting about?

The Gillises had been arguing over their trip to Portland. After Gillis and Honeybee finally stopped their bickering, they came over to see Riley. It was to be Riley's task to guard the Gillises' house while they were on vacation.

GILLIS: Just take care of our mail, Rile, that's all.
RILEY: Leave it to me. I'll take as good care of your house as I do my own.
HONEYBEE (aside): That does it. Let's call off the trip.
GILLIS: Now, Honeybee! What could Riley possibly do to our house?
HONEYBEE: You wouldn't think a couple of termites could eat half our porch but they did. And Riley's bigger than they are.

Chester A. Riley was the image of the typical 1950s American, albeit without the brains of most. He liked nothing better than to watch the ball games on television with a nice cold beer. Perhaps he was an innocent and endearing prototype of today's Archie Bunker. In those days when Communists were supposedly hiding in every shadow, anyone who didn't like such a complete American as Chester A. Riley simply was not a good American. The series continued for a prosperous five years until its cancellation in August 22, 1958.

Make Room for Daddy, which premiered on ABC-TV on September 29, 1953, was one of the early shows produced by Lucille Ball and Desi Arnaz' company Desilu. The theme song of the program was appropriately "Danny Boy" since it starred entertainer Danny Thomas as night club singer Danny Williams. Make Room for Daddy did not feature a stupid father, although Danny did manage to encounter countless humorous problems. Usually Danny's troubles focused upon his job forcing him to stay away from his family, which consisted of his wife Margaret (Jean Hagen), his daughter Terry (Sherry Jackson) and little son Rusty (Rusty Hamer). The theme closely paralleled his off-screen life; the warmth that Thomas conveyed in his role of Danny Williams consequently seemed real and was experienced by everyone watching the program at home. The Williamses were another ideal television family, though they still had their problems. Often Danny found himself the target of a three-person attack by his wife and children, as when Margaret was trying to impress her husband with her new hairdo.

MARGARET: Victor is not just a hairdresser. He's an artist. Haven't you noticed what he's done with my hair?
DANNY: It looks the same to me.
MARGARET: Everybody talks about it. They say it's never looked lovelier. People say to me, "Margaret, I've never seen your hair so beautiful."
DANNY: Name me one people who said that. (*Terry enters from living room.*) Hi, sweetheart.
TERRY: Mother!
MARGARET: What?
TERRY: I've never seen your hair looking so beautiful.

Danny began to suspect that a plot had been launched against him when his red-haired son Rusty, always quick with a wise remark, entered the room.

RUSTY: Mother, I've never seen your hair looking so lovely.
MARGARET: Thank you, thank you very much.
RUSTY: It's a regular knockout.
MARGARET: That's sweet of you to say so. Run along, dear.
RUSTY: No, really, I've never seen your hair look so lovely.
(*Margaret looks uncomfortable at this.*)
MARGARET: Run along, dear. Help your sister set the table.
(*Terry enters.*)
TERRY: Mother, I just can't get over the way your hair looks. It's beautiful.
RUSTY: Yeah, it's so chic.
DANNY: All right. All right. That's enough. Now, what's with this hair routine?
RUSTY: Haven't you tried to swing it yet, Mother?
DANNY: If there's going to be any swinging, I'm the one that's going to do it. All right, kids, get lost. I want to talk to your mother.
RUSTY: Do you think you can handle this alone, Mother?

MARGARET: I have a feeling I should have handled it alone from the beginning. You overplayed your parts.
TERRY: What did you expect for fifty cents—Lunt and Fontanne?
MARGARET: Get lost!

By anyone's standards the Williams kids could be considered brats for the way they spoke to their poor father. But the hugs and kisses they and Danny exchanged at the end of the shows atoned for giving their father headaches. *Make Room for Daddy* was one of television's more popular series and all of us loved the Williams family, snotty kids and all. It was a major television event when Jean Hagen, after portraying Margaret Williams for three seasons, left the role.

Danny Thomas was then faced with the problem of how to continue the popular series. Rather than merely substituting a new actress for the part of Margaret, Thomas decided upon a more logical solution. Sherry Jackson was maturing into a lovely young lady. Rusty Hamer was also getting older. The original format of the show, which included a very young Rusty, worked well. On October 1, 1956, the program received a new name: *The Danny Thomas Show*.

Other changes had been made. Danny was now a widower. He became engaged to a pretty Irish widow named Kathy (Marjorie Lord), who had a very young daughter named Linda (Angela Cartwright). Danny and Kathy inevitably married. Terry went off to school, leaving Rusty and Linda to enact the roles of Danny's sarcastic children. Danny's Lebanese personality contrasted with Kathy's fiery Irish personality. The series, though retaining the old format and energy, had been given something new. On October 7, 1957, *The Danny Thomas Show* was transferred to CBS, where it continued its long television run, occasionally guest-starring the medium's First Family, the Ricardos.

One episode had Danny trying to dissuade Kathy from attempting a career in show business.

DANNY: But you have no talent!
KATHY: *What?!*
DANNY: I didn't mean that! Don't get excited now. I just meant you have no theatrical talent.
KATHY: Well, let me tell you something, Mr. Smarty. You're skating on very thin ice. I haven't told you this before, but I've had offers to go into show business.
DANNY: To do what? Be the new Lassie? What offers have you had to go into show business? What a silly statement to make.
KATHY: I suppose you don't remember the party we went to with the people from the television agency last month?

DANNY: I remember it quite well, yes.

KATHY: Well, Stanley Cooper, the television producer, told me that I ought to be in television.

DANNY: Pure parlor talk, that's all.

KATHY: It was not parlor talk. You remember I was playing charades.

DANNY: I remember you playing charades.

KATHY: Well, when I acted out "see no evil, speak no evil," everyone was very impressed.

DANNY: How come nobody guessed it?

Kathy boasted that she could secure a job in show business and Danny dared her to proceed with her little plan. Naturally Kathy could not evade the dare. And naturally Danny could not let her get off without a lesson. Using his influence in the business, Danny arranged a screen test for Kathy in which she was subjected to every physical inconvenience the director could concoct. Eventually Kathy learned the truth about her husband's interference and her Irish blood almost exploded. Danny finally got her a small part in a real television commercial and the minimal taste of stardom immediately inflated her ego and her acting ambitions. Accepting his defeat, Danny put on Kathy's apron, a type of white flag in those days.

The joke about *Father Knows Best* when it was a radio program was that he *didn't* know best. On radio, insurance man Jim Anderson (played by genial Robert Young) was the typical bumbling hubbie who required the sensibility of his wife Margaret to bail him out of his jams. When *Father Knows Best* moved to television on the CBS network, October 3, 1954, Jim really *did* know best. Jane Wyatt portrayed Jim's wife, Elinor Donahue played his older daughter Betty, Billy Gray was his teen-age son Bud and Lauren Chapin played his younger daughter Cathy. The stories centered upon the problems indigenous to the various members of the Anderson family, many of which seemed impossible to solve until Father intervened with a warm piece of advice and encouragement that could obviate any problem. Jim was the ideal father, whether counseling Betty on her latest romance, advising Bud as to whether or not to enlist in the Air Force or helping Cathy compose a paper for school.

When the children's comments about old age began to gnaw at Jim and Margaret, they decided to recapture a bit of their youth by attending the reunion of Father's college graduation class of 1933. But even in their respective fraternity and sorority houses, the nostalgic couple could not escape the comments about their allegedly advanced age. Jim and Margaret were finally able to enjoy some privacy together on the university campus.

JIM: Remember the last time we sat here, Margaret?

MARGARET: It was the night before you graduated.

JIM: I remember you cried.

MARGARET: I know. I was a sophomore. I was afraid you wouldn't wait for me.

JIM: Well, it was a long three years.

MARGARET: Where does time go, Jim?

JIM: I don't know, honey. I only know it seems to go faster as we get older.

MARGARET: Would you like to be back in school again?

JIM: I suppose I would if it weren't for three reasons.

MARGARET: What are they?

JIM: A very noisy character by the name of Bud, an impressionable young lady who reminds me very much of her lovely mother . . .

MARGARET: And a little pixie by the name of Cathy.

JIM: No, Margaret, I like things just the way they are. Oh, youth is wonderful. But middle age has its compensations. (*Gong sounds steadily.*)

MARGARET: Eleven o'clock.

JIM: Eleven o'clock?

MARGARET: Does that bring back memories?

JIM: It certainly does! I've just upset the schedule of the entire fraternity house.

Father Knows Best was canceled by the sponsor on March 27, 1955, after which an outraged public demanded its reinstatement. The show returned by "popular demand" over NBC on August 31 of that same year. The Andersons are still popular on television reruns and somehow seem only slightly dated when viewed during our more sophisticated 1970s. Robert Young's portrayal of Jim Anderson is timeless even with two decades separating the program's initial run from today. Perhaps in these so-called enlightened times there remains that nostalgia for a simpler day when a father could indeed know best.

The Kingfish and the Sergeant

Television's *Amos 'n' Andy*, which debuted on June 28, 1951, was originally a popular radio program starring Freeman Gosden and Charles Correll. This team of white performers had a background of minstrel shows and were accustomed to the then common practice of Caucasians appearing in blackface to portray Negroes on the stage or in films.

Gosden and Correll created a set of lovable characters that everyone seemed to love, regardless of their race, in those innocent times.

There was Amos Jones, the epitome of all that was good in a human being. Amos was intelligent, honest and a down-to-earth family man. His partner, Andrew H. Brown, however, was a different matter altogether. Andy was shiftless, lazy and not very smart. Most of his energies seemed to be trained upon watching the gals and making feeble attempts at going after the fast buck. Andy was just not crooked enough and Amos was simply too naïve and wholesome to provide sufficient contrast between the two. A third character was then written into the story line and given the name of George Stevens, best known by his official title of "Kingfish." Stevens was the president of the local Harlem lodge of the Mystic Knights of the Sea. It was Kingfish's job to organize the club's various functions. But he liked collecting the dues most of all. For the Kingfish was an outright confidence man who would go to great lengths to make a dishonest dollar. The gullible Andy was usually the inadvertent supplier of those dollars. Kingfish was such a strong character that he eventually eased Amost out of the spotlight.

When *Amos 'n' Andy* moved over to television it was basically the adventures of Kingfish and Andy. Amos maintained his old job as a cab driver with the Fresh-Air Taxicab Company but his role on television was minimal. Although the voices of Freeman Gosden and Charles Correll did introduce the television espisodes, they did not appear in blackface for the new series. The cast of TV's *Amos 'n' Andy* were black actors who did their best to imitate the radio voices and Southern dialect. Amos was portrayed by Alvin Childress, who appears on occasion as the minister on the more recent, more "relevant" black comedy series *Sanford and Son*. Overweight Spencer Williams played the new Andy while the role of Kingfish was assigned to Tim Moore. Only Ernestine Wade, who on radio portrayed Sapphire, Kingfish's nagging wife who incessantly shrieked at her husband to get a job, carried her radio part over to television.

Kingfish's plots to swindle Andy were always outrageous in their execution. One time Stevens learned that Andy wanted to acquire a pilot's license and convinced him that he had the power to offer such a document providing certain requirements were fulfilled. Kingfish called Andy over to his office at the Mystic Knights of the Sea lodge hall and sat him in a chair, giving him a stick, like the type in a plane cockpit, to grasp. This was in compliance with the regulation that an applicant for a pilot's license have a prescribed number of hours of solo flying. "You be flyin' so low you ain't even goin' to leave the ground," Kingfish told him with assurance. Stevens' scheme got out of hand, however, when a blindfolded Andy, trying to fulfill the "flying blind" requirement for the license, accidentally soared into the sky in a real plane.

One of the better episodes of television's *Amos 'n' Andy* was entitled "The Rare Coin." Amos, in the voice of Gosden, provided the opening narration after the fade-out of the show's perennial theme, "The Perfect Song."

AMOS: Ladies and gentlemen, this is Amos. I just want to tell you about somethin' that happened to my friends Andy and the Kingfish. Andy found a nickel in an old trunk. It was dated 1877. So Andy writ a letter to Mr. Wilson, a rare coin dealer, and right now Mr. Wilson is answerin' Andy's letter.

Mr. Wilson estimated the value of Andy's rare coin at $250 and immediately wrote him a letter of reply. But as usual, such an opportunity for Andy to make some unearned money was intercepted by the Kingfish, who got hold of Wilson's missive. Kingfish opened the letter and began to read. Then his eyes opened wide.

KINGFISH: Holy mackerel! Andy is got a nickel worth $250!
SAPPHIRE: George Stevens, it was bad enough openin' Andy's letter. You ain't thinkin' 'bout gyppin' him outa that coin, is you?
KINGFISH: Who, *me?* Innocent Stevens? Ha, ha, ha . . . I'll say I is!

The Kingfish had to deduce a way to get Andy to remove his pants so that he could take the coin out of his pocket. No scheme to get Andy's money was too bizarre for the con man because the "big dummy," as Kingfish frequently called him, would apparently fall for anything. The Kingfish knew that a man takes off his pants while undergoing a medical examination. Before much longer the executive office at the lodge hall resembled a doctor's office. By now Andy should have been suspicious of the Kingfish when he stopped by the office to retrieve his letter.

ANDY: Kingfish, I been expectin' a letter that was supposed to . . . uh, uh, uhhhh . . .
KINGFISH: 'Scuse me, Andy. Can't you see I'm takin' a blood count heah? That's four, subtract two. Hmmmm. Dat's the most anemic blood I ever did see. Well, Andy ol' pal, it's good seein' you. Uh, 'scuse the rubber glove. I just come from a big operation.
ANDY: Kingfish, you mean to say that you is an actual doctor?
KINGFISH: Well, I ain't been blabbin' it around but I been takin' a

correspondence course in doctorin' from that, uh, big medical school down dere in, uh, Baltimore.

Through a series of inane operations, Kingfish managed to convince Andy that he needed medical attention. Part of "Dr." Stevens' examination required Andy to put on a blindfold and take off his pants. After securing the rare coin, Kingfish dashed to a nearby telephone booth to call Mr. Wilson. But, displaying only slightly more intelligence than Andy, he dropped the valuable nickel into the telephone coin slot.

Amos showed Andy that the Kingfish had swindled him yet another time. Before Andy could hit Kingfish in the jaw, the con man's mind had already concocted another plot. All Andy had to do to regain the coin was to break into the pay phone. Kingfish, naturally, would stand guard outside. But when a plainclothes detective wanted to use the phone while Andy performed his illegal act, the two well-meaning "criminals" were taken to jail.

Defending Kingfish and Andy in court was their crooked lawyer Algonquin J. Calhoun (played by Johnny Lee). Before Calhoun's actual appearance in the courtroom, Kingfish spoke to Andy. "What we gotta do is stick together," Kingfish insisted. "And don't forget. We's all brothers in that great fraternity, the Mystic Knights of the Sea. We got to be loyal to each other. Face this thing with a united front. All for one and one for all!" Even in the courtroom Kingfish's crafty mind was clicking. As he approached the judge's stand he said emphatically, "Your Honor, he's the one what done it!"

Finally Calhoun boisterously entered the courtroom.

CALHOUN: Your Honor, I'd like to enter a plea of not guilty for these two crooks.

JUDGE: On what grounds? According to the report, these two men were caught trying to break into a telephone coin box in the presence of a witness who also was a police officer in this city.

CALHOUN: W-e-l-l, yes, sir, Your Honor. But they done learned their lesson. They ain't n-e-v-e-r gonna break open nothin' in front of a cop no mo'!

JUDGE: Isn't your name Calhoun?

CALHOUN: That's right, Your Honor. Algonquin J. Calhoun.

JUDGE: And didn't I disbar you three years ago?

CALHOUN: Woooooooooooo . . . So long, boys!

Only the intervention of Amos and the arresting officer managed to convince the judge that the defendants' intentions were good. The judge dismissed the case with a stern warning. But even though the case was closed, Kingfish had not given up trying to inveigle the rare coin from Andy. Outside the courtroom Kingfish told Andy to call up Mr. Wilson. Andy slipped his nickel into the telephone coin slot and then began to shake. Again the 1877 coin had been slipped into a public telephone. Kingfish derided Andy, then stormed off puffing angrily. But this time Andy had shown that he was not the "stupid bum" and "big dummy" Kingfish thought him to be. Andy smiled triumphantly and spoke to the telephone operator.

OPERATOR: What number did you dial, please?
ANDY: Eldorado 0-6353.
OPERATOR: I'm sorry, there is no such number.
ANDY: I know dere ain't. Uh, would you please ree-turn my nickel?

Andy retrieved the rare coin from the return slot and kissed it, his face beaming now that he had finally outsmarted George "Kingfish" Stevens.

All of the conniving and scheming of the Kingfish was laid aside for a special Christmas telecast of *Amos 'n' Andy* in 1953. Andy had taken a job in a Harlem department store to enact the role of Santa Claus in order to buy a Christmas gift for Amos' daughter Arbadella (twelve-year-old actress Marie Ellis). The episode included a traditional scene taken from the *Amos 'n' Andy* radio program. Amos tucked his daughter into bed and then eloquently interpreted the meaning of the Lord's Prayer. Freeman Gosden and Charles Correll, who had decided never to appear on camera in the television series, were so moved by the episode, particularly Childress' explanation of the prayer, that they appeared in the opening to introduce the Christmas show.

Amos 'n' Andy continued on television until June 11, 1953, and then went into countless reruns. In the 1960s the program brought complaints from the National Association for the Advancement of Colored People that it produced a distorted and stereotyped image of black people. We can argue that only a few of the characters on *Amos 'n' Andy* were stupid or shiftless and that there were certainly characters of this nature on all-white television comedy series. Alvin Childress himself once stated, "I didn't feel it harmed the Negro at all. . . . Actually the series had many episodes which showed the Negro with professions and businesses like attorneys, store owners and so on which they never had in TV or movies before. . . ." We might also add that the program was and is legitimately funny and that the performances of the main actors were superb. But we must also consider the fact that *Amos 'n' Andy* presented virtually the *only* image of the black man in those early days of television. It was this fact that brought on the resentment of the black community just as they were finally emerging from so many centuries of white domination with a pride deservedly all their own. As a result of such protests *Amos 'n' Andy* was withdrawn from the rerun circuit.

Now that we are in an evolving process by which we can hopefully look back upon ethnic humor objectively and historically, and now that black people are appearing in both heroic and villainous roles in motion pictures and on television, perhaps the innocence of *Amos 'n' Andy* might someday return to television screens. Both of the present writers hope that one day, as in the past, everyone will again love Amos Jones and Andy Brown and a con man called the Kingfish.

Whatever schemes the Kingfish failed to concoct must have been hatched by Sergeant Ernest G. Bilko, as portrayed by comedian Phil Silvers. Bilko was the staff sergeant of the motor pool at Fort Baxter, a nearly forgotten outpost of the United States Army in Kansas. The program which featured Sergeant Bilko premiered on CBS-TV on September 20, 1955, and was entitled *You'll Never Get Rich*. Bilko apparently never believed that, for he spent week after week organizing his get-rich-quick schemes in the firm belief that he would inevitably emerge from the Army a wealthy man.

You'll Never Get Rich originated as a fluke. Phil Silvers had been searching for the proper format for his new television series, rejecting a number of ideas until he decided to do a show focusing upon Army life. Everyone can identify with soldiers, Silvers contended, whether he himself had ever been a member of the armed forces or had known someone in uniform. The gimmick of the new program was that it was really not about Army life but about a confidence man in uniform whose platoon of loyal accomplices aided him in his attempts to prove that you *can* get rich without working.

Bilko's platoon included such cast regulars as Harvey Lembeck as Paparelli, Allen Melvin as Henshaw and Maurice Gosfield as the fat slob of the group, Private Duane Doberman (so named because of the actor's supposed resemblance to a Doberman pinscher). With such a grouping of loyal and unscrupulous stalwarts, Bilko provided numerous headaches for the commanding officer of Fort Baxter, Colonel Hall (Paul Ford). Bilko virtually ran the fort himself, for Colonel Hall knew that to interfere with the Sergeant's machinations could prove disastrous for everyone on the base.

When *You'll Never Get Rich* premiered it was scheduled opposite Milton Berle's hour-long comedy show. Naturally Berle clobbered

Silvers in the ratings. But eventually the adventures of Sergeant Bilko began to amass a sizable audience of fans. Silvers was stealing away much of Berle's audience just as Bilko was raking in the dollars on the air. On November 1, 1955, Silvers' popularity had mushroomed to the extent that CBS rewarded him with a name change for his series. Now it was *The Phil Silvers Show*, with its star assuming the position of one of the true giants of television.

In a classic episode entitled "The Motor Pool Mardi Gras," written by Nat Hiken, who created the format of the show, the men of Bilko's platoon were transforming a jeep into a float for the gala event. Among the soldiers working on the float were Corporal Fender, Corporal Rocco, and Privates Gander, Kadowski, Fleishmann, Paparelli, Mullen, Zimmerman and, of course, Doberman.

DOBERMAN: You guys make me sick. This is the Army. Who needs a Mardi Gras?

PAPARELLI: Look, Doberman, just because you can't get a date . . .

DOBERMAN: Aw, cut it out.

KADOWSKI: Come on, Duane. The Mardi Gras is the only affair in the whole year where Bilko doesn't make one cent profit.

ZIMMERMAN: Imagine, Bilko doing something without making a profit.

PAPARELLI: Even the Chaplain is stunned. He's using it for the subject of next Sunday's sermon. (*They all laugh. Bilko and Henshaw come in.*)

BILKO (*barks*): All right, what's going on here? On the ball, everybody. Remember, boys, this Mardi Gras has gotta be the biggest thing. We gotta make them forget they hold one at New Orleans. How are the tickets going, Rocco?

ROCCO: Sold out, Sarge. Every guy on the post is coming.

BILKO: Good boy.

ROCCO: I wonder what they're gonna say when Marilyn Monroe doesn't show up?

BILKO: We'll cross those bridges when we come to them.

Bilko then took charge of the drawing by which the annual King Rex of the Mardi Gras was selected. The lucky winner was entitled to a number of honors including attending the festivities with the girl of his choice. Everyone gaped in disbelief when Doberman won the drawing and the girl of his choice was the debutante Joy Landers, wealthiest girl in Kansas. Bilko sent a few of his hirelings to announce the "good news" to Miss Landers while he himself coached Doberman as to the proper behavior with women. But Joy laughed off the honor of becoming Queen of the Motor Pool, saying that she would never consent to becoming a "Miss Grease Pit." Naturally Bilko would not accept defeat, especially considering Joy Landers had insulted his platoon.

BILKO: Men, Doberman selected a queen. It's up to him to turn *her* down.

ROCCO: But, Sarge, Doberman turning down Joy Landers?

BILKO: Exactly. She's going to know how it feels to be laughed at herself.

MULLEN: But, Sarge, Doberman's going to turn *her* down?

BILKO: She gonna pant for Doberman. She gonna want Doberman like no woman has ever wanted a man.

ZIMMERMAN: Sarge—Doberman?

BILKO: Yes, Doberman. Men, this will be the masterpiece of my career.

Maintaining the honor of his outfit meant as much to Bilko as swindling some poor jokers in the next platoon. Thus began his plan to discredit the spoiled Joy Landers. First he visited Joy in her opulent home, begging her *not* to become Queen of the Motor Pool. The internationally famous Duane Doberman was plagued by too many women already, he told her, and unable to enjoy even a moment's respite. When Bilko left the Landers home Joy could think of nothing other than this mysterious playboy Duane Doberman. Bilko did not relent in his brainwashing of Joy Landers. Wherever she ventured the name of Doberman arose until, just as Bilko predicted, Joy begged to be chosen as his Queen. So successful was Bilko's incessant suggestion that the inevitable meeting between Joy and Doberman defied belief.

BILKO: To describe him you must take a leaf from the Orient where love and beauty are mysteries they have mastered . . . short, dark, with that pulse-quickening plumpness. A Buddha . . .

JOY (*agreeing, mesmerized*): Yes. Yes . . . short and fat.

BILKO: . . . and his face shining as if anointed by the mysterious oils of the East . . . swarthy, greasy if you will, with the inscrutable smile.

HENSHAW (*enters*): Here comes Doberman.
    (*Voices all over the room echo: "Here comes Doberman."*)

JOY (*clutching Bilko for support*): Sergeant.

BILKO: Courage, my child. (*Doberman comes through the door petrified. He is smoking with a long cigarette holder. A cape is draped casually over his shoulders.*) Miss Landers, this is . . .

JOY (*completely under Bilko's spell*): You don't have to tell me. He's exactly as you described him . . . he's magnificent.

BILKO: Private Doberman, this young lady would like to meet you. (*Doberman can hardly walk. He inches along. Bilko starts bringing him forward.*) She insisted. After all, she was offered the crown as your Queen. This is Joy Landers.

JOY: This is the happiest moment of my life.

BILKO: Duane, the lady spoke to you. Haven't you something to say to her? (*Doberman looks imploringly at Bilko.*)

JOY (*out of her mind with anticipation*): Yes. Say it. Say it.

BILKO: Say it.

DOBERMAN (*flippantly*): Get lost!

Bilko mused that honor had been restored to the platoon and he had enjoyed the last laugh. But Joy eventually humbled herself and became the Queen of the Motor Pool with Doberman as her King. As she squeezed the round cheek of Doberman's fat face, the private blushed and dropped unconscious to the floor.

Ernie Bilko continued trying to get rich until June 19, 1959, when his show went off the air.

Situation comedies continue to occupy time slots on television that the critical members of the viewing audience wish were reserved for more meaningful programs. With the exception of a few "sit-coms," as they are called today, the majority of these domestic comedies do little to spark genuine laughter from the viewer. Most of the guffaws that are heard originate in the recording studio where "canned laughter" or "laugh tracks" are cued in over the allegedly humorous actions or dialogue (a carry-over from the days when radio listeners actually heard the laughter of a live studio audience) so that the apparently dense viewer is told what is funny.

In the early and middle fifties many of the situation comedies *were* funny, whether they were embellished by prerecorded laughter or not. Further proof of the durability of these old programs is that they are still on the air, usually playing in the mornings or afternoons on the rerun circuit. Thankfully, Lucy Ricardo, Sergeant Bilko and others of their breed are still with us.

The Great One

On the Saturday evening of March 6, 1954, Jack Lescoulie, the smiling and smooth-talking emcee of *The Jackie Gleason Show,* addressed the studio audience and the viewers watching the comedy variety show at home.

LESCOULIE: And now it's time for another visit with two of your favorite characters, Ralph and Alice Kramden, better known to you as the Honeymooners. Usually our visit with the Kramdens is a short one depicting one brief incident in their daily lives. But tonight something has happened to Ralph and Alice that will take a little longer to tell you about. What is it? Well, suppose we look in on the Kramdens, as played by Jackie Gleason and Audrey Meadows, and see for ourselves.

This particular *Honeymooners* sketch was "A Letter to the Boss," written by Marvin Marx, Walter Stone, Syd Zelinka, Howard Harris, Leonard Stern, Bill Hackett and Bill Shelley. It remains one of Jackie Gleason's favorites.

Ralph Kramden had come home from work with a dejected look on his round face. His pretty wife Alice looked at her husband, standing like an overstuffed retired soldier in his Gotham Bus Company driver's uniform. It was his regular bowling night, but this time Ralph had no desire to go out with the boys. Ralph had been told not to show up in uniform the next day, because he wasn't driving a bus for the company any more. "I been fired," he said, wrinkling his brow.

RALPH: I'm not letting my friends know I'm out of work. And have them stand around saying, "Poor Ralph." And getting their phony sympathy. . . . Not me.

ALICE: Oh, Ralph. That's carrying your pride too far.

RALPH: Never mind. That's the way I want it. Remember I don't want any of my friends to know I'm out of work. When I get another job I'll tell them I quit to get a better one. But in the meantime, I'm not tellin' anyone!

(*Door opens. Norton enters carrying bowling ball in carrying case.*)

Ed Norton was Ralph's closest friend. He worked in the sewers of New York where he gave himself the more appealing title of "underground engineer." Norton, usually dressed in a T-shirt and vest and wearing a shapeless felt hat, always had words to soothe Ralph when he was in one of his terrible predicaments. Ed's words did not, however, always produce the desired effect.

NORTON: Hello, Alice. . . . H'ya, Ralphie boy!

RALPH (*unconcerned*): Hiya, Norton. (*Almost in tears.*) I lost my job today. I was fired!

NORTON: Come on, Ralph, you're not gonna let this get you down . . . where's the old spirit? At a time like this you gotta keep your chin up. You gotta smile. Come on, boy, let's have a little smile. (*Ralph awkwardly tries to smile.*) There, that's my boy . . . Bigger, bigger, that's it! That's the way you gotta stay even if it takes you a whole year to get another job. Even if you never get another job!

RALPH (*loses his smile and looks angry and throws Norton's arm away*): How can you expect me to keep smiling with you talking like that!

NORTON: I was only trying to cheer you up.

RALPH (*bitterly*): A fat lot I've got to smile about. Nine years on a job. Today I'm fired and by tomorrow I'm forgotten. They won't even remember what I look like.

NORTON: That's great. . . . Go right back tomorrow morning and ask for a job.

RALPH: Norton, you are a mental case.

The Honeymooners was the brain child of Jackie Gleason, the heavy-set comedian who played Ralph Kramden. His career had spanned radio, night clubs, burlesque, Broadway and a number of motion pictures, none of which made him a star of any caliber. Gleason's brand of humor was scarcely sophisticated and appealed to virtually everyone not a part of high society. In 1949 he left New York for Hollywood after receiving a call from his agent offering him the role of Chester A. Riley in the television situation comedy *The Life of Riley*. Gleason was beginning to discover his medium.

His distinct character and humor emerged when Dumont starred him in *The Cavalcade of Stars* in 1951. There he could ad-lib according to his own personality and get away from the literal interpretation of script which doomed his characterization of Riley. He began to create his own cast of characters, each marred for the better by some human tragic flaw, and each somehow expressing Gleason's own personality. There were loudmouths, alcoholics, and imbeciles in the Gleason line-up. But his ultimate and best-remembered characters premiered the following year, when CBS signed him to *The Jackie Gleason Show* on Saturday evenings, with an appealing weekly salary of $10,000. It was there that *The Honeymooners* was created.

It is doubtful whether Ralph and Alice Kramden ever actually went on a honeymoon. Their home was on Chauncy Street in Brooklyn, a cheap apartment that reminded one of a flophouse with only one bed. A telephone, at least to penny-pinching Ralph, was an outrageous luxury, far beyond the means of a man earning barely $60 a week. The apartment was stripped to the barest minimum in furnishings—a table, chairs, bureau, and an incredibly ancient stove, kitchen sink and icebox. (The iceman kept complaining about traveling across town in the hot summer to deliver one melting block of ice.)

Certainly *The Honeymooners* was Gleason's most realistic creation. Almost everyone knew someone who constantly roared off such colorful phrases as "Oh, you're a regular riot, Alice! Har-de-HAR-de-harhar!" or "You're askin' for a knuckle sandwich, Alice!" or the classic "One of these days, Alice . . . *one of these days* . . . POW! Right in the kisser!"

But Alice put up with Ralph, whose scatterbrained schemes to get rich always resulted in tragedy. She loved Ralph but could raise her own voice enough to put him in his place and leave him speechless. In the end Ralph always realized his blunder, admitting, "You know why I did that, Alice? 'Cause I'm a BLABBERMOUTH!" Then, before the final fade-out, he'd give his wife a big hug and kiss, saying, "Baby, you're the greatest!"

Much of the humor of *The Honeymooners* resulted from Ralph's weight problem. Apparently Ralph was only concerned with his weight when someone made a remark about it. Otherwise he and Norton were never reluctant to go to the local pizza parlor or Chinese restaurant. The Ralph Kramden "fat" jokes became as familiar as the "cheap" jokes made about Jack Benny.

RALPH: Alice, your mother is not stepping foot in this house!
ALICE: Why not?
RALPH: Before you know it, she'll be starting in with the cracks. Remember what she went around telling everyone at our wedding? "I'm not losing a daughter, I'm gaining a ton."

Another time Ralph had come home early from a meeting of his lodge, the Royal Order of Raccoons. His uniform resembled that of a doorman with a coonskin cap. Alice was babysitting, but the always jealous Ralph believed her to be seeing another man. Storming toward the bedroom, he was preparing to fight his adversary when a small boy appeared, rubbing his sleepy eyes, and said, "Gee, I never knew Davy Crockett was so fat!"

Most of the scenes of *The Honeymooners* involved Ralph and Norton. Art Carney, a former impressionist, announcer and singer, who had been with Gleason since the second *Cavalcade* show, played Ed Norton. The characters of Ralph and Norton totally complemented each other. Actually the characterizations of the two were not entirely the creation of Gleason. He based the entire series on an old burlesque routine called *Friendly Neighbors* and made Ralph and Norton Brooklyn versions of Stan Laurel and Oliver Hardy.

Norton, like Laurel, was the skinny idiot whose humor involved a lot of broad hand and arm gestures. Both were stupid and made no pretext at being intelligent. Ralph, like the rotund Hardy, was barely smarter than Norton. But Ralph's trouble was that he thought himself to be quite a brain, even though his past life's blunders should have informed him otherwise.

As usual, Ralph relied on Norton to help set straight the situation of losing his job by writing a snide letter to the boss.

RALPH: Look, Norton, I'm too nervous to write this letter. You sit down and I'll tell you what to say.

NORTON: Okay, Ralph.

RALPH: Now let's see . . . Put this down, Norton. . . . "You dirty bum."

NORTON: Wait a minute, Ralph. Don't you think that's a little strong for a starter?

RALPH: Maybe you're right. . . . Take this. . . . "Dear Mr. Marshall . . . (*Ralph pauses, trying to think of something nicer to say but can't.*) You dirty bum!"

NORTON: That's better, Ralph.

RALPH: "After giving you the best years of my life, you fired me, you miserable low life. A man like you should turn in your membership card in the human race."

NORTON: That's a nice touch, Ralph.

RALPH: Thanks, Norton. . . . "After what you did to me, I can safely say that you are the meanest man in the whole world, you dirty bum" . . . uh . . . uh . . . I can't think of anything else to say.

NORTON: Maybe this is a good spot to hint around getting your job back!

RALPH: Don't be an idiot. . . . Now look, while I get a stamp, finish writin' that up, and end it with somethin' like "Sincerely or Very truly yours, etc., etc." You know.

After Norton took the letter to be mailed, Ralph learned that he had misunderstood the man at the bus company. He wasn't fired but promoted to traffic manager. The rest of the episode involved Ralph's attempts to retrieve the letter. Finally he stood before Mr. Marshall himself just as the mail arrived. For a laugh, Marshall decided to read this crank letter, although most of them ended up in the wastebasket unread. Ralph squirmed until Marshall came to the end.

MARSHALL: Kramden, do you know how this is signed? It says, "Sincerely yours, etc. etc." . . . He didn't even have the nerve to sign his name.

RALPH (*does big reaction*): "Sincerely yours . . . etc. . . . etc. . . ." Oh no . . . (*Ralph falls on floor and faints.*)

The Kramdens were about to celebrate when Norton, attracted by the smell of the Chinese food they were having, came into the apartment.

NORTON: I felt so rotten about your losing your job and everything, I thought about it all day. So when I finished work I went down to the bus company. I saw your boss and explained the whole thing to him.

RALPH (*takes deep breath*): You explained the whole thing??

NORTON: That's right. I told him you didn't mean that stuff in the letter about him being a big bum.

RALPH (*sinks into chair*): You didn't??

NORTON: Sure. And believe me you got nothing to worry about. He said he wantsa see you first thing in the morning. (*Norton opens door and speaks from doorway.*) And remember, if you're ever in trouble again, Ralphie old boy (*indicates upstairs with finger*), I live right upstairs.

Once again Ralph's troubles resulted from his own big mouth and his reliance on Ed Norton.

The first actress to portray Alice Kramden was Pert Kelton, who could give Ralph the perfect "I told you so" look when he managed to get himself into trouble. She was eventually replaced by Audrey Meadows (Jayne's sister), who stayed with the series through the end of the old *Jackie Gleason Show*. Joyce Randolph enacted the part of Trixie, Norton's wife.

The Honeymooners was sandwiched in between the other acts on the show. Because of its popularity, it made the show's ratings skyrocket even more, beating Milton Berle in the ratings and giving Gleason the title of "Mr. Saturday Night."

Eventually *The Honeymooners* became so popular that it spun off into a half-hour filmed series of its own in 1955, performed before a live studio audience. Gleason's technique involved little rehearsal and much improvisation of lines. In doing each scene from beginning to end with no intercutting, the filmed series retained all the excitement and spontaneity of the live show.

Almost every one of the episodes in a classic, as funny as it was originally regardless of the number of times viewed in rerun. Ralph repeatedly put his foot into his, as he so often put it, "BIG mouth." In one episode, after telling his boss he knew how to play golf, when he had never swung a club in his life he had to learn in a day. Another time his mouth got him into a fight with a neighborhood bully who could break him in half. One of the best episodes occurred when Ralph talked himself into an appearance on the television quiz show *The $99,000 Answer*. This show was written by Leonard Stern and Sydney Zelinka and was presented on Sunday, January 28, 1956.

A very nervous Ralph walked onto a television stage adorned by a curtain heralding the name of the show, *The $99,000 Answer*.

MC: What kind of work do you do, Mr. Kramden?

RALPH: I brive a dus.

MC: You brive a dus?

RALPH: I mean I dus a brive.

MC: Oh, you drive a bus!

RALPH: That's what I said, I'm a dus briver!

MC: Mr. Kramden, I can understand you being nervous, but it will be to your advantage to relax and calm yourself. Just remember we're all friends and I'm here to help you. (*Ralph smiles appreciatively.*) Are you married, Mr. Kramden? (*Ralph nods "yes."*) What's your wife's name?

RALPH: Mrs. Kramden.

MC (*helpfully*): Her first name.

RALPH: Her—oh!—Alice!

MC: And you're from Brooklyn . . . have you lived in Brooklyn all your life?

RALPH: Er—not yet.

Ralph managed to muster the courage to select "popular music" as his category of questioning. But luckily the bus driver had appeared during the closing minutes of the program, thereby winning a full week to brush up on his subject and to overcome his flusteration. Ralph then rented a piano and hired Norton to play it, spending the week learning every popular song imaginable. Norton continued to grate on his nerves by prefacing each rendition with a few bars from "Swanee River," as he put it, "to get warmed up." Yet despite Norton's continual aggravation of the new television celebrity, Ralph managed to endure. All the while his ego and self-confidence expanded to match his physical proportions. When Ralph again appeared on the television quiz show, he was smiling and waving confidently to viewers across the nation. The master of ceremonies' explanation of the rules was hardly more complicated than those of the real show being satirized, *The $64,000 Question.*

MC: I have here your first question. Now, Mr. Kramden, you know how the $99,000 answer works. We start with the first question, which is our lowest hurdle. You get that right and get $100. Then you go over our second hurdle, which is worth $600. After that our hurdles become higher and our questions naturally a little harder. Our third hurdle is worth $6,187.50, and if you answer that right, you will have a total of $12,375. Then we keep doubling until you finally get to the $99,000 hurdle. Any time you feel like stopping you can do so and keep whatever you have won. Of course if you miss, you go home empty-handed. Is that clear, Mr. Kramden?

RALPH: Yes, sir. But if it's all right with you I'd like to make a statement.

MC: Certainly. Go right ahead.

RALPH: I've made up my mind I'm going for the $99,000!

But Ralph's prediction was destined not to materialize. The very first question, the one paying $100 if answered correctly, was "Who is the composer of 'Swanee River'?" " 'Swanee River'?" Ralph asked, confused, acting as if he had never heard of the song before. As the familiar piano strains of "Swanee River" sounded through the studio, Ralph's large eyes bulged.

RALPH: *That's* "Swanee River"?

MC: Yes. Now who wrote it? (*Ralph is speechless.*) Your time is almost up. Make a stab at it. Take a guess!

RALPH: Homma . . . homina . . . Ed Norton?

MC: Oh, I'm terribly sorry, Mr. Kramden, the right answer is Stephen Foster. But at least you have the satisfaction of knowing you have been a good contestant and a good sport. Good-by, Mr. Kramden.

Ralph stammered with disbelief, not wanting to leave the stage. The always jovial master of ceremonies continued his attempts to get him to walk off camera range.

MC: Well, Mr. Kramden . . . I'll be seeing you. (*Ralph, half dazed, automatically answers what he thinks of as a song title.*)

RALPH: "I'll Be Seeing You." A hit song written in 1938 by Irving Kale and Sammy Fain!

MC: But, Mr. Kramden . . . it's all over now.

RALPH: "It's All Over Now," words and music by Bazzy Simon, 1927.

MC: Good night. Mr. Kramden, good night. (*MC motions off to girl assistant to come and help.*)

RALPH: There are two good nights. "Good Night, Irene" written by Lomax and Leadbetter and "Good Night, Sweetheart" by Rudy Vallee and Ray Noble and . . . (*The girl now has Ralph by arm.*)

GIRL: Please. This way, sir. Please.

RALPH (*as he is being led off*): "Please" sung by Bing Crosby in *Big Broadcast of 1933.* By Robbins and Rainger. (*As they lead poor Ralph off camera.*)

On his regular variety shows, Gleason would walk onto the stage following a number by the June Taylor Dancers. The Great One, as he became known in later years, would then deliver a comedy monologue, climaxed by his cue to orchestra conductor Ray Bloch, "A little traveling music!" Gleason would then dance about the stage, waving his arms in his characteristic fashion. Before he dashed behind the curtains to assume the role of one of his myriad characters, the Great One would exclaim, "And awa-a-a-a-a-y we go!!" On one particular night in the 1950s, Gleason's "Away we go" proved a bit too much for even this energetic performer. He stumbled forward and broke his leg. When he next appeared to open his television program he was hobbling on crutches. Not even a broken limb could prevent Gleason from appearing before the cameras.

Gleason is one of the few television performers whose distinct personality dominates every aspect of his show, including the music, the boisterous reactions from his live studio audience, the flavor of the commercials and the bevy of elegantly dressed beauties who cater to his every whim. But Gleason's personality is reflected mostly in his characters such as Ralph Kramden. Gleason's contention is that there must be tears in laughter and this belief has been manifested in his line-up of personages.

There was Charley the Loudmouth, wearing equally loud clothes and straw hat and smoking a cigar. Charley was the terror of the meek, bespectacled little man played by Art Carney, who always opened the sketch by attempting to eat his food. "Oh, I only hope that loudmouth Charley doesn't come in today before I'm finished eating," he would say only moments before Charley himself burst into the place. "Hiya, pal!" Charley would roar, slapping Carney on the back so hard that he knocked the food from his spoon. "What's that slop you're eatin'?" Carney would then explain that his delectable dish consisted of pickled prunes in buttermilk before getting bombarded with the Loudmouth's vociferousness.

When the television camera dollied through the swinging doors of a tavern, Joe the Bartender would be singing "My Gal Sal" inside. Joe the Bartender was Gleason's one-man sketch in which the camera became the never seen Mr. Dunahee who listened while Joe poured him a beer and related all the humorous neighborhood gossip.

Perhaps Gleason's most sympathetic character was the Poor Soul, a slow-witted yet lovable innocent wearing tweed. The Poor Soul would go about searching for and doing only good, clapping one hand atop the other when something, however slight, pleased him. But though he sought out good, what he invariably found was trouble.

A typical Poor Soul comedy routine of the early fifties was one that found its way into numerous television programs of that early era. The hapless character managed to acquire a job in a bakery shop run by Art Carney. The shop utilized some modern conveniences including a conveyor belt that transported cakes across the room. All the Poor Soul was required to do was casually squirt some whipped cream onto each cake, then drop a handful of chopped nuts and finally a cherry. The finished cake was then picked up before it could reach the end of the belt and smash against the floor. The Poor Soul was then to place the cake in a cardboard box, run up the stairs and ascend the ladder that led to the overhead shelf. Finally he would ring a bell. Yet when the Poor Soul performed so simple a task the forces-that-be seemed out to interfere.

The Poor Soul did as he was instructed to the strains of "Tenderly," theme song of the sketch. But then the inevitable bad luck of the character caused the conveyor belt's speed to increase . . . and increase. The reader may well imagine the numerous catastrophes that followed, culminating with the Poor Soul's discharge from the job by Carney. But even though the Poor Soul had lost again and was exhausted almost beyond human endurance, he managed to give Carney the same decorations he had attempted to give each cake. Carney sat dumfounded, his head covered with whipped cream, chopped nuts and a cherry, and with a sign hanging over his chest with the inscription "Crumb Cake."

Pathos of yet another kind was elicited for Gleason's most tragic character, Reginald—or, more affectionately, Reggie—Van Gleason III. Reggie was the spoiled playboy son of the wealthy Van Gleason family. He was usually attired in formal wear, including a cape and incredibly tall stovepipe hat. There was almost always an insipid smirk beneath his bushy black mustache. Yet despite this amusing exterior Reggie Van Gleason was possessed of a severe problem. He was an alcoholic. And although the word "alcoholic" was never used until a more "relevant" Gleason television special of 1973, Reggie's drinking problem was obvious and the source of most of the character's humor.

In a typical sketch telecast in the winter of 1957, Reggie Van Gleason III was to be interviewed on the air in a spoof of the popular interview program, Edward R. Murrow's *Person to Person*. The Van Gleasons' butler had entered the opulent living room of the family's stately mansion as the roar of a mighty engine resounded from outside. "Oh, that must be Mawster Reggie landing his helicopter on the lawn." Reggie's pompous and doting (not to mention overweight) mother merely returned delightedly, "Ohhhhhhhh!"

As always, Reggie's entrance was likened to that of royalty. The sketch's theme song "Shangri-La" blared as Reggie stepped into the room, an alert and waiting serving maid in a short sexy outfit standing to one side. Reggie turned slightly, removing his enormous hat and giving it to the maid. Then with a theatrical gesture he raised his arms slightly, letting his black cape fall into her waiting hands. A clever manipulation of his cane sent it into the maid's grasp. Reggie completed this undressing by removing each white glove, finger by finger, then handing them to the girl and following her exit with licentious eyes. Then he turned to behold his beaming and overly proud mother. And when she spoke she seemed to be singing opera.

REGGIE: Ooooo, hello, dear Mom.

MRS. VAN GLEASON: Oh, Son, I'm so glad you got here in time. Remember you're going to be on television tonight.

REGGIE: Ooooo, did they accept my application for the Mousketeers?

MRS. VAN GLEASON: Oh, Reggie, you have forgotten. You're to be interviewed by *People to People* tonight. It's Friday!

REGGIE: It's Friday? What happened to Monday, Tuesday, Wednesday and Thursday?

MRS. VAN GLEASON: Oh, Reggie! I'm going to go and freshen up a bit before the program. I know you're going to make your mother very proud of her dear, darling little boy tonight! (*She waits expectantly, looking exaltedly at Reggie. Reggie looks her up and down.*)

REGGIE: Mmmmm, boy, are you *fat!*

When Reggie said that line the entire studio audience exploded with laughter. The line took no one by surprise. Reggie said it every sketch and it was awaited with fondness whenever the cavalier playboy made his appearance. Equally anticipated was Reggie's subsequent action as he "prepared" himself for the interview that was to come. He pushed a concealed button which caused a fully equipped liquor cabinet and bar to emerge from the wall. With the skill of Joe the Bartender, Reggie mixed his drink and downed it with one gulp. The audience waited. Reggie's eyes bulged and his head snapped in the fashion of the double-take. "Ooohhhh!" Reggie would always exclaim. "That's good booze!"

Art Carney, who usually played the part of Reggie's father, did his best impersonation of Edward R. Murrow when he introduced this latest installment of *People to People*. Carney addressed the audience directly, with total sobriety.

CARNEY: Ladies and gentlemen, this is *People to People*. It's all on film, not live. We take no chances. Tonight we're taking you to the home of a man who's been the subject of gossip columns and whose escapades have often made the front pages of your newspapers. That man's name is Reggie Van Gleason III. The Van Gleasons live in a town house in the East Sixties, Seventies and Eighties. This is the Van Gleason living room where we hear Reggie spends very little of his time. I don't see anybody about. Perhaps Reggie is in another one of the rooms. I'll call him. Ah, Reggie? Uh, Reggie?

REGGIE (*entering the room*): Oooooo . . .

Naturally Reggie shocked not only his family but a nation of *People to People* viewers as he revealed to them his extravagant and unorthodox life style.

It was always Art Carney, usually in his role of Ed Norton, who rivaled Gleason himself in popularity. When Carney eventually quit the show, Gleason's ratings went along with him. Despite new shows with such talented costars as Buddy Hackett and Frank Fontaine, the latter enacting his Crazy Googenheim characterization to straight man Joe the Bartender, Gleason was unable to recapture the magic of his earlier sketches, all of which included Carney. Gleason and Carney worked together with a success that neither was able to duplicate on his own. For a while Gleason became a motion picture actor and, as always, traces of his familiar television characters were evident in his new roles. *Gigot* (1962) was heavily influenced by his Poor Soul while characteristics of Reggie Van Gleason III affected his starring role in *Papa's Delicate Condition* (1963).

In the late 1960s *The Honeymooners* returned with Gleason's new television series for CBS. Costarring the incredible Art Carney, who had been lured back to the fold, and with Sheila MacRae as a more mellowed Alice and Jane Kean as Trixie, the new series was the result of a one-shot revival of the sketch done with the old cast. Gleason had previously vowed to quit television for good. But *The Honeymoon-*

ers and its unending popularity gave him good reason to stay. For a while Jackie Gleason and Ralph Kramden were back on top. In a way it seemed as though *The Jackie Gleason Show* of the early 1950s had returned.

When the reruns of the filmed *Honeymooners* episodes are shown, as they still are in various cities, I recall the line Gleason made famous in his late 1960s variety series, *The American Scene Magazine:* "How sweet it is!" Yes, that line may well apply to *The Honeymooners* and the other creations attesting to the genius of Jackie Gleason.

Comedians,

Cowboys,

the Private Eye

and Live Drama

PART II

by Jim Harmon

CHAPTER 10

The Champion Clowns

The four men in uniform with the stars on their caps sang, "We are the men of Texaco . . . from Maine to Mexico . . ." and then he came out. He was a presentable-looking fellow—could have been a whiz in real estate—and he was wearing a nice, frilly dress. He walked on the sides of his ankles. "Good evening, ladies and germs," he said. "I'd call you ladies and gentlemen"—his strapless gown began to slip alarmingly and he adjusted it—"but you know what you really are."

He was Milton Berle, Mr. Tuesday Night, Mr. Television.

Berle's comedy was in startling contrast to most of the other programming on early television. It has been theorized that the dawn era of the TV age was designed to appeal to a higher intellectual standard because the only people who could afford the first, expensive TV sets were of the wealthy, better-educated class. If so, Milton Berle was the magnet to those potential set owners hanging around bars and pressing their noses to the windows of appliance stores.

It was Berle who was the subject of conversation among adults—in the way the kids talked about Howdy Doody's adventures.

Did you see that show the other night where Berle came on dressed up like Superman?

Did you catch that routine with Basil Rathbone as Sherlock Holmes? Holmes was looking for a corpse, and naturally when he saw Berle standing there, he went up to him and said . . .

You know he came out dressed up like the Easter Bunny and with those two front teeth . . .

He came out in a dress the other night—looked just like my Aunt Edith. . . .

They wheeled him out in this stroller, see, and he was dressed like a baby, but he was smoking this cigar. . . .

Berle was wearing this ballerina's outfit and tiptoeing to "Swan Lake." My wife went into hysterics, I tell you. . . .

So they don't laugh and he says, "What are you, the Nuremberg jury? You didn't have to pay to get in here, you know."

He was wearing this old lady's dress . . .

And then they hit him right in the kisser with the biggest damn powder puff you ever . . .

And he was wearing a woman's dress all through this!

The program during its greatest popularity was called the *Texaco Star Theater.* (The title had been used before for Fred Allen's radio show in the thirties, and for Berle's own radio series.) The quartet marched onto the stage to open the show with a rousing chorus:

> "Oh, we're the men of Texaco,
> We work from Maine to Mexico.
> There's nothing like this Texaco of ours.
> Our show tonight is powerful,
> We'll wow you with an hour full
> Of howls from a shower full of stars.
> We're the merry Texaco men.
> Tonight we may be showmen.
> Tomorrow we'll be servicing your cars."

After Berle made a spectacular entrance—this night he wore a sequined evening gown—Uncle Miltie would do one of his original routines.

The "originality" may have been open to question. There were sketches showing Berle sneaking into Red Buttons' living room and sandpapering his fingertips to have a go at the safe where Red kept his jokes. As with many legends, there was a grain of truth in all this.

In the early days of his vaudeville and radio career Berle or his writers actually did lift the jokes out of other comedians' shows. It used to be said during the radio era that if you missed Fred Allen's show you could hear all the best parts of it a few days later on the Berle program.

But mainly Milton Berle stole from himself. He used the jokes and routines that a long career had taught him audiences appreciated.

One of his favorites—one of the favorites of his audience—concerned Berle posing as a stunt man for a star making a movie. (The star was any one of a number of people over the years—Mickey Rooney, Donald O'Connor, Hopalong Cassidy and others.)

The picture was usually a Western. The star had been stranded out on the desert, crawling through the sands, dying of thirst. He came to the outlaws' ranch and croaked, "Give me a drink. Give it to me."

A bearded heavy would scowl down at the star. "What did you say?"

"I said, 'Give it to me!'" the star repeated.

"Cut!" yelled the director. "Stunt man!"

Berle would rush onto the set eagerly and be hit in the face by the make-up man with the biggest powder puff the world had ever seen. Then he would get down into the star's kneeling position and repeat the line: "Give it to me."

The bearded outlaw would let him have a bucket of water in the face on top of the white powder.

In another scene the "star" of the movie would attempt to stop the villain from stealing the schoolmarm's prize apple pie. "Unhand that pie. Give it to me."

"Cut!" yelled the director. "Stunt man!"

Berle got into place and repeated the line. "Give it to me."

He got it.

The process would go on and on, with Berle reeling and collapsing from the punishment and finally seizing the mother of all powder puffs and wildly flailing the star and the director.

The audience loved it. They always did.

Classic comedy writer Goodman Ace recently revealed the philosophy behind Milton Berle's humor. Uncle Miltie liked his jokes not to be sappy but to be "lappy"—to be laid right in the audience's collective lap. "The peoples won't get it if it isn't lappy."

The "peoples" laughed in rhythm. If you got them to laugh at two jokes in a row, you really didn't need a third joke. Double-talk would do. "She was fat—so fat when she tried to sit down, she just clyde."

The depressing thing to Ace about the "lappy" theory was that it worked. The "peoples" laughed.

At least it worked and they laughed for some years of steady viewing. That pragmatic creature, the public, still takes out Milton Berle from time to time for a rare airing, like taking a dribble glass or a whoopee cushion from a box on the top shelf. The old jokes bring a fond laugh, a kind of tribute to a time when they *really* seemed funny.

Another comedian, Sid Caesar, said, "The American people uses people. It uses them up, and then discards them. That should not happen to a human being."

Of course, some talents are too significant for fate to deal them that final indignity. The movement to discard *everything* of yesterday, the good and the bad, for the uncertain newness of today is there, but the great ones swim steadily against the tide.

Caesar was great by being small—the classic Everyman. Charlie Chaplin was the Little Fellow, but specifically he was the Little Tramp. Most of us are not literally tramps. We have to hold down some kind of a job to support a wife and children, to pay for having the kitchen painted and the grass cut, to pay for the car, pay the taxes, pay, pay, pay. We may fantasize about being a tramp without obligations, but we know we have to work for a living.

Sid Caesar had a job—it varied from being a plumber to being a part of a mechanical church steeple clock—and he had a wife. Invariably, she was Imogene Coca, appealing but decidedly not movie-star-pretty. Caesar would come home in his 1950s suit (wide lapels and broader shoulders than Rosalind Russell's) and find his 1950s wife with a timeless problem—she had done something wrong and she had to break the news to her husband. (For Women's Liberation troops —yes, it works the other way too.) She had had a little trouble with the car getting out of control. How to break the news? How? "Dear," Coca said to Caesar, "remember that charming little old-fashioned store run by Tony down on the corner—the one that . . . used to be there . . ."

Caesar sensed nothing wrong. He had done a good day's work. He was tired. He was looking forward to a glass of beer and watching wrestling on TV. "The store's still there. I saw Tony in the doorway just yesterday, dear."

"It was there yesterday," Coca said. "But not . . . today."

"How could it be there yesterday and not today?" A faint glimmer began to appear in Caesar's eyes. Was there something wrong? "Something happen to Tony?"

"Oh no, not a scratch," she said. "Just the store. It was wiped out by a car going right through the front window and out the back door."

Caesar burst out in uncontrollable laughter. "Right through the store! Right through it! How could anybody do anything as dumb as that! It must have been a woman driver, right, dear?"

"Yes."

Terrible stark suspicion, mounting dread in Caesar's chubby, pliable face. "A woman driver. It wasn't . . . No, it couldn't have been. That's impossible. It couldn't . . . *YOU* DID IT!"

Seldom has any comedian had such brilliant support as Caesar in cast and crew. Besides Miss Coca, there was smooth, affable insurance-salesman type, Carl Reiner, and handsome, little, shy-nervous Howard Morris. Reiner was always trying to get Caesar to do something stupid (buy a house or a car or a statue he couldn't afford) and Morris was always trying to do the stupid thing first, to prove that people couldn't shove him out of line just because he was short.

Reiner was also one of the writers, along with Mel Brooks, the very youthful Woody Allen, Lucille Kallen, Neil Simon, Mel Tolin and others. Max Liebman was the producer who assembled this group. Putting all these mammoth talents together in a working group was possible, but a *smoothly* working group it was not. It was yell and scream time, the writers performing their own material brilliantly (only a Sid Caesar could have improved on those script conferences, I imagine). It was soggy half-eaten pastrami-on-rye time—cream soda bottles, cigars, pickles on mustard-smeared wax paper, and Mel Brooks walking on his knees to simulate a midget for the tired eyes of Carl Reiner and the others. But in the end it all jelled. A script was created.

Sid Caesar was perfect for a visual medium but he could also handle dialogue and dialect. Reporter Carl Reiner would often interview scientist Ludwig Von Fossil (Caesar looking rather like a burley-que comic in crushed hat and baggy pants).

REINER: What is the greatest discovery you've made as an excavator and archaeologist?

CAESAR: You know, the greatest secret in archaelogy is the Secret of Titten-Tottens Tomb and I decided to make it my life work. After many years, I found the Secret of Titten-Tottens Tomb.

REINER: What was it, Doctor?

CAESAR: I should tell you?

REINER: . . . What is the most revolutionary discovery you made in all your travels?

CAESAR: I found an old civilization. It was a matriarchal society where the women were the important people—the men were nothing. The women were the rulers, they were the heads of government. They were in charge of everything.

REINER: Where was this, Doctor?

CAESAR: In Cincinnati.

Of course, it is impossible to reproduce Caesar's dialect and his facial takes; they have to be seen to be believed. The incomparable Caesar is no longer on television for free, but millions have *paid* to see Caesar and Coca and the gang in a movie anthology of some routines from their old show, *Ten from Your Show of Shows.* Eventually, the movie may be shown on television and Caesar will be back where he belongs.

Many of the better comedians came to television from the films, stage and radio (as opposed to Sid Caesar, who seemed to have been *born* there). Ed Wynn, "the Perfect Fool," Red Skelton (Clem Kadiddlehopper and Junior, the "mean widdle kid"), ski-nose Bob Hope, baggy-eyed Fred Allen (too verbal in his unequaled wit for the visual medium) and, of course, Jack Benny.

Some of them went and some stayed. Jack Benny remains forever in our memory and shows up too seldom in a special.

Benny came to TV with a point-by-point adaptation of his radio show. For television he still had announcer Don Wilson, tenor Dennis Day, Mary Livingston and his black man of all work, Rochester (Eddie Anderson). Now, to his character of the old tightwad who claimed always to be thirty-nine years old, Benny could add his famous takes— his look at the audience with spread hands, the man befuddled but accepting his fate and asking for just a little sympathy in his plight.

He got plenty of chances to use his "look" when Benny visited another great, ventriloquist Edgar Bergen, on an early show and was perplexed to find Bergen's famous dummies, Charlie McCarthy and Mortimer Snerd, walking around like real people and Bergen's wife, Frances, casually accepting it.

FRANCES: Mortimer, this is Jack Benny, star of stage, screen, radio and television.

MORTIMER: Jack Benny, the big movie star, eh?

JACK: Yeah.

MORTIMER: And you're on the stage, too?

JACK: Yes, yes.

MORTIMER: You've got your own television show, eh?

JACK: You've heard of me?

MORTIMER: No.

FRANCES: Mortimer, what do you mean you never heard of Jack Benny? How did you get so stupid?

MORTIMER: Er . . . What did you say?

FRANCES: I said, how did you get so stupid?

MORTIMER: Well . . . er . . . I got a good deal and I couldn't turn it down. . . . Well, see you later, Mister . . . Mister . . . oh, the heck with it. (*Mortimer exits.*)

JACK: Frances, I just can't get over it. I mean, if I didn't see Charlie and Mortimer walk in here with my own eyes, I would never believe it. Imagine Charlie and Mortimer actually being—

EDGAR (*entering*): Jack! I'm sorry I kept you waiting.

JACK: Edgar!

EDGAR: Now sit down here with me, Jack. I've got a wonderful idea
for the show. . . . I'll come on with Charlie and do a five-minute
routine . . .

JACK: But, Edgar, I don't understand. I . . .

EDGAR: Then I'll bring on Mortimer Snerd. Just leave it to me. It'll be
a wonderful show.

It was a wonderful show.

Those early days of television were ablaze with talent. And some
of the talent was burned up like firewood. Yet the solid oak among
them continues to burn brightly.

CHAPTER 11

When Television Brought Us the Greatest Shows We Ever Heard

The first night we had our TV set I saw for the first time Steve Wilson of *Big Town*. For years I had been listening to the crusading newspaperman on the radio. The role had been created in the late thirties by Edward G. Robinson, but I'm not sure whether or not Mr. Robinson's screen image was the one I saw in my mind. A crusading editor who took on all the crooks in Big Town with his bare fists had to be a big, broad-shouldered galoot in athletic condition. A later radio actor, Ed Pawley, added another element of gritty toughness when he took over the role, sounding as if he had a flint-ridged jaw like Dick Tracy. (As a matter of fact, he actually did have a jaw like that in publicity photos.) But now, on the dim blue blur of the TV screen, Steve Wilson appeared in the person of actor Pat McVey, a gentle-faced man well into—perhaps past—middle age. He was not even the editor of the *Illustrated Press* any longer—he had been demoted to being only a reporter.

Caught up in the excitement of the new medium, my disappointment in these changes in the *Big Town* format were fleeting, of course. *Big Town*, alterations aside, was a pretty well done series for early TV.

Steve Wilson (in the person of Pat McVey) was not overly given to punching guys in the jaw. I recall a time or two he knocked the gun out of some character's hand just as the boys in blue rushed in and took charge. Most of the time he was listening to people's troubles, Wilson-McVey's sympathetic Irish face rather resembling Pat O'Brien's in a priest role. Some poor middle-aged, frazzled housewife sobbed out that her paroled, ex-con husband could not stand the neighbors throwing overripe fruit at him or turning their sprinklers on when he went near, so he had skipped town. Steve Wilson listened, his eyes like poached eggs. He would help—the *Illustrated Press* would help. "Good gravy, Lorelei," he would say to his pert blonde fellow reporter (actress Jane Nigh), "there's a story here. Men like Sam who have paid their debt to society and who are now trying to make a place for themselves in it again—they deserve a chance. The *Illustrated Press* is going to see that they get it."

On TV, Steve Wilson listened to people's problems better than anything else. The show was practically an anthology series, with Steve and Lorelei Kilbourne just touching at other people's lives, perhaps being in at the pay-off. A policeman would stand accused of using excessive force. "I'm alone out there, Mr. Wilson. They got guns and knives, and blackjacks, and brass knucks and broken bottles. I've got my two good fists. Patterson attacked me with a sledge hammer. Sure, I broke his jaw and put him in the hospital. Can't an honest cop defend himself against punks in Big Town any more?" Steve Wilson listened. He sensed a story there. "Lori"—he called her that sometimes—"Lori, they are out there day and night, defending you and me and all the folks in Big Town safe in their beds. Are we going to let down one of the guardians of justice when he's in trouble?" No, the staff of the *Illustrated Press* would not do that.

Steve Wilson listened to the mothers of men on Death Row. "Sure and me boy stuck up that candy store and shot the old man and woman. Don't me boy have a right to make a livin' too?" He listened to sad-eyed chorus girls. "You said I was a nice girl, Mr. Wilson, for telling you how Rocky murdered that little crippled girl. It's been a long time since anyone said that to me. You start out with hopes and dreams. But your shoes get run down and your stockings get a run. Then you let some guy put his arm around you and buy you a beer. Then it's a lot of beers. Then you find yourself drinking this stuff. Whiskey. Yes, Miss Kilbourne, *whiskey*. No, no, I'm not crying. Just go. But I'll always remember what you said."

Finally, Steve Wilson heard another speaker with another message. "You're fired!"

We in the viewing audience never heard that message but we saw its results. Easygoing, middle-aged reporter Steve Wilson (Patrick McVey) was replaced with youngish managing editor Steve Wilson (Mark Stevens).

This gaunt, rather grim Steve Wilson was perhaps a bit closer to

the old radio version, but the style of the program was now semidocu-
mentary with just a touch of relevancy—landlords were gouging tenants
for outrageous rents and the *Illustrated Press* would not stand for that
going on in Big Town. It seems to me that this version did not last
long. I can't recall Mark Stevens' Steve Wilson *ever* slugging a crook,
although he psychoanalyzed a few into giving themselves up.

Apparently not even a movie star like Stevens could keep the circu-
lation of the *Illustrated Press* up, and Big Town became a ghost town.

Other radio mysteries made it to television. Some like *The Man
Called X*, with Barry Sullivan replacing radio's Herbert Marshall, bore
so little resemblance to the original that all that was left was the title.

At least one pioneer television mystery retained the same set of
voices we were familiar with from the radio—Jay Jostyn in the title role
as Mr. District Attorney, Len Doyle as the tough detective, Harrington,
and Vicki Vola as the faithful secretary, Miss Miller. I'm talking about
the very, very early live series circa 1950. We did not have television
yet in our area, but I saw publicity stills of the series in such magazines as *Radio (and Television) Mirror*. It looked okay. But later
stories frankly admitted that the viewers were disappointed in Jay
Jostyn's *youthful* appearance. On the radio he sounded like a white-
haired father figure, such as Lorne Greene. But on the tube he appeared as a young man, possibly still in his late twenties. The stories
even had to be changed on TV. On radio, Harrington always did the
rough stuff—fighting the crooks with his bare hands, three or four to
his one. Now the younger "chief" seemed much more capable of that
kind of action.

When Ziv bought the rights and the series moved to Hollywood,
David Brian, appropriately white-haired, took over the title role. In the
unkindest cut of all, Brian even took over the *radio* series. Jay Jostyn
changed offices at the city hall and became police commissioner on a
short-lived radio series, *Top Guy*. (Come to think of it, at that, the
show lasted until about the end of major nighttime radio programming.) Later, Jostyn achieved a logical progression to become a judge
on *Night Court* on the visual medium.

The David Brian *Mr. District Attorney* series soon developed a
"documentary" style. That is, in order to achieve realism all the characters ceased to behave like human beings. No longer did Harrington
burst into the D.A.'s office yelling, "Chief—me and Murphy machine-
gunned two of Killer McGurk's boys as they was trying to knock over
the First National, but McGurk hisself got away. And, Chief—that
ain't all! McGurk forced Tommy, the mayor's son, into the getaway
car with him!"

No, now Harrington would submit a typed report to D.A. Brian, who would read it over, and for a dramatic curtain to Act I, Brian would lift his snowy eyebrow in marked concern. (The report was about a ring of fraudulent washing machine repairmen who were overcharging on faulty or unnecessary repairs, an evil that the D.A. swore to wipe out. This was, of course, no reflection on the vast numbers of honest washing machine repairmen who operated within our community and helped make it a better place in which to live.)

Much of this documentary quality given to *Mr. District Attorney* and *Big Town* in the early days of the tube came from Jack Webb's *Dragnet*. Even before it got to TV itself, its image from the unseen but image-making medium of radio was having its impact.

Remember big, beefy Ben Alexander as Frank Smith, brooding Joe Friday's jovial sidekick? I do too, but I remember also Friday's *first* partner, Ben Romero, played by Barton Yarborough, one of the finest actors on radio. Ben Romero was of Mexican-American extraction, hailing from Texas. The crooks he and Friday questioned would make frequent comments about Ben's drawl, referring to him as "Dixie-mouth" or "Cottonhead." Did Ben ever kick their teeth in, or tell them that he was going to add an "assaulting an officer" charge to their sheet? No, no police officer on a program from the official files of the Los Angeles Police Department would do a thing like that. Instead, Ben's partner, Joe Friday, would tell the wise-lipping hood, "Just stick to the facts."

Ben Romero appeared only in the first three *Dragnet* television shows. The first one concerned a maniac who was wired up with dozens of sticks of dynamite and was determined to blow up City Hall unless his brother was released from jail. Joe and Ben made several nerve-racking attempts to disarm the walking bomb, before Friday got the dynamite into a bucket of water and dashed madly out of the building with it, only to—Remember how that one ended?

After only two more episodes, actor Barton Yarborough died of a heart attack (the same fate for Ben Romero in the script). Stock footage from those few shows was used as flashbacks in several other *Dragnet* episodes over the years.

Briefly, Joe Friday had an older man for a partner, Ed Jacobs (played by Barney Phillips), and then the chubby Frank Smith (Ben Alexander). (Years later, of course, he would have a much older partner, Bill Gannon—veteran character actor Harry Morgan—one who was retiring from the force in the initial pilot episode, but who went back into service for the rest of the new color films.) The average viewer still remembers Officer Frank Smith best, if he or she is old enough to have seen the original series.

In a recent *TV Guide* interview, Jack Webb discussed the early series. "When I designed *Dragnet* with Jim Moser, we decided . . . the way to go for a documentary approach: the people aren't as important as the overall idea. . . . Maybe it was the infinite patience with which Moser and I built up the detail in *Dragnet* that they liked. Then, perhaps the lack of histrionics in all areas gave it a different look. . . . The so-called monotone disappeared after about the third season, but for some reason it stuck in people's minds. . . ."

The "so-called monotone" could hardly be said to have "disappeared" by most viewers—but it did become *modified*.

How many comedy and variety shows presented a take-off on *Dragnet* with wooden actors droning, "How's your mom, Joe?" (Often, the "satire" wasn't much of an exaggeration of the performer's own acting style. Though he's never appeared on the show, Robert Stack *always* seems to have just stepped out of *Dragnet;* an element perhaps in the success of his own *Untouchables* series.) Garry Moore has the perfect, expressionless *face* for *Dragnet* parodies, and he and Durward Kirby performed countless such skits. "Frank, go to the P.D.C.L. and run a P.M.R.X. on the D.C.T. and make it P.D.Q. And, Frank—how's your bursitis?"

Sometimes it is the comedy exaggerations we remember instead of the real show. When the program was revived in color a few years back, it seemed to have changed a lot. Or had *we* merely changed from those days of the Fab Fifties? An examination of one of the early scripts reveals much of the actual—not burlesqued—style.

FRIDAY: We want to ask you some questions about this man you called the police about. The one who took your money and disappeared. We think he's a confidence man, the same one who's been taking money from a lot of women in this territory lately.

MRS. WILSON: You're quite mistaken about Mr. St. George. He's a charming British gentleman, very polished, distinguished—so much like my first husband.

SMITH: St. George. So that's the name he used.

MRS. WILSON: That is his name. William Eric St. George, from Manchester, England. I'm sure he's not one of those confidence men.

SMITH: Then why did you notify the police, ma'am?

MRS. WILSON: Well . . . He's been gone three weeks now and I think perhaps something has happened to him.

FRIDAY: Did this William St. George propose marriage?

MRS. WILSON: I can't see how that's germane to his disappearance.

FRIDAY: It's part of his M.O., his modus operandi, Mrs. Wilson. He always proposes marriage.

MRS. WILSON: Well, he did propose, yes. But, Sergeant, this can't possibly be the same man. He's so cultured. Shakespeare, Goldsmith
—the words flowed from his mouth in a smooth, steady stream.
SMITH: Same guy, Joe.

Needless to say, this story was true, with only the names changed to
protect the innocent.

Other crime fighters besides detectives were adapted from radio—
the heroes of the afternoon adventure shows for kids. (But how many
parents also listened in with covert interest?)
    One of the earliest to appear was Captain Midnight, stalwart leader
of the Secret Squadron. According to the legend, during World War I
a young American flier completed a dangerous mission on which the
whole course of the war depended and flew back to his base just as the
steeple clock struck twelve o'clock—Midnight. After the war he became
leader of an undercover group of fliers and espionage agents. They
fought master spies and criminal geniuses the world over—notably that
fiend among fiends, Ivan Shark.
    Beginning in syndication on radio in 1938, and going to the Mu-
tual network two years later, the good Captain made an abortive television appearance about the start of 1950. This could not exactly be
said to be a *series* in the precise sense of the word, since Captain Midnight made only *one* appearance which was run over and over every
week. (Today TV producers have lowered the number of original
episodes made for a year of some shows to twenty-two. Despite pre-
emptions for specials, some few episodes are run three times in one
season. The maker of the first Captain Midnight improved on this
situation—they ran one episode all year long.)
    Of course, the Captain's part only served as an introduction to other
fare—a frame. Behind the title *Captain Midnight's Adventure Theatre*
we saw a modern jet plane coming in for a landing. The screen faded
into a view of a handsome young man in flying togs walking into a
room. "Hello, Secret Squadron members. We'll get right to our thrilling story in a moment, but first let me tell you how Ovaltine builds
strength and health. . . ."
    After the commercial, the promise of a "thrilling story" was certainly
delivered.
    I remember the first time I saw the Captain Midnight TV show
after listening to it on the radio since I was a very small boy. After seeing this opening of the impossibly handsome young pilot (the unidentified actor looked like the proverbial collar-ad type—no other phrase

could describe him as well) there was an immediate cut to a masked Westerner hanging grimly to the tongue of a runaway wagon, while bands of horsemen rode around the careening vehicle, shooting at each other in a fury of gunsmoke and trail dust. I blinked in complete disorientation. Television was new to me. We had only had our set a few days. Had the channels changed inadvertently? Had the station somehow switched on the wrong show? What did this Western scene have to do with the air adventures of Captain Midnight? The abrupt cut to this Western scene simply did not make sense. I was familiar with the technique of sometimes starting a story in the middle to grab the audience's attention, but this was total confusion. It didn't make sense. But then I thought, maybe TV doesn't have to make sense. Maybe they just put on anything to sort of hold the viewer's eye—like those endless closed loops on toy movie projectors of Betty Boop dancing or Popeye hitting the punching bag. Of course, that was only a very early impression of TV formed by a dumb, inexperienced kid.

After I watched this battle out West for a minute or two, it dawned on me that this was an old Zorro movie serial. (I got a clue from all the characters constantly referring to the masked man as "Zorro.") I pieced reality together. I got my head straight. "Captain Midnight" was merely the filmed host of a showing of an old movie serial. (I had already seen celebrities like the TV weather man introducing a package of ancient mystery talkies on the *Eleven O'Clock Crime Theater.*)

While I was disappointed not to see a picturization of the adventures of Captain Midnight, his young aides, Chuck and Joyce, and the faithful mechanic, Ichabod Mudd, in their encounters with the evil Ivan Shark, I was certainly pleased to see the great movie serials I had seen in theaters as a very small tyke.

The Zorro serial was *Zorro's Fighting Legion* with Reed Hadley, and as the weeks went by it was followed by *The Mysterious Doctor Satan, King of the Texas Rangers, Daredevils of the Red Circle* and other well-made Republic chapter plays. Since the package contained all Republic productions, the series (to my knowledge) never ran Columbia's *Captain Midnight* serial. (Of course, Dave O'Brien in the title role would not have matched up with the collar-ad host Captain Midnight.)

After a few years there was a full-flown Captain Midnight air adventure series, made especially for TV. Richard Webb played the stalwart Secret Squadron commander. Added to the cast was the good, mad (or at least eccentric) scientist, Tut, played by Olan Soulé, who had played various parts on the old Midnight radio series (although not this one, which was created especially for TV).

A typical script was "Electronic Killer" by Dane Slade. In the story, the Secret Squadron leader had traced a group of spies to their lair. The actual shooting script reveals the following description.

Exterior in front of house
It is a deserted-looking house "out in the sticks." There is no other house in sight. The sedan comes into scene and stops. Fred and Marius get out, go into the house. Door closes behind them.
Closer shot at car
Midnight slips out of the car from where he had been hiding, goes toward the house.
Close shot at side window of house
Midnight comes in, looks through window.
Interior house through window
Group shot Bart Marius Fred (Captain Midnight's point of view)
No dialogue can be heard, but the action is self-explanatory— Bart is giving Marius the formulas and Marius is giving him a wad of folding money.
Closer group shot inside room
The three men look up in astonishment as the window crashes in. Framed in it is Captain Midnight, gun in hand.
CAPTAIN MIDNIGHT: Hold it! Just like that!
They freeze—but as he starts through the window Bart picks up a chair and hurls it at him. Midnight fires, the bullet presumably hitting the chair. The chair hits him, knocking him off balance, and the men are on him.
Several angles of fight
The four men fight all over the room. They are three to one, and Bart is a giant in size and strength—but Midnight is Captain Midnight. . . .

Later in the story, Midnight rescues a young scientist named Derek Savage from imprisonment in a plane in the air, intended to be the target of a Nike test rocket. The Secret Squadron officer leaps out of the plane wearing a single parachute but holding onto the dazed man of science.

The script also reveals the interesting sidelights that Tut's real name is Aristotle Jones, and that Captain Midnight's first name is Jim. On the radio, his secret identity had been revealed to be Captain Albright, but this was a first to learn his given name was Jim.

The television series carried on the traditions of the radio series and offered premiums—Shake-Up Mugs for cold Ovaltine, drinking cups for hot Ovaltine, arm patches, and codeographs for decoding messages.

These plastic codeograph badges were shiny and pretty but not up to the solid metal badges I could still remember from the Midnight radio show.

These TV giveaways were marked "SQ" as an abbreviation for Secret Squadron. The radio premiums bore the letters "S.S." But S.S. had gained a somewhat unfavorable connotation from Hitler's elite Nazi troops of that designation. Midnight himself was no longer SS-1 but now was SQ-1. He must not have been No. 1 in the ratings because the show did not last long.

Another early series adapted from a popular radio serial was Sky King. The original radio show has been described as a cross between Captain Midnight and Tom Mix, and the same could be said for its video counterpart.

Despite the flying motif, the Tom Mix radio show was perhaps the primary source of Sky King. Set in a fictional never-never land of the "modern West," Tom Mix and His Ralston Straight Shooters had cowboys on horseback existing side by side with foreign spies in airplanes. Tom Mix himself often left Tony's saddle to take the controls of a trusty biplane. When Sky King came on the air, he merely chalked up more hours in the air than Tom Mix. His crew was much the same as Tom's Straight Shooters. There were Sky's young aides, Penny and Clipper (Jane and Jimmy on Tom Mix), and a crusty old sidekick, foreman Jim Bell (the Old Wrangler on Tom's show). Tom had his TM-Bar Ranch, and Sky King was ramrod of the Flying Crown Ranch.

Tom Mix never made it to TV, except in reruns of the early talkies made by the cowboy star who served as a basis for the radio show (although, as late as 1972, I was asked to do a pilot script for an unsold Tom Mix television series by a producer). Since Tom Mix was one of my favorite radio shows, and since it never came to the TV screen, I looked on Sky King as a surrogate for the Straight Shooters' show.

If Sky King on TV was not better than the Tom Mix radio show (and it wasn't), the Sky King television show was better than the Sky King radio show. I can think of few, if any, other programs that I considered better in their video versions than on radio.

The radio show had all the right elements, but they worked better on TV. The whole concept of old West situations with cattle rustlers and gunfighters existing in a present-day period with cars and airplanes can get pretty silly, but the Sky King series made such things as believable as possible. If there was a stagecoach involved in the story, it was because there was a Frontier Days celebration in the town of Grover. Sky himself (played by Kirby Grant) did not routinely tote

17. Ricky Ricardo (Desi Arnaz) waits for his wife Lucy (Lucille Ball) to announce when she is ready to go to the hospital. Virtually the entire nation awaited the birth of the Ricardos' son on *I Love Lucy*. Off screen, Lucy gave birth to a real son who never appeared in the series.

18. Jackie Gleason as Ralph Cramden is warning Audrey Meadows as Alice (off screen) that she is risking a sudden trip right to the moon, while Art Carney as Norton looks on in this scene from *The Honeymooners*. Originally one sketch on *The Jackie Gleason Show*, the popularity of *The Honeymooners* grew to the point where Gleason's many talents were almost drowned in this one *shtik*.

19. The disarmingly youthful Walter Cronkite and the primitive studio conditions (is that a desk or an orange crate?) show how much things have changed in television since this photo was taken, about 1955.

20. A very artificial "great outdoors" graced the set of *One Man's Family* on September 22, 1951. Marjorie Gateson and Bert Lytell as Father and Mother Barbour and Lillian Schaaf as daughter Hazel were beginning their third season of the program created by Carlton E. Morse on radio in 1932. Like most writers, Morse liked getting paid for reruns. In 1949 he began tele-vising his radio scripts from the thirties, giving youth back to his then middle-aged characters.

21. Gertrude Berg brought *The Goldbergs* to TV from radio, still successfully portraying Molly Goldberg, a char-acter she had created as actress and author over twenty years before.

22. The Hansens pose for a family photograph on the 1950 Mother's Day episode of *Mama*. The show concerned a Norwegian family living in the United States and starred Peggy Wood as Mama, Judson Laire as Papa, Rosemary Rice as big sister Katrin, Richard Van Patten as brother Nels and Robin Morgan as little sister Dagmar.

23. In an era when situation comedies seemed to concentrate on the antics of the bumbling husband, it was refreshing to watch *Father Knows Best*. Robert Young portrayed Jim Anderson, an intelligent insurance man, while Jane Wyatt played his wife Margaret. There was an earlier radio version in which Jim did fall into the bumbling husband syndrome. But on TV Father really *did* know best.

24. There have been many Lassies and many young boys have portrayed Lassie's master. On television, this was the most fondly remembered combination. Here Tommy Rettig smiles, posing alongside his male collie costar of the first TV incarnation of *Lassie,* now seen in syndication under the new title *Jeff's Collie.*

25. Tuesday nights were once dominated by Milton Berle, known to his adoring fans as "Uncle Miltie." Berle was notorious for going to extravagant lengths to get laughs, a policy which has not changed even in more recent years, as shown here.

26. Comedy teams were often created on television. Sid Caesar and Imogene Coca constituted perhaps the greatest of such teams, debuting in 1949 on *The Admiral Broadway Revue* and eventually going on to star in the popular *Your Show of Shows*. This photograph shows Sid and Imogene reunited after a four-year split, together again for ABC's *Sid Caesar Invites You* in 1958.

27. Garry Moore made the crew cut and bow tie his trademark on television. In 1950 alone, the easygoing and affable Moore hosted a total of three different variety programs and in 1954 began moderating the panel of the quiz show *I've Got a Secret*. His last regular series, *The Garry Moore Show*, which premiered in 1958, introduced Carol Burnett, who went on to become one of the medium's biggest female stars.

28. No one ever provided more problems for her father than Margie Albright, played by Gale Storm, on *My Little Margie*. Charles Farrell, a former matinee idol of the movies, was Vern Albright, a handsome widower who spent most of his time squirming out of the situations that Margie invariably stuck him in.

29. Apple polishing was still fashionable when Connie Brooks taught English at Madison High. Here Eve Arden, star of *Our Miss Brooks*, turns the apple on student Walter Denton, a typical teen-ager of the early 1950s as played by Dick Crenna. (Crenna later became known as "Richard" and starred in a number of TV series and motion pictures.)

30. William Gargan, once a real private detective in Brooklyn, New York, was aptly suited to star in the NBC mystery series *Martin Kane, Private Eye*. This 1949 photograph reveals the economy of studio sets during the early days of television.

31. Richard Denning and Barbara Britton, as Pam and Jerry North, on the half-hour series *Mr. and Mrs. North*. The show, which added a dash of humor to the weekly murder stories, was about a mystery writer and his wife who regularly solved some very real crimes.

32. One of the numerous shows that made the transition from radio to television was *Big Town*, a series chronicling the adventures of the crusading reporter of the *Illustrated Press*. Pictured here are Patrick McVey as Steve Wilson (played on radio by Edward G. Robinson) and Jane Nigh as his loyal partner Lorelei Kilbourne.

sidearms, although he would relieve a crook of his gun after a fast knockout punch to cover the other hoods rushing into the room. His niece Penny (Gloria Winters) was no supergirl, felling men twice her size with a judo chop. No, she was a pretty normal teen-age girl, thankfully not a demeaning female clown the way radio and TV portrayed most girls of her age. She outsmarted some adult males on occasion, but girls have been doing that a long time.

The airplane incidents were realistic, thanks to writers Dorell and Stuart McGowan. No wing-walking or dogfights—just take-offs over rocky terrain, flying on instruments through a stormy sky. The downgrading of glamor was probably necessary for a more sophisticated, though still juvenile, audience.

All in all, Sky King seemed to be aware that he was in a new decade, on a new medium. He changed with the times and survived into the sixties. Most other adaptations of radio adventure shows were not improvements.

The Lone Ranger radio series always dealt with vast landscapes, matters of destiny on which the growth of a young nation depended. There were armies of cavalry, tribes of Indians, spectacles of mighty railroad engines going down with collapsing bridges. It was easy with radio sound-effects men and a handful of skilled actors. It was too costly for television. The Lone Ranger's personal frontier became a desert, populated by ghost towns. The Masked Man and his faithful Indian companion usually fought one villain and his single henchman. It offered too small a challenge to such a godlike super-hero.

Clayton Moore gave his all to the role of the Lone Ranger, but he had powerful competition from the towering figure created in our imaginations by the booming voice of radio actor Brace Beemer. Moore, particularly in the early episodes, copied much of the Beemer style in his speech. Yet he himself had his own style and presence. In the end, he convinced us. We accepted him as the Masked Man. Jay Silverheels as Tonto never had any problems—he was perfect.

Another series which, like *The Lone Ranger*, was also created by radio producer George W. Trendle and his chief writer, Fran Striker, was less effective in its transition to television. *Sergeant Preston of the Yukon* had tales of the gold rush which involved the heroic Mountie and his champion lead dog, Yukon King, attractive enough to younger viewers. But a more mature eye could see that some stories were shot almost entirely on one trapper's cabin set, virtually all from one camera angle. The films had all the disadvantages of a live TV drama, with few, if any, of its virtues.

Aside from adaptations from radio, there were a handful of shows that appeared on radio and TV at exactly the same time, designed jointly for both media.

Wild Bill Hickok appeared in the early fifties with the deadly law officer of history converted into the typical B-Western do-gooder portrayed by the A-Western star, Guy Madison. The contract must have been incredibly lucrative to lure Madison from serious roles in important theatrical films to play in a children's show. The radio series filled the 5:30 P.M. slot (in all time zones), Monday, Wednesday, Friday, on the Mutual network vacated by *Tom Mix* only a couple of years before. The TV show was generally seen on Saturdays, rubbing shoulders with *Space Patrol* and *Kit Carson*.

The Kellogg's cereal company was behind the advertising campaign and they also managed to acquire the services of Andy Devine as Hickok's deputy, Jingles. As with many B Westerns, the comedy sidekick seemed to be the whole show. Guy Madison was merely handsomely stalwart, modestly claiming to be "James Butler Hickok, mister." But Jingles would waddle forward enthusiastically. "That's *Wild Bill* Hickok, mister! The bravest, strongest, fightingest U.S. marshal in the whole West!" Jingles was warm, human, and given to making mistakes—like mistaking Raymond Hatton, playing an outlaw leader, for a kindly old rancher. But Wild Bill's guns and fists were always there to rescue him from any trouble.

Another series appearing on both radio and TV in 1949 was Duncan Renaldo's version of *The Cisco Kid*. One of the pioneer Western series for television, it was the first made in color (at a time when black and white reception was hard enough to receive). The man behind the show was Duncan Renaldo, not only as star, but in many creative and business aspects as well. Renaldo had been a producer and director, and romantic leading man, since the days of the silents. During a hectic career with improbable ups and downs, he also played character parts, doubled in stunts for stars (he leaped the Fremont Pass on horseback for Tom Mix). But his talent and intelligence always brought him back to the top.

In 1943, he began his association with the Cisco Kid in a series of theatrical features. In 1949, he appeared in the first of the 156 episodes that brought O. Henry's Robin Hood of the Old Southwest to television. Well, perhaps not O. Henry's unwashed bandit. Renaldo's vision was of a clean, youthful Don Quixote and his faithful Sancho Panza setting out to right the world's wrongs.

What better sidekick could he find than Leo Carrillo? Carrillo had been a popular character actor in movies for decades, was one of the finest horsemen in films, and a leader of the Spanish surnamed community of California. He played the character of Pauncho for humor, but he was never the fat *bandito* stereotype.

Renaldo was in his fifties, and Carrillo was seventy-five years old, when they were doing the hard-riding necessary for the Western series. (Pressure of time caused Renaldo and Carrillo to give up their radio roles to Jack Mather and Harry Lang.)

While Carrillo did much of his own action, he had a stunt double in the person of George DeNormand. DeNormand had been the dean of stunt men for decades. He introduced such other well-known stunters as Dave Sharpe and Tom Steele to the business. In some of his last talkies, George DeNormand doubled Tom Mix riding and fighting. In the Rough Riders movie series, DeNormand did stunts for both Buck Jones and Tim McCoy in the same film. For thirty years he was Spencer Tracy's regular stunt double in every film. He even doubled Boris Karloff in *The Bride of Frankenstein*. His work for Leo Carrillo came after he officially retired, and it was hard work for a man supposedly taking it easy.

One *Cisco Kid* episode called for Pauncho to be caught in a tumbling stream. DeNormand took the dunking for Carrillo, but unfortunately he cracked his head on a floating log. After a moment, Duncan Renaldo saw that DeNormand was nowhere in sight. Renaldo dived in the water and successfully pulled DeNormand to safety in a bit of real life heroism.

Dave Sharpe was another stunt man in evidence on the filming of the *Cisco Kid*, sometimes playing a bad man that Cisco-Renaldo fought. They had been doing such screen fights together since the days of the old F.B.O. studios in the thirties. Renaldo, Sharpe and DeNormand are still friends to this day.

Film-making can be dangerous. In one episode, Renaldo was supposed to dodge a fake boulder being rolled down a cliff at him. Although a fake, the "boulder" weighed sixty-five pounds, being made of a wooden frame, canvas, *papier mâché* and filled with bed springs to make it bounce. Unfortunately, the supposed bad man threw the boulder directly at Renaldo, instead of *rolling* at him, slow enough for the actor to dodge. It struck him directly on the head, breaking the fifth and sixth vertebrae of his neck. He was hospitalized, paralyzed for two months. But nature, or Renaldo's fighting spirit, prevailed and slowly feeling and movement returned.

The episode in which the accident happened was completed with the use of doubles, but an announcement about Duncan Renaldo's hospitalization was made, and he was flooded with thousands of get-well cards.

While the *Cisco Kid* show was filled with action, Renaldo always took a stand against violence, as he does in his current lectures and public appearances. "I didn't believe in my heart if you are going to play in television, particularly, and go into the people's homes, you ever have to let the protagonist become a killer," he told me in a recent interview. "We used the guns—to shoot the guns out of the *banditos'* hands, that sort of thing. . . . I only used *one* gun—that's enough for anybody. . . . Any time you point a gun at anybody you only have one meaning to the gesture—'I want to take your life.'"

Renaldo pointed out, "On my gun I inscribed on one side: 'Do not touch me.' The other side says 'I don't want to hurt you.' It has a rattlesnake on the line of sight, with the head up for the sight. It bites like a rattler without giving you a chance."

The convictions of Duncan Renaldo are sincere—simple but thoughtful. "It's a dastardly thing to paint our people who worked so hard to leave us this beautiful West as criminals and brigands. . . . They were not that. They were hard-working people. . . . We have killed more people on television than populated the Old West!"

The makers of Sano cigarettes were behind another sales campaign putting a series called *Martin Kane, Private Eye* on radio and TV at the same time. The series was the quintessence of all private detective shows, owing a lot to Dashiell Hammett's Sam Spade of fiction, film and radio, and similar characters created by Raymond Chandler, James Cain and even Mickey Spillane, who was beginning to appear on the scene.

Many of the shows that were television contemporaries of *Martin Kane* might as well have been adapted from the horde of radio detective shows, although they were not literally that.

Rocky King, Detective starring Roscoe Karns appeared on the Dumont network Sunday nights. Karns had mostly played good-natured Irish sidekicks in the movies, companion to Fred MacMurray and such stars. But the added years seemed to give him enough authority to be believable as a dogged, efficient police detective—if not quite a brilliant one. The cases he was called upon to solve rarely called for brilliance. A furrier had faked a robbery to collect on his insurance. Rocky and his assistant discovered the second warehouse where the furrier had stored the supposedly stolen coats, and engaged in a perfunctory gun fight with a couple of underlings. (There were no flashes from the guns—just recorded gunshots played when Rocky poked his gun in a dramatic gesture.)

The bits of humor made the show quite appealing. The program usually began with Rocky at the breakfast table, talking with his wife Mabel. Mabel was never seen, always off stage. The device had been used on radio with characters who never spoke (such as Myrt the telephone operator on *Fibber McGee and Molly*). The character who never spoke on radio, and the character who spoke but never appeared on TV (another later example was John Beardsford Tipton on *The Millionaire*), was a transparent, inside joke—an attempt by the producer to save money. *Nothing* was paid a non-speaking (and therefore non-existent) actor on radio, and *less* was paid an actor on TV who did not appear and only spoke lines. At least the device began this way, although it often developed that a certain viable commercial appeal was developed in the "mysterious" unseen speaker.

Certainly such an interest developed in Rocky's wife Mabel.

Rocky would talk with Mabel about getting the sofa reupholstered (Rocky had probably carelessly shot a hole in it while cleaning his service revolver). Mabel was busy whipping up Rocky's eggs in the kitchen while he sat in the dining alcove, but she spoke insistently about needing the upholstering job. Then Rocky's assistant would show up and tell him he was needed down at headquarters to question that witness in the First National robbery. Throwing a kiss to Mabel, Rocky would put on his trench coat and rush off into action.

After the case was wrapped up, Rocky would phone Mabel at home and try to tell her about it, while she told him about *her* trouble with the upholstery man. "Yes, dear . . ." Rocky would say complacently. "Yes, dear . . . I'll be right home." Then, with a wave to his fellow workers, Rocky King would disappear into the night.

Viewers became insistent on *seeing* Mabel, not realizing that this would spoil their fun of trying to imagine what she looked like. (And as if such a prototypical 1950s housewife could look anything but relentlessly average.) Finally, Rocky announced Mabel would be shown the next week. But when the big moment finally arrived, it proved too great a strain for the camera—all that could be seen was the cracked lens. Some weeks later, in answer to continuing letters, the show finally did show a view of Mabel—but a very out-of-focus one. Wisely, the producers had decided not to let the viewers' demands spoil the audience's fun.

As with most live TV series, *Rocky King* had its bloopers. My colleague, Don Glut, recalls that one of Rocky's several handsome young assistants came back on the set a bit late after a commercial break. "Well, where have you *been?*" Roscoe Karns ad-libbed. The assistant's face colored. *"You* know!"

Another radio-type detective show (although "original" to TV) was *Man against Crime* with Ralph Bellamy as Mike Barnett. The show was on film and had a lot of chases and fisticuffs, somehow a lot more believable than when live. "Mike Barnett . . . with two Ts" (as he introduced himself) was seen in such diverse places as a slain anthropologist's laboratory laden with skulls and bones, and a litter-strewn subway tunnel dodging hoods' bullets behind cigarette machines (which seemed to be stocked exclusively with his sponsor's product, Camels—Ralph Bellamy read the list of veterans' hospitals that got a dole of the health product each week at the end of the show).

But the authentic radio-TV joint venture remained *Martin Kane, Private Eye.* The vigorous effort of doing a live half hour each week took its toll of middle-aged leading men. The series began with William Gargan, but he was followed by Lloyd Nolan, Lee Tracy and finally by a more youthful Mark Stevens. The live series ended, and nearly a decade later Bill Gargan came back in a brief *Martin Kane* series that had been filmed in Europe.

One of the problems of the original live series was covering for the lead getting from one set to another—from his private investigator's office to the library of an eccentric millionaire, for instance. One technique was having the supporting character—the kooky millionaire—talk into empty air as if Martin Kane was really there—until the lead could actually get into position and be seen as the camera pulled back. On one show—I believe Lee Tracy was doing it then—the star somehow got on the wrong set and the murder suspect had to keep talking to a blank wall for a *long* time. "So you have more of your infernal questions for me, do you, Mr. Kane? I'm getting tired of this constant harassment. I'm not going to put up with it much longer. No, not much longer at all. Not much more. I'll tell you that. Not much more at all. . . . Well, I suppose you're going to ask me what I know about Cousin Herbert's death. All I know is that he died Wednesday night at nine o'clock. Now I suppose you want to know where I was at Wednesday at nine. I was home alone and—"

"What do you know about your cousin Herbert's death?" Martin Kane gasped out breathlessly.

An actual episode of the show began with the billboard:

ANNOUNCER: Martin Kane, Private Eye . . . presented by Model . . . Dill's Best . . . Old Briar Pipe Tobacco . . . and their new teammate . . . Sano cigarettes for full smoking pleasure, yet only one per cent nicotine. . . .

KANE: This is Martin Kane with a story about a dime-a-dance girl, a Broadway joint, a niece named Irma Field, and her uncle, a distinguished old gent named Brooks Field who currently has his Brooks Brothers parked in my guest chair. . . .

BROOKS: That's the story, Mr. Kane. Irma disappeared earlier that night. I haven't seen or heard from her in two months.

KANE: Did you notify the police, Mr. Fields?

BROOKS: No, I haven't—and for a good reason. Irma is the recipient of a trust that falls due shortly. If the trustee finds she isn't home with me, she could incur a penalty.

KANE: I see—you want to protect her.

BROOKS: I'm very fond of my brother's daughter even though she seems to have fallen into the wrong company.

KANE: Do you have a reason for making that remark?

BROOKS: No . . . except for her attitude before she disappeared. She became—shall we say—hard. Position meant nothing. She acquired sort of a . . . bebop outlook on life.

KANE: She began to "dig it," huh? Okay, Mr. Fields, I'll take on the job. . . .

Kane grimly began his search for this girl with a dangerous "bebop" attitude toward life, finding her "digging it," working at a dime-a-dance joint. The manager (known as the Hacker) waltzed him out the door when Kane tried to speak to the girl. As always, Kane took his troubles to his friendly neighborhood tobacco salesman.

KANE (narrating): First stop was Hap McMann's tobacco shop. The ex-police captain was engrossed in the morning news. . . .

MCMANN: Hi, Marty. . . . Isn't this a little too bright—plus a little too early for you?

KANE: I wouldn't say so.

MCMANN: You wouldn't, huh?

KANE: No. . . . Hap, what's your opinion of the various dime-a-dance joints along the main stem?

MCMANN: Comme ci, comme ça.

KANE: Do you know a character called "the Hacker"?

MCMANN: A thoroughly bad citizen—although nobody ever got anything on him.

KANE: Thoroughly bad in what way?

MCMANN: One second, Marty— Yes, sir?

CUSTOMER (approaching): Do you have Sano cigarettes?

You could bet that Hap did have Sano cigarettes, and that he would explain to the customer that they delivered full smoking pleasure yet contained only one per cent nicotine. And you could bet that Martin Kane would find out just how bad the Hacker was in his search for the dime-a-dance girl which would lead him onto murder, a smidgin of violence and a neat solution.

Martin Kane was selling cigarettes right in the middle of his show. But then so were Arthur Godfrey and all the Little Godfreys in the middle of all their singing and dancing and ice skating Wednesday nights and every weekday morning.

The years rolled by and more and more radio stars and radio shows came to television. Perry Mason turned out to be monumental Raymond Burr (radio's Mason, John Larkin, was another lawyer on another show—*Edge of Night*). *Our Miss Brooks* with Eve Arden and Marie Wilson's *My Friend Irma* started on radio but almost seemed to have been cast with TV in mind. *Fibber McGee and Molly* were unsuccessfully impersonated by Bob Sweeney and Cathy Lewis when the originals, Jim and Marian Jordan, did not care to move into the new medium. But *The Great Gildersleeve* came to TV with almost all the radio cast. Willard Waterman had been playing the pompous Gildy, the middle-aged, lady-chasing water commissioner of Summerville, for years on the non-visual medium, taking care of his little nephew, "Lee-roy" (although the Gildersleeve role had been created by Hal Peary).

The programs from that other form of broadcasting came to television, and some were successful with an audience too young to associate anything with radio except music and news. But those shows from radio were simpler—with exaggerated characters, simple values, often repetitious situations. They were designed for a time of innocence and non-questioning.

Some radio favorites arrived incredibly late. *The Green Hornet* did not appear until 1966 when the *Batman* craze made a series about a masked crime fighter acceptable. But some viewers complained that the show about the idealistic crusader really wasn't nearly as funny as *Batman*.

The most beloved adventure show from radio did not hit TV until 1973 in a two-hour pilot film made years before at the height of *Batman*'s popularity. *I Love a Mystery* made fun of its soldier-of-fortune heroes, Jack Packard, Doc Long and Reggie York, ridiculed the whole concept of mystery or adventure stories, and told the audience—correctly—that they were fools for watching this piece of trash.

Carlton Morse's original *I Love a Mystery* was a fine show. Nostalgia is not a full explanation for the appeal of its genuine character humor, chilling atmosphere and transcending imagination. But, like so many of the shows created for radio, *I Love a Mystery* required a willing suspension of disbelief. That is, it required belief.

As the fifties unfolded, we were no longer in the age of belief. We were in the age of television. We had to be shown it all. And for better or worse, we were shown it.

CHAPTER 12

"*A Window to Other Lives*"

"Joanne, you can't let that woman take Patti away from you," Marge Bergman insisted.

Joanne smiled bravely. She did that best of all. She patted the bun on the back of her head and liberally doused a bowl with a lot of baking powder. "Marge, you know my mother-in-law is—ill. I don't believe Patti or any other child should be placed in the hands of one who is criminally insane."

"That's true," Marge agreed. "That's very true. I wish I had the vision to see things as clearly as you do, Joanne."

"I see what a mother must. Where's my big spoon?"

"The big spoon is behind the spice rack."

Joanne picked up the big spoon from behind the spice rack. She frowned. She was thinking about something, something that made her sad but determined.

That was the way things were, approximately, near the beginning of *Search for Tomorrow* in 1951. (The first episode was shown on September 3.) From the first show, Joanne has been played by Mary Stuart, who is still baking and burning with various passions.

I remember those stirring words of the title floating against the clouds in those early days. The show was only a quarter hour then, but it seemed to pack in as much misery as the thirty-minute serials of today.

The program was done live in the beginning. Doorframes floated phantomlike in thin air like a set from some avant garde play, but all the housewives and unemployed, ill, or malingering males at home took it in stride. The performers made mistakes. Sometimes they would start talking like real people and making a lot of sense—then you knew they had lost their place in the script and were making up their dialogue as they went along.

Miss Stuart, who plays Joanne Barron Tate, has been in the same role longer than any other performer in television. Dave Garroway, Howdy Doody, Jerry Lester, Dagmar, *Rocky King, Captain Video,* Red Skelton, Ed Sullivan, *Maverick,* have all come and gone, but Mary Stuart remains. Considering all the grief she has endured, it is a tribute to the tenacity of the human spirit.

Joanne lived through the death of her first husband, Keith Barron, only a short time after the serial went on the air. A car crash took him out of the story, leaving Joanne a youthful widow with a daughter, Patti. Patti was a cute kid—rather tall for her age, then again short, blonde, brunette, chubby, lanky—all depending on the child actress portraying her at any given moment.

The nutty mother-in-law fought Joanne for custody of the child, won for a while, but finally lost and flipped out. She kidnaped Patti and the police made a desperate search for the girl and her kidnaper through the woods—or at least through a maze of music stands with branches tied to them. Mary Stuart recalled in a 1972 *TV Guide* interview that director Charles Irving made an exciting chase out of it in those days of live TV with a lot of close-ups and intercutting.

Everything was done live on camera. Mary Stuart ran a sewing machine right on the show and made curtains for the set. She mixed up batches of corn muffins for the lunchroom she ran on the show. Some viewers complained that she used too much baking powder in the muffins but they forgot she was supposed to be baking for a café, not a family. She was making twelve dozen muffins at a crack.

With all that baking, it is perhaps understandable that at times Joanne looked like Betty Crocker. She was impeccably neat in a starched apron, her hair in a bun. But as the years went by she let her hair down. The public came to accept that a twice-married woman did not have to look virginal.

In fact, by the time of her second marriage in the story, the actress, who was happily married in real life, was eight months' pregnant. Camera angles tried to hide it, but there may have been shocked whispers out there in middle America.

Her second husband was businessman Arthur Tate. The strain of being married to Joanne and running a business proved too much for him, and a fatal heart attack followed.

It was probably a case of sinking ratings rather than a sinking illness. A new leading man was called for and he appeared in the form of Robert Mandan, playing the part of Sam Reynolds. Arthur had been portrayed by Terry O'Sullivan, who had the unpleasant task of reading a script in which he died. That has always been the saddest scene for soap opera performers to perform. It means they are out of the story and out of their pay checks for appearing on the series.

According to Miss Stuart, O'Sullivan merely packed up his car, loaded in his new bride, a girl some years his junior and six feet tall, and drove off into the sunset, toward California.

Sam Reynolds was not destined to become Joanne's third husband. For personal reasons, actor Mandan left the show. The fighting then going on in Biafra gave the writers a chance to finish him off in topical fashion. While on a United Nations mission, Sam Reynolds' canoe capsized and he was not seen again. At least not until the character reappeared, played by George Gaynes, later played by Roy Schuman.

The valiant searcher for tomorrow, Joanne, had become entangled with someone new but Sam Reynolds' return from the apparent dead ended that.

Of course, Joanne's troubles are hardly over. Most recently, she has had trouble with her eyes, suggesting she may be heading toward blindness.

Blindness is one of the classic trio of problems that have beset soap opera heroines since radio days. Besides the prospect of going blind, soap opera leading ladies are most often subjected to amnesia and being tried for murder. (Romantic difficulties are omnipresent, of course.)

Even longer-lived than *Search for Tomorrow* is *Guiding Light;* the show has been on the air more than thirty-five years, twenty of them on TV. (For several years in the early fifties, the show was on *both* radio and TV.)

Two of the cast members have remained the same since the days of radio. They are Charita Bauer as Bertha Bauer (a coincidence of last names) and Theo Goetz as Papa Bauer.

The program was created by Irna Phillips, one of the legendary writers of radio soap opera. Miss Phillips was one of a select group including Elaine Carrington, Sandra Michael and Frank and Anne Hummert who created the majority of the daytime serials of radio. Irna Phillips was the only one of this group to achieve much success in the new field of television, and she soon became the overseer of the story lines for *The Guiding Light* and other TV serials.

The light that guided on the famous serial was originally the light of religion or faith. Most radio soap operas were created to fill definite categories, such as folksy (*Ma Perkins* or *Just Plain Bill*), or humorous (*Vic and Sade* or *Lorenzo Jones*). *Guiding Light* was originally intended as a religious soap opera. Several ministers had running parts through the early stories, but the concept soon changed and the Bauer family became the central focus of the drama.

Theo Goetz commented in a recent interview that the early days of live telecasting were the most hectic. Since these serial episodes stand little chance of being rebroadcast, the only reason for putting them on video tape recordings is for the convenience of the actors and production staff. Mistakes can be corrected but, production time being as valuable as it is, mistakes are usually left in. Any day's viewing can see garbled lines of dialogue, actors calling each other by the wrong character name, and the omnipresent shadow of the boom microphone hanging overhead to pick up actors' voices. (They were so familiar on the recent supernatural serial, *Dark Shadows,* that it was suggested by some critics the show might better be called *Mike Shadows*.)

However, in the 1970s, two serials were still being telecast live on most occasions—at least, in the Eastern time zones. Those shows were *As the World Turns* and *The Edge of Night,* both of which began the same day, April 2, 1956. Like many TV soap operas, they have their roots in radio.

The Edge of Night is what amounts to a TV version of the old *Perry Mason* radio serial. Mystery novelist Erle Stanley Gardner owned the character names on the series, but the radio show was written by Irving Vendig. Gardner reserved the *Mason* title for a prime-time TV series, so Vendig merely started a new TV show about another crusading lawyer, Mike Karr (played by John Larkin), and moved many of the radio actors and production staff to the TV show.

The live quality of the TV series did present problems. On one occasion Larkin was supposed to burst dramatically through the front door of a home for a confrontation with principals in the plot. The door refused to budge when the cue came up. Not wishing to shake the whole set down, Larkin rushed around behind another wall and came dashing out of a closet. The viewers were supposed either to have forgotten that it was a closet or to think he had been hiding there all the while or, better still, not to think about it at all.

On the same series, Mandel Kramer plays a chief of police, a role that should come naturally to him after having played David Harding's assistant on *Counterspy* and the title role of *Yours Truly, Johnny Dollar* on radio for years.

The TV police chief had a crook trapped in a liquor store in one episode. The script called for a blazing, bottle-busting shoot-out between the two of them. Kramer was willing, but his revolvers were reluctant. They would not fire their blanks on cue. The special-effects man did not miss his signal, however, and the wired liquor bottles began blowing up in response to Kramer's noiseless shots. The gunman suspect was lucky. He could get out of the scene by falling dead.

In spite of such difficulties, producer Erwin Nicholson preferred live performances. Television was not intended to be merely a second-run house for old films. Actors have agreed. TV has none of the advantages of either movies or stage—the only element it has unique to itself is instant communication. "It is a matter of adrenalin," Nicholson says. If the actors and technicians know the show must go on at exactly three-thirty, with no hedging, everybody *has* to be at his best to make it go.

On *As the World Turns* the role of Nancy Hughes has been played by Helen Wagner for the better part of two decades. Most of those years have been spent in a TV kitchen set with pots that boiled over, dishes that cracked and oven timers that screeched like banshees—none of which were called for in the script.

The cast of *As the World Turns* reveals what an inheritance video soap opera has from its radio counterpart. The featured players have included Don MacLaughlin (once Dr. Jim Brent on radio's *Road of Life* and the title-role star of *David Harding, Counterspy*); Bill Johnstone (who took over Orson Welles's role in *The Shadow*); and Fran Carlon (Lorelei in *Big Town*), among others.

One of the earlier radio soap operas came to the dawn of television as well. It was *One Man's Family,* written and produced by Carlton E. Morse. The first series, shown once a week at night circa 1949, starred Eva Marie Saint as Claudia Barbour. It was during one of these live shows that Claudia was talking to a fellow passenger on an airplane. The actor "went up" completely on his lines, looked around at the rows of passenger seats, said, "Excuse me—this is my stop," and walked off the plane.

A few years later, in the middle fifties, the famous title was tried again in the more conventional five-afternoons-a-week format. Morse, the creator of the show, had the universal desire of writers to get paid for "reprints" of his earlier work. The TV series used scripts originally done for the radio series twenty years earlier. All the characters well known to listening audiences were given back their youth. The eldest son, Paul Barbour, was now brooding over his experiences in World War II (instead of World War I as he had done on radio). He was portrayed by the ruggedly determined but mature Russell Thorson. "I went through hell in the war," Thorson explained. "I'm thirty-five but I look forty-five." (When the original radio Paul, Michael Reffetto, retired, Thorson also took over on the air.)

The TV series showed scenes that older viewers had only heard decades before. We saw the twins, Claudia and Clifford, sitting by the sea wall overlooking San Francisco Bay and talking about the problems of growing up. With those two, most of the problems sprang from entanglements with the opposite sex. Their rendezvous was a shiny new snapshot of a conversation overheard in the twilight decades before.

Father and Mother Barbour were around as well. Fanny Barbour rather took a back seat to her husband, Henry, like most of the Barbour clan. Henry Barbour was a stockbroker and very much the head of his family. He meant well, and he meant to have his way. In a recent interview, Carlton Morse mused, "Father Barbour was 'Mr. Republican' and his son, Paul, was a liberal Democrat. The same kind of arguments they had are going on today."

For some reason, the daily *One Man's Family* television show lasted only one season. (The radio series went on for twenty-eight years.) When *Peyton Place* was a popular nighttime serial on the home screen, there was talk of reviving the *Family* show, but it never happened. It is a pity. There were always enough implications of sex in the Barbour saga, which could be made specific for today's jaded audiences. What's more, there were strong characterizations and literate writing, enough to earn the radio series a Peabody Award. Some television soap operas have also won awards but it is difficult to perceive in what way they are superior to their competitors.

One Man's Family's dialogue speaks for itself.

HENRY: If a child's world is wrecked before his eyes, what has he to cling to? It immediately colors his conception of the whole world. Immediately his mind forms the belief that there is nothing solid, nothing stable, nothing that he can ever quite believe in, and he grows to manhood a cynical, unbelieving citizen, certain that the only law of the universe is "Every man for himself."

CLAUDIA: I see . . . and if a country's citizens believe it's every man for himself, then that nation's going to be an aggressive, belligerent country.

HENRY: Yes, believing in the law that it's "every nation for itself."

PAUL: I think you've stated your case very well, Dad. And your solution to the world's ills is the maintaining of a high type of family life?

HENRY: Exactly. Bring back the old-fashioned type of family built on true affection and discipline!

Perhaps those sentiments were better on 1930s radio than repeated (slightly embellished) for the 1950s TV audience, especially the TV soap opera audience, which rapidly became less interested in international affairs than in extramarital ones.

Today soap opera deals with abortions, adultery, homosexuality. It was different in the good old days of the fifties. Not even once did an episode of *Mama* deal with Katrin being molested by her schoolteacher, Mr. Peepers. It was a different world. Better? At least different.

CHAPTER 13

The Buckeroos' Gold Mine

"Howdy, all you little buckeroos out there in Televisionland, and have we got a real treat for you today!"

He said it, that host of the afternoon old Western movie. Pretty often he was some old prospector type with a beard that did not look quite real. He was different in different cities, but on the NBC-TV network coast to coast he was a gent with a *real* beard, and a real connection with Western films, Gabby Hayes.

Gabby would come on the screen, after firing the famous Quaker cannon that puffed up the Puffed Wheat that was "Shot from Guns." Then Gabby would scratch his beard and mutter something like "Now let me see, whar in thunderation did I leave off yesterday? Sometimes I do get a mite forgetful. I recollect the morning I went out and saddled the cow, and made my horse madder than blue blazes. . . . Wait a tick now. . . . Seems to me my pal Johnny was riding after the stagecoach . . ." The scene faded into one of Johnny Mack Brown on horseback, from one of his movies of twenty years before.

The Gabby Hayes Show cut up old features, serializing them against their original intention, stretching them out over a week of daily fifteen-minute episodes. Locally, some hosts, such as the Masked Rider, a version of the Lone Ranger who never made it outside of Evansville, Indiana, introduced complete sixty-minute features each afternoon, close to original length. There were only a few minutes out for commercials, sometimes only two or three minutes in an hour (not that the stations would not have liked to get more if they could have in those early days). Other stations ran the cowboy pictures in two half-hour segments, one a day, or worst of all, padded out one feature in a two-hour time slot, with the movie interrupted for as much as fifteen minutes while the small fry of the audience displayed their pets, their model planes and their own well-scrubbed faces to the cameras.

It was the old Western film itself that I tuned in to see. What great action films, what great stars there were in those days of the 1950s TV showings of Western movies. These were not the series made for TV, which were just getting started, but the authentic old theatrical B Westerns. No matter that these films had been made twenty, even thirty years before. No matter that some of their stars were dead. As much as Milton Berle or Robert Montgomery or Kukla, Fran and Ollie, the early stars of television were Tom Mix, Buck Jones, Tim McCoy, Ken Maynard, Bob Steele, Hoot Gibson and, in just a bit, Gene Autry and Roy Rogers.

When the grim facts of mortality permitted, these monarchs of the plains would make appearances *live* on the programs showing their old movies. (They received no residuals, but the renewed publicity often rescued them from obscurity, gaining them paid appearances with rodeos and circuses and royalties from toys and comic books. These cowboys promoted their old films as diligently as if they were being paid directly, because they were benefiting indirectly.) Sometimes the side-by-side comparison with the living man and his image of twenty-five years before was shocking. Crash Corrigan showed up in front of the live cameras, seemingly having doubled his weight. It has been reported that the late Whip Wilson made one appearance barely able to stand, after having rehearsed a barroom scene for too many times.

However, other stars of the era were so little touched by time that they could actually film new scenes to match up with old footage of themselves from decades before. William Boyd did this for his Hopalong Cassidy series, although mostly concentrating on off-screen narration for the condensations of his feature films into a half-hour format. Lash LaRue also did a new frame for his old films, matching his old image almost perfectly. (But he had been a late-comer, and there was only a five- to ten-year gap for him to bridge.) James Newill contributed new introductions to his *Renfrew of the Mounted* features, not completely masking the fact that Renfrew kept gaining and losing twenty years from one scene to another.

Tim McCoy

Of course, the greatest host of old Westerns on TV, the man introducing his own feature films of an earlier era, was Colonel Tim McCoy. McCoy has been called "the greatest living figure of the

American West." The title does not refer just to the cinematic West but to the West of history and tradition. McCoy represents a living link, uniting the *real* American West to the motion picture. Later stars, younger men, of course, could not have the advantage of living through those last days of a fading frontier simply because the era was over before they were born.

While few men alive saw the "Wild West" during the classic period of the 1880s, men like McCoy were there around the turn of the century when there was still plenty of wildness left. While working near Lander, Wyoming, rounding up wild horses (and learning Indian traditions on the Wind River reservation), McCoy proposed a new regiment of Rough Riders to former President Theodore Roosevelt at the outbreak of World War I. Although the plan was not formally accepted, McCoy and his cowboys did enter the Army. He became a captain and in France met Major General Hugh L. Scott, an officer in the Indian wars of some thirty years before. Soon McCoy was a colonel, and a firm friend of the general.

After the war the two officers traveled the West together, learning of Custer's Last Stand from some of the survivors on the Indian side, as well as other lore of the frontier. Tim McCoy then traveled with William F. Cody (Buffalo Bill) during the last season of his Wild West Show. The two men were much alike—dynamic, heroic showmen who wanted to show the world what the West had been, legendary figures in their own time.

Tim McCoy was perhaps the foremost expert in the use of guns to appear on the screen, the top gun fighter. He went West after the time of the classic shoot-outs of Wyatt Earp and Wild Bill Hickok, but more than once a mere demonstration of McCoy shooting the spots out of a falling playing card quelled would-be troublemakers. (Although at other times his fists finally had to quiet matters.)

While a man of action, McCoy was primarily a man of learning and leadership, the image he projected on the screen. It was too formal an image for some, who preferred the earthiness of Buck Jones or John Wayne, or the sense of fun projected by Hoot Gibson or Ken Maynard. It was for his knowledge that McCoy was brought to Hollywood in 1923. He supervised the Indians used in making the silent film, *The Covered Wagon*. Unfortunately the film's director, James Cruze, called on little of McCoy's knowledge of how Indians (or pioneering whites, for that matter) actually behaved, in making a movie that reduces epic grandeur to lifeless posing, always seen from a great distance. The film was successful, however, and McCoy went on to become an actor in silents. In the twenties he made a series of elaborate historical Westerns for MGM, including *Winners of the Wilderness,* directed by W. S. Van Dyke, in which McCoy played an Irish officer in the British Army in pre-Revolutionary America during the French and Indian War. Others in the series were more conventional Westerns, but McCoy always seemed too dignified for the fun of the cowboy-action pictures of Tom Mix, Buck Jones, Ken Maynard and others. The brooding, sentimental, inner-directed silents of William S. Hart, from *On the Night Stage* to *Tumbleweeds,* were in a class by themselves, the art of a solemn man. Along with Harry Carey, Tim McCoy gave the silent Western the figure of a mature man but a friendly, healthy one.

Of course, it was not his silents that Tim McCoy hosted in person on early television, but his B pictures of the thirties and early forties.

Tim McCoy would appear by the corral fence on the old sound stage, little touched by the years, and often would begin by explaining something about Indian sign language:

MCCOY (*He makes two fingers of his right hand into a V shape, and forks it over his straightened left hand*): Now this is the Indian sign for "horse"—straddling sign for an animal that is ridden. . . . An Indian and his horse were inseparable. . . .
(*He points two index fingers to his eyes.*)
When an Indian wanted to express sorrow, he pointed to his eyes like this, then with his fingers, he showed the path of his tears. . . . The Indian had cause to shed many tears in his dealings with the white man. . . .

After a bit of Indian lore (and often a few serious words about the "bad shake" given the red man) McCoy would lead into the showing of one of his earlier films.

One such film was *The Westerner,* an epic title for a solid little B picture centering around a rodeo. The 1936 Columbia picture, directed by David Selman from an original story by pulp writer Walt Coburn, told of how Tim Addison (McCoy) had to contend with gamblers trying to throw the fix into the bucking horse contest. In one scene Tim's father, Zach, took him into his office for a serious talk.

ZACH: They tell me you're going to ride a horse called Bad Medicine, Tim.
TIM (*reacts in surprise*): Bad Medicine? Why, I broke him when he was a colt. He's no outlaw.
ZACH: Maybe you're lucky.
TIM: Wait a minute, Dad. How does anyone know what horse I'm going to ride? The drawing hasn't come off yet.

ZACH: I was just telling you what I heard.

TIM. There will be no sport to that. I can ride Bad Medicine blind-folded. I'll be heartbroken if I draw that horse.

ZACH: So will the gamblers, if you don't. They're betting a lot of money on this contest and they're laying everything on you to ride Bad Medicine.

Tim did not like things being made too easy for him. (This was characteristic of the hard men who carved out the West, personified today in the public utterances of actor John Wayne.) He was being given a horse he knew he could ride to make him a sure thing for gamblers. Tim deliberately let himself be thrown from the bronc and limped away to the jeers of the arena, but confident in his own heart he had done the right thing. This was, of course, only the first step on a long, dangerous trail to put an end to these spoilers of the West.

The Rough Riders

Tim McCoy's last starring pictures were for Monogram in a series made around 1942. In these he joined with two silent veterans, Buck Jones and cagey old-timer comedian Raymond Hatton, to form the Rough Riders. It was a landmark series, since it featured *two* of what a critical consensus often considers the *seven* greatest Western stars of all! (The Big Seven would be William S. Hart, Tom Mix, Buck Jones, Ken Maynard, Hoot Gibson, Tim McCoy and John Wayne.)

The Rough Riders series was very well designed, with a tight format and a number of trademarks like such successful radio shows as *The Lone Ranger*. Jones, McCoy and Hatton portrayed three veteran United States marshals who always worked undercover at first to break up the bandit gangs that plagued the West. It was Jones who was the top hand, given both more prominent billing and a larger piece of the action. Tim McCoy often posed as a preacher or gambler in clawhammer coat to get information, while Jones stuck to more colorful cowboy outfits and did the rough stuff. One or the other of them often worked himself into the gang, allowing for scenes of conflict where the two friends supposedly would be close to settling matters with their guns or fists.

Of course, Raymond Hatton as Sandy Hopkins was always on hand to aid "Buck Roberts" and "Tim McCall." Whether the old lawman was posing as a medicine show man or as a horse trader, Hatton gave a depth of warmth and reality to the comedy relief that no other

Western comic even tried to match. It was only for the showdown that the three lawmen dropped their poses and went into action together. "This here is whar the Rough Riders ride again!" Sandy would vow. And ride they did—with Jones and McCoy still doing most of their own riding and other stunts, though well into middle years. What foolhardy gang would dare to stand its ground against *both* Buck Jones and Tim McCoy? But many tried—Harry Woods, Charles King, even that new menace of the forties, Roy Barcroft. They tried, and failed, falling beneath Buck Jones's fists or under Tim McCoy's guns.

When the mess of trouble was over in those parts, the three men on horseback would say good-by before heading back to their respective states, to await another assignment that would bring them together again. Each one in turn said to the other, "So long, Rough Riders!" Then the three would ride out down three separate trails, and you heard the "Rough Riders' Song," which opened and closed each picture.

> The Rough Riders ride—beware!
> The Rough Riders ride—take care!
> There's no finer bunch of fighters in the land,
> Chasing every outlaw and guerrilla band.
> The Rough Riders watch the trail!
> The Rough Riders never fail!
> They keep law and order everywhere they go,
> Without a fear of any foe,
> And it's ten to one they're on *your* side,
> When those old Rough Riders ride—
> When the Rough Riders ride!

No other Western series developed such a well-knit and faithfully followed format. Other series might have more technical polish at Republic, but the cast, the characterizations, the time period were constantly changing; not so with the rock-solid Rough Riders. Much of the credit for this was due veteran producer Scott R. Dunlap.

After a stirring conclusion to one of his films and a few more lessons in Western lore, Colonel Tim McCoy would close his show, but there were hundreds of other Western hosts from coast to coast on local stations—Sheriff John, Bob Atcher, Uncle Johnny Coons and countless others.

It was the pictures these hosts showed that were really the important thing. Even some of the smallest fry got impatient with the time-consuming palaver on the part of the host and were chomping at the bit to get down to the action. There was plenty of action those afternoons. During the fifties kids and even young adults could see a great panorama of Western programs—"B" pictures, budget Westerns, cowboy pictures—whatever one chose to call them, you recognized one when you saw it. Stars and their films separated by as much as thirty years still managed to rub shoulders comfortably in that early evening time spot, usually four to five, or five to six.

At no other time, has the average person been able to see so many and so varied an assortment of these cowboy Westerns. It was a feast, a bonanza, a gold mine.

Buck Jones

There were many, many cowboys riding their broncs out of rodeo stalls in those days. Probably the top favorite (always excepting Hopalong Cassidy, who had a series of his own) of these rerun wranglers was Buck Jones. The square-jawed costar of Tim McCoy in the Rough Riders series won the popularity poll on his own merits—good looks, appealing style, and ability at stunting and acting—and partly because he outnumbered the competition ten ways from Sunday. Because of his lasting quality, Buck Jones made hundreds of sound Westerns and virtually all of them turned up on television. Many stations ran nothing but Buck Jones films on three days of the week. One station ran nothing but Jones oaters for several months, a new one a day, with no repeats.

Buck Jones accomplished what no other Western star of his time was able to do: he was a major star of Westerns in the silent era, and he remained a major star of Westerns in the sound era. Almost every important Western star of the silents appeared in talkies, but those appearances were either very few or were in films of steadily declining importance. Buck Jones stayed near the top. (He took second billing in one B production, a serial, and a supporting role in a major production.)

His background was colorful and authentic. Born in 1891 in Indiana, he and his family soon moved to a ranch in Oklahoma where he grew up. When hardly more than a boy he became a trick rider with a Wild West show. After that he entered the Army, serving first in the Philippines and later as an aviator. He did stunt work in Tom Mix pictures at Fox and then was made a young rival star to Mix at the studio. In Westerns like *Western Speed* and in many non-cowboy roles, Jones became a top name in the movies.

The advent of sound slowed Buck Jones down only a bit, as it did every other major Western star. Sound ended forever big-budgeted "fun" cowboy pictures. A complex situation reduced some of the biggest names in motion pictures—such as Jones, Tom Mix, Ken Maynard —to appearing in second-string B pictures for the first time in their careers.

Buck Jones, at least, made a success of his lower-budgeted films. He did not have the voice of a trained actor, but his vocal delivery was masculine and sincere. In early pictures such as *Men Without Law* and *Range Feud* (costarring boyish John Wayne), Buck Jones came off well.

A significant early picture was *White Eagle,* directed by Lambert Hillyer. In the picture Jones played an Indian brave, the title role. All through the film Buck fought the heavies and worshiped the heroine with a "hopeless" adoration. Finally, in the last reel, it was revealed that Buck had been raised by the Indians but was really white. Thus he could marry the girl. It cast a sour note into the proceedings. All through the picture one was made to admire Buck and his Indian companions, but now we were supposed to see that the only truly admirable people always turned out to be white. The old perennial, *Ramona,* had long ago made interracial marriage between Indian and white acceptable to a mass audience, but perhaps it was thought that this would not be acceptable in a movie primarily for impressionable children.

The same title and theme were used much later for a serial starring Buck Jones, with vast amounts of stock footage from the earlier feature.

Although he was not responsible for this story line, Jones often wrote his own vehicles and sometimes directed them (*Law for Tombstone*). He had a weakness for comedy, casting himself as the dumb cowpoke. Despite some of his admirers' praise for this modesty, Jones did not do comedy well. He was too formidable and quietly brooding ever to seem funny, unlike more cheerful, fun-loving men such as Hoot Gibson and Ken Maynard.

In an interview I had some years ago with screen villain Roy Barcroft, that actor gave a couple of insights into Buck Jones's personality. "When you had a fight with Buck Jones, he *really* hit you." Of course, in movie stunt fights, both men are supposed to just narrowly miss, so that it *looks* as if they connected. Barcroft did not seem overly concerned. "That was just Buck's style," he explained.

Barcroft told of one occasion when the director told Buck Jones to climb a high, rock-strewn cliff. Jones refused. He told the director to get a stunt man. Barcroft went on to say, "Buck told him: 'They couldn't see it was me way up there, and if they can't see you do it, why do it?'"

Buck Jones was heroic enough when it really counted. Trapped in the Coconut Grove night club fire in 1942, he went into the flames time after time to bring people to safety, suffering fatal burns in the process.

His final film was not a Rough Riders picture with Tim McCoy as is sometimes reported, but actually a Monogram "special," *Dawn on the Great Divide* with Raymond Hatton and Rex Bell, a good Western performer making an infrequent appearance before concentrating entirely on politics; he eventually became lieutenant governor of Nevada. The picture contained many elements of what would later be called the "adult Western"—romance, pathos, a complex cast of characters. One could say that the picture was returning to the realism of William S. Hart but, more accurately, it was only anticipating the soap opera elements of the little Westerns that were to be made especially for the TV screen.

Perhaps if he had lived Buck Jones would have been given some of the minor A Westerns such as those starring Randolph Scott. Yet Jones did not have the slickly professional polish associated with such entries. Probably he could have lasted out the B cycle into the early fifties, possibly as second lead to a younger man, a singing cowboy such as Jimmy Wakely (grim as that thought might be). Thereafter, he would have had the guest-star cameos for the productions of Mike Todd, A. C. Lyles and Alex Gordon. Whatever pictures he might have been in would have been better for Buck Jones being in them.

Despite his death, television gave Buck a new generation of fans, many as dedicated as their fathers had been. Sometimes people with no show-business connections can be incredibly naïve about its workings, and more than one middle-aged man of my acquaintance, marveling at how well he had kept his looks, thought Buck Jones was back making new films for TV.

Hoppy

The so-called "trio" Western perhaps best realized in Buck Jones's Rough Riders series was developed earlier almost simultaneously in the Three Mesquiteers and Hopalong Cassidy series in the early thirties.

While the Hopalong Cassidy pictures took their title from a single character, they were much in the mold of the trio films, since they featured the mature hero (Cassidy), the youthful hero (James Ellison, later Russell Hayden and others), and the comic old-timer (Gabby Hayes, later Andy Clyde).

Based loosely on novels by Clarence E. Mulford, the moving pictures altered Cassidy from a gimpy-legged, heavy-set, elderly, red-haired man to a tall, slender, handsome man with distinguished silver hair, dressed in tailored dark blue riding clothes (which photographed black) as portrayed by the former romantic idol of the silent screen, William Boyd.

During a period heavily influenced by radio listening, it was perhaps Boyd's *voice* that enabled him to establish the Cassidy character so successfully. It was rich and deep, commanding and expressive. It belied the apparent age suggested by his white hair, indicating that certainly his vigor was not diminished by the years. He asserted instant authority over the rest of the cast, and comes out on top when compared in memory with such competitive Western stars as Ken Maynard and Gene Autry, whose speaking voices all seemed too light and unschooled.

Another strong element of the series was the father-son relationship between Hoppy and his young sidekick, Johnny Nelson (Ellison) or Lucky (Hayden). Young audiences always seemed to be looking for a father figure, but one with the "curse" of actually being a commanding father taken off by being only an uncle (Uncle Jim in the *Jack Armstrong* radio series) or only a mature, fatherly man as here or in many Harry Carey Westerns. Hopalong Cassidy gave orders as foreman of the Bar 20 ranch, but he also gave his trust and loyalty to his younger friend. In *Sunset Trail*, Lucky deliberately throws a stagecoach race and joins a gang of outlaws. "Lucky go bad? Not that boy!" Hoppy vows, and is of course proven correct.

Boyd was not a Western performer in the sense of being a rider, stunt fighter, et al. at first, but rapidly gained much ability in that line. In the above-mentioned picture, Boyd can be seen almost in close-up deftly sliding from a moving stagecoach to the saddle of his white horse, Topper. While not spectacular, it was a feat involving some skill and risk, one not likely to be performed by a star in a picture today. (In the same line, in one of his last TV half hours Gene Autry can be clearly seen actually grabbing the reins of a runaway wagon team from the saddle of his own horse and bringing them to a stop. We're so used to more extravagant feats by stunt doubles that it is not easy to fully appreciate that the star was working a lot harder than he really had to in order to give the audience a bit more.)

Adding much to the Cassidy films were the comic sidekicks, first Gabby Hayes and later Andy Clyde. Hayes was an accomplished character actor and can be seen in some early John Wayne pictures as a very dignified elderly law officer or as a clean-shaven bandit leader and swindler. Of course it was as the talkative old codger, *sans* store teeth, that he won his greatest fame. His role of Windy in the Hoppy series was well conceived and seldom interjected comedy bits or numbers but only supplied touches of comedy arising naturally out of the situation.

Andy Clyde as California Carlson was a later replacement. With a career going back to the silents, Clyde was a master of "takes" and falls, and conveyed much the same warmth as Hayes.

More humor came from the lovesick moonings of youthful heroes Ellison and Hayden. (The two ex-sidekicks of Hopalong Cassidy got together in later years and made a series of their own. This particular series is often attacked by some critics for a repetition in cast and settings for economy, giving each film much the same look. As a matter of fact, the films are so charmingly done, with a kind of tongue-in-cheek lightness, that they are some of the few old B Westerns acceptable to a modern audience and still being shown.)

Hoppy's own romantic interludes, with an old flame or with a woman gone wrong, were more serious—in fact, usually tragic. Of course, he was the only cowboy hero of the era who was able to get away with a romance of any intensity whatsoever.

It was producer Harry Sherman's vision of the series that prevailed through a number of directors and distributors. Originally he designed the films as basically character studies following the Mulford novels, with only the final reel blazing into large-scale action in which Hoppy either led a large posse to the rescue or was rescued in turn by Lucky and the others. A stirring *agitato* (often "Dance of the Furies" from Gluck's *Don Juan*) accompanied the action, sending a stirring thrill through the youthful audience.

As time went on the format was liberalized, with action occurring naturally within the story. Some of the later films, when the series switched from Paramount to United Artists were among the best. *Forty Thieves* featured handsome Kirk Alyn (later a hero of serials, notably *Superman*) as a crook out for election as mayor at any cost. (Alyn was not a rider in those days and had trouble even sitting on a horse for medium shots. He reports the horse sensed his unease and kept reaching around to bite his toe.)

The very last Hoppy pictures were produced by Boyd himself on the cheapest possible budgets. Nevertheless, the Boyd-Cassidy personality made even these films enjoyable.

With the revival of his films on television, Boyd at first only added narration to the condensations of his theatrical features. Then he made a series of half-hour television films with none of the old cast but himself, and added Edgar Buchanan as a character called Red. By contrast, Hoppy was now the ostensibly young hero after nearly twenty years in his role. (The films were reasonably well produced within TV limitations, looking a bit more expensive than some of the last theatrical films.)

Both the TV and theatrical Hoppy films have played off and on for years on TV. About 1962 there was a strong campaign to revive the popularity of the series and return it to its old fame. But the series was withdrawn within a few weeks. Again, in 1972, a Los Angeles station, KTLA, tried bringing back the Cassidy pictures, one feature a week, at five o'clock Sunday afternoon. Seventy-four-year-old Bill Boyd was even induced to pose for new color publicity stills in his old outfit and to do new voice-over promotional announcements for the series. (No, he did not still look and sound the same—but still pretty damned good.) Unfortunately, mixed reaction resulted in spotty, irregular scheduling after a few weeks. One wonders if a "right" time can ever be found to revive the Hopalong Cassidy series for modern, cynical audiences.

Three Mesquiteers

The other trio Western to appear about the same time as the Cassidy films was the Three Mesquiteers series. The films were freely adapted from stories (actually, just the characters) by William Colt MacDonald, with, it need hardly be said, a tip of the sombrero to the immortal Alexander Dumas. There was a long-running series from Republic Studios, but the initial entry was produced by RKO under the title *Powder Smoke Range*.

This 1935 production was termed in advertising "the Barnun & Bailey of Westerns." It starred Harry Carey, Hoot Gibson and Guinn "Big Boy" Williams as the Mesquiteers and featured Tom Tyler and Bob Steele (both of whom, coincidentally, were later to play Mesquiteers in other films) and such other old-time cowboy favorites as Wally Wales (Hal Taliaferro), Buffalo Bill, Jr., Buddy Roosevelt and Art Mix. (The last three named were *not* relatives of Buffalo Bill Cody, Teddy Roosevelt or Tom Mix—they just hoped one would think so.)

Carey, Gibson and Williams were cast, respectively, as Tucson Smith, Stoney Brooke, and Lullaby Joslin. Harry Carey, an extremely dignified, mature man, was clearly the leader of the group as Tucson.

(In most, not all, of the later pictures, the character Stoney Brooke was top hand.) Hoot Gibson's role of Stoney was a relatively thankless one, only a step above a comedy relief such as Gabby Hayes. It was not a generous treatment of one of the great pioneers of Western films. Big Boy Williams' Lullaby was a character of about equal importance, but Williams was doing what he did best, lending comedy support. (He was painfully miscast as the hero in some primitive talkies.)

The story of *Powder Smoke Range* was another working of the father-son relationship. Harry Carey had successfully persuaded the Guadalupe Kid (Bob Steele) to give up the outlaw trail, but he had more trouble convincing Tom Tyler as Sundown Saunders.[1]

Sundown had been hired by the local kingpin to kill Tuscon in a gun fight, so that he could not interfere any further in the crooked business going on. The Kid (Bob Steele) went to Sundown, to talk to him earnestly.

KID: I'm not looking for trouble, Sundown. I just want to talk to you. I offered to take on Tucson's fight with you. He laughed at me. You can laugh too if you want to. But I'm telling you if anything happens to Tucson, you'll have me to face.

SUNDOWN: Whoever gets me will have to get me in the back, and that ain't worrying me. Life don't mean anything, anyway.

KID: I used to think that way too, back in the old days when I knew you, I didn't care a hang about living or dying. I think different now. Tucson changed me. I wish you could talk to him. . . .

SUNDOWN: Cut it out, Kid. . . . A year from now you'll forget where you buried Tucson Smith.

When it came to the classic shoot-out in the street, Tucson used a pair of specially procured guns, thirty-two-twenties on forty-five frames. The other Mesquiteers, Stoney and Lullaby, as well as the Kid, argued desperately with Tucson not to use such light guns against the hardened killer. Those "dinky" little slugs would hardly upset his digestion. Tucson persisted. At the hour of sundown the two men walked toward each other down the deserted street. Then, abruptly, when they were separated by the considerable distance of sixty yards, Tucson went for his gun. Sundown outdrew him but

[1] Tyler was a fine western type, a hero in silents and talkies. But the lanky, tight-lipped star played a wide variety of other roles—a villain as here or in *Stagecoach*, the monster called the Mummy, and superhuman Captain Marvel. With his modest acting ability, the list is more incredible than impressive.

blazed away wildly, inaccurately. Tucson's light-caliber bullets sang true. Sundown was down, but not fatally wounded. The graying Mesquiteer rushed to him.

SUNDOWN: You took me by surprise, Smith, shooting at that distance. How'd you know I wasn't accurate over fifty yards?
TUCSON: Your name's Sundown, isn't it? I figured you always planned your fights for when the light was bad so you could draw up close.

Sundown recovered, but eventually lost his life helping Tucson win his battle against the local headman.

Republic took over after this single entry from RKO, and the first of the regular series was *The Three Mesquiteers*, starring Bob Livingston as Stoney Brooke (now the stalwart leader), Ray Corrigan as Tucson Smith (a lighter character now, but still a heroic one), and Syd Saylor as Lullaby. Saylor, a rather urban (though not urbane) comedian, left immediately and was replaced by Max Terhune, a country music entertainer.

This first entry took place just after World War I, but the series shifted time periods with a startling disregard for continuity, all the way from the old West of the 1870s to the then contemporary world of the 1930s and 1940s. *Covered Wagon Days* dealt with an early period, but *Pals of the Saddle* and *Valley of Hunted Men* dealt with foreign spies in modern America.

The cast seemed to change almost as fast as the setting. John Wayne took over as Stoney Brooke for a time. Of course, Wayne was an excellent Western star, from his first movie in 1930, *The Big Trail*, through such primitive Lone Star productions as *Randy Rides Alone*. However, he seemed too mature and too realistic a figure for these extravagant pictures, basically for small boys. He seemed a tough guy, rather than an "action ace," and some of his dialogue to his heroines actually sounded sexually suggestive, something absolutely unheard of in B Westerns. One of the best of the Mesquiteer films with Wayne was *Overland Stage Raiders*. The "stage" in this one was a bus, and mixed up with rustlers on horseback were crooks in modern airplanes. This Western greatly resembled some of the outlandish serials Republic made so well (such as *King of the Texas Rangers*). Despite Wayne's realistic figure in the midst of the fantasy, it emerged a great "fun" picture. (Within about a year John Wayne would be in *Stagecoach* where he more properly belonged. Other John Ford-directed vehicles would follow, including *She Wore a*

Yellow Ribbon and the other cavalry epics. Mesquiteers fans probably never could have foreseen his one-eyed, aging lawman in *True Grit,* but even then, many could see he was cut out for more than chasing airplane-riding rustlers.)

Other stars to be included in the series were Tom Tyler, Duncan Renaldo, Bob Steele and, for one picture, Ralph Byrd (star of *Dick Tracy* and other serials). Bob Steele played Tucson Smith when Bob Livingston resumed his role of Stoney. Eventually Tom Tyler took over as Stoney, but Steele continued as Tucson, now assuming top billing and apparent leadership of the band, according to story lines. Steele gave the illusion of being only about half as tall as Tyler, but he proved the value of being a very good little man.

The comedy relief Mesquiteers included Rufe Davis, Jimmy Dodd and the best (as usual), Raymond Hatton.

Even the leading ladies in this great series were outstanding: Carole Landis, Rita Hayworth (then known as Rita Cansino) and Jennifer Jones (then Phyllis Isley).

The Trailblazers

Republic offered an exceptional series in the Three Mesquiteers pictures, but the smaller Monogram presented two different "trio" Western series of greater historic and nostalgic appeal: Buck Jones and Tim McCoy in the previously mentioned Rough Riders series, and Ken Maynard, Hoot Gibson and Bob Steele in the Trailblazers series.

The contributions of Ken Maynard to the Western film can hardly be overestimated. More than any other individual, it may be argued, he kept the Western film alive at a time when it seemed about to become as extinct as the traveling medicine show.

The foremost element of his on-screen performance was his horsemanship. He is often said by surviving early Western film people to have been second only to Tom Mix as a rider, and some say he was as good. His first screen appearance was in the silent spectacular, *Janice Meredith,* in the role of the most famous American horseman, Paul Revere.

From this small role, Maynard soon became the star of a series of cheap, but interesting, Westerns for one of the countless independent producers, the Davis Corporation. These included *The Grey Vulture,* in which Maynard pictured himself as one of King Arthur's knights in a dream sequence. It was prophetic in that Ken Maynard today has literally become a legendary figure, his name and the fables of his derring-do known to thousands of people too young ever to have seen him in a film, and who would be surprised to learn that he was living in a tiny trailer in the San Fernando Valley until his death in 1973.

Bigger things were ahead for Maynard than inconspicuous Westerns such as *The Grey Vulture*. In 1926 he joined First National and began to make big pictures. *The Red Raiders* from this period is probably more often shown by film societies as an example of the so-called program Western of the silents than any other. It is a good picture, but not really typical of the silent Western in that it is too expensively made and it has a very specialized plot: the Indians on the warpath.

There are no personalized villains in *The Red Raiders*, only the Indians as a kind of force of nature, resisting invading civilization. Massive arrays of Indian forces are seen, as well as impressive shots of Maynard on horseback escaping the raiders and warning the settlers.

These First National films were the peak for Ken Maynard. In these silent days, expensive showcases were mounted for cowboys dedicated to showmanship such as Maynard and Tom Mix. After the introduction of sound, major budgets would be allowed only for those following to some degree the pattern of grim realism offered by William S. Hart. Indeed, in the first few years of sound, it looked as if there would be no place whatsoever for the more colorful cowboys.

Tom Mix was disinterested. The movies were only a part of his life, not all of it, and he wanted to do other things, to travel with his own circus, following the pattern of Buffalo Bill. But Ken Maynard protested in the trade papers: "The Western is not dead!" He committed much of his personal fortune to ironing out the problems of putting sound to outdoor dramas. "I never regretted spending that money developing sound," Maynard told this writer. "Somebody had to do it, and it seemed up to me."

Unfortunately, the earliest results of Maynard's dedication were not good. *Lucky Larkin* only offered scenes of low comedy in a barroom setting for the sound sequences, scenes that stopped the story development dead. Moreover what sound scenes there were proved of such poor quality that they were almost inaudible and poorly synchronized with movement. To top it off, exhibitors persisted in offering these pictures as "all-talking" when there really were only a few static sound sequences, thus angering and alienating the movie-goers.

Eventually Maynard did go on to genuine all-talking films such as *Fargo Express* and *Dynamite Ranch* (both exceptional films, among the best program Westerns ever made). It remained for a big A picture, *In Old Arizona,* directed by Raoul Walsh, with Warner Baxter as the Cisco Kid, to demonstrate the possibilities of sound for the Western film. (As well as the excitement of gunshots and pounding hoofs, small touches such as the sound of bacon frying added atmosphere impossible to the silents.) Yet it was Maynard who stubbornly proved that the "streamlined" Western, the cowboy action film, could also be made in sound. It was the small Western that preserved the whole corps of actors, directors, cameramen, stunt men who formed the heart of the Western film (since until *Stagecoach* in 1939 "big" Westerns were few and far between).

Unfortunately, the low-budget Western utilized sound very poorly in the beginning. There was no background music, especially desirable in the chases.[2] After the *agitato* was introduced, kids could not ride their imaginary horses in play without it. ("Dum-de-dum-dum-dum," we hummed rousingly back in the forties.)

The use of sound effects was equally lacking in the early days. The fights were often staged very poorly visually before choreographed fighting was developed by Yakima Canutt and others. Added to this, when a wild swing missed by a mile and there was no hardy "smack" of fist to confound the eye, the cowboy falling down from a non-existent punch was hard to accept. Generalized scuffling was sometimes heard, or often no sound at all.

Worse still, fights and chases were often still being filmed at silent speed, 16 frames, not 24 a second, giving a jerky, unrealistic speed some film makers thought—inaccurately—would give an exciting illusion of maddened pace.

Slowly, these defects were overcome by such companies as Republic and such film makers as Ken Maynard.

Maynard had his own production company, often in effect directed

[2] To make some primitive sound Westerns more palatable to television viewers, a few have been redubbed with lively music. It is a good idea but, so far, extremely poorly executed. Only two pieces of music were secured, one slow and moody, one fast and furious, and one or the other was inserted over every foot of film in some Guinn "Big Boy" Williams pictures, among others. The repetition was bad enough, but with two choices before him, the unknown scorer often chose the wrong one, putting chase music over the love scenes and slow mood music over the fights.

his own films (without taking screen credit), and more often wrote
them. This was a mistake. While Maynard's formal education was
spotty, he was self-educated, with all the blocks of surprising knowledge and empty holes that produces. He argued points of Latin with
bartenders, and the planets of the solar system with science fiction
writers. The story lines Maynard composed were often bizarre and
incredible in the extreme. The plot of *Smoking Guns,* 1933, was
described by William K. Everson in his book (with George N. Fenin),
The Western:

> In a scuffle the villain is killed by a henchman; Maynard is
> blamed, but manages to make his escape. He is next seen, bearded
> and white-haired, in a crocodile-infested jungle swamp, presum-
> ably in South America. Hot on his trail is Texas Ranger Walter
> Miller, who captures him. They become firm friends during their
> trek back to civilization. As they paddle through swamps, Miller
> suddenly becomes wildly delirious and shoots at a swarm of croc-
> odiles; the canoe overturns, and Miller is badly mauled by a croc-
> odile. Then, in an incredibly written sequence, Maynard casually
> announces that, having lived with the jungle Indians, learned
> many of their medical secrets, it will be a simple matter for him to
> amputate Miller's leg with a red-hot iron before gangrene sets in.
> Miller, understandably skeptical, shoots himself.

After this, Maynard discovers that he is an exact double of Miller
(an opinion the audience can hardly concur in). Going back as Miller
(after shaving and dyeing his hair), he fools everyone completely, and
finally clears himself of the false murder charge.

(Maynard was especially talkative about his "exploration" of the
Central American jungle when he flew his own plane down there in
the twenties. Some of his own experiences were undoubtedly used to
fabricate the plot for *Smoking Guns.*)

Ken Maynard sang in many of his early talkies, and took pride in
being the "first singing cowboy." While he might respect the amount
of money Gene Autry made with the gimmick, the singing cowboy
was a dead end in Western films, and Maynard made more lasting
contributions than that. As for Maynard's singing itself, it was too
undistinguished (although pleasant enough) and too casually presented
to make an impression on audiences.

The 1935 Mascot special, *In Old Santa Fe,* presented the singing
voices of both star Ken Maynard and guest star (so to speak) Gene
Autry in his first screen appearance (except for a tiny part in a

Maynard serial). In the early part of the film, Maynard sang casually on horseback and was insulted by sidekick Gabby Hayes as being the "worst he ever heard." Later, Autry and his sidekick, Smiley Burnette, were spotlighted in a musical short plopped right into the middle of the picture while Maynard looked on passively and turned down a drink of hard liquor as "not for me" (which should have earned him a stunt check). This picture with its dude ranch setting and its modern racketeers was a blueprint not for Maynard's later films but for Autry's.

Ken Maynard continued to make routine Westerns for years, until he was teamed with Hoot Gibson in the Trailblazers pictures.

Maynard and Gibson were much alike, fun-loving and action-seeking in real life. They both flew their own planes in transcontinental air races in the twenties and thirties. Hoot Gibson was probably the less serious of the two. He had been a cowboy and rodeo champion, like Maynard, but earlier, being somewhat older. (Maynard expressed respect and something like hero-worship for Gibson.) But while Maynard may have had strange ideas about the art of the Western film, Gibson never expressed *any* opinion of art himself. He was only in films for the fun and glamor of making them, and to make money.

Many of Gibson's films were bright and enjoyable, from his two-reelers for Universal in the silent era to early talkies such as *Clearing the Range*. His personality has become a stereotype for a constantly recurring screen character—the fun-loving, carefree, roving cow hand. But Gibson never seemed to have a sense of his personal identity, or that these films were more than just a fairly pleasant, well-paid job. Like the character he portrayed (or, more accurately, *was*), he was quite capable of drifting on to something else—dealing in real estate developments, playing minor roles on screen.

Hoot Gibson was teamed with Ken Maynard in *The Law Rides Again*, *Blazing Guns* and *Wild Horse Stampede*. Both men were obviously quite mature by this time, and neither really looked heroic. (Maynard seemed to be strapped into a corset so tight he could hardly move.) They seemed to be more character actors than stars. (Gibson can be seen doing much of his own riding and a few minor stunts. Maynard seems completely doubled in anything requiring fast movement by Cliff Lyons.) The plots of the pictures were routine but offered large amounts of action.

Monogram added a third star to the series, Bob Steele. Steele was younger than the other two, having first entered movies in 1927, but appeared much younger, almost boyish, due to his short stature and tousled, curly hair. Steele joined Maynard and Gibson for *Death Valley Rangers, Westward Bound* and *Arizona Whirlwind.*

These three films are especially interesting in that they are the only so-called "trio" Westerns to actually feature three *heroes.* (In the others, one of the three is a comedy relief.) These pictures were designed to spotlight each of the stars in turn, in fights and chases. There was also a bit more character development, with Maynard presented as the serious leader of the group, Gibson offering moments of comedy (but not on the level of a bumbling sidekick) and Steele as a ladies' man. (Maynard and Gibson were too old for that sort of stuff.) One trademark was Gibson saying, "Say, I've got *another* idea," while Maynard and Steele groaned "not again!"

Maynard was difficult to work with in those days and was dropped from the series. Gibson and Steele went on to make several more pictures together, some with Chief Thundercloud (Tonto of *The Lone Ranger* movie serials) being given costar billing.

Hoot Gibson went on to play smaller roles in several pictures, usually in what amounted to a guest-star role, as in John Ford's *The Horse Soldiers,* until his death in 1962. He had had a full life, and seemed to enjoy every bit of it.

Bob Steele continued starring in pictures for another decade. He played several serious roles, such as Curley in *Of Mice and Men,* and played them well. He was a regular in the comedy-Western TV series, *F Troop,* and still does featured roles in TV and movies.

If the Trailblazers series does not represent the peak of the careers of these three remarkable men, the pictures were at least a thoroughly enjoyable highlight for their fans.

Ken Maynard starred in only one other picture after the Trailblazers series. That was *White Stallion* for Astor. After that, he made a modest living appearing at rodeos and fairs.

Television brought renewed fame for Maynard in the early fifties. It also brought a moment of humiliation. Milton Berle, Mr. Television, discussed the popularity of old Westerns on his show and showed film clips of the youthful Maynard, roping and riding. "Now meet Ken Maynard today," Berle cried. Ken walked out, having grown quite stout, and swept off his sombrero to reveal his balding head for the hoots and jeers of the studio audience.

In the 1970s, Ken Maynard made another screen appearance in *Bigfoot,* a low-budget horror film under the direction of Robert F. Slatzer about the legendary monster of the northern California woods. Maynard played a storekeeper and did quite a creditable job in scenes with another grand old-timer of another genre, John Carradine. Those who love the movies (not merely for the money that can be made in them) will always respect Ken Maynard and those like him.

Tom Mix

Tom Mix was, almost without a doubt, the most admired Western star of all time.

He made only nine talking feature films and one fifteen-chapter sound serial. It was enough to make his name a household word again in the early 1950s, thanks to TV. A new series of comic books was begun by Fawcett, picked up by Charlton, and went on for nearly ten years. Once again, you could buy Tom Mix boots, Tom Mix T-shirts, Tom Mix home movies.

To a great extent, the fame of Tom Mix had been kept alive by the *Tom Mix and His Ralston Straight Shooters* radio series. The broadcast began in 1933, but "Tom Mix was impersonated," as the identification tag went, by a long list of actors including Russ Thorson and Joe "Curley" Bradley. No real attempt was made to imitate Mix's actual voice—a nasal baritone drawl, masculine and Western enough, but unschooled in diction. The radio performers only tried to sound heroic in their natural tones.

The radio series took place in the fantasized "modern West," a never-never land with wild Indians and cattle rustlers on horseback co-existing with cars and airplanes. Contrary to some sources, even a slip on the part of Olive Stokes Mix in her brief but moving book, *The Fabulous Tom Mix*, many of Mix's own films also took place in this allegedly contemporary setting, from the silent *Sky High* through the talking feature *Flaming Guns* to his final film, the sound serial, *The Miracle Rider*. Tom Mix always tried to get the most fun and action out of his movies, not historical accuracy. Cinema shorthand capsulizes his contribution as "showmanship." Every critic has followed the first who used the term. To put it another way, Tom Mix contributed the exact opposite of William S. Hart's realism—Tom Mix gave fantasy to the film Western.

The life he had lived off screen was a fantasy itself, one partly created by his press agents. Certain facts of his official biography are constantly in dispute, and some of them are unquestionably fictitious. However, it appears that much of his fabled life as an adventurer, peace officer, and soldier of fortune can be documented. But never mind. As the newspaperman in John Ford's *The Man Who Shot Liberty Valance* said to James Stewart about John Wayne and Stewart himself: "When the legend becomes fact, print the legend."

The legend of Tom Mix runs to the effect that he went West (from his father's horse farm near DuBois, Pennsylvania) and as a teen-ager had a run-in with rustlers. War broke out between the United States and Spain, and Tom Mix was soon in the Regular Army (not Teddy Roosevelt's Rough Riders). He became involved with the Moro uprising in the Philippines, the Boxer Rebellion in China, and even the Boer War in South Africa. (One event alone should give Mix a claim to immortality: he saved the life—and the comic genius—of W. C. Fields in a bar in South Africa. Fields often told the story, and Mix was one public hero he never tried to deflate.)

After soldiering, Tom Mix returned to serve as a peace officer in Kansas, Oklahoma and Texas. His titles seem to be obscured by the dust of history—sheriff or deputy sheriff? Town marshal or United States marshal? Was he really only an *honorary* Texas Ranger? Nevertheless, he did arrest many criminals and killers.

He also was a hand on the Miller brothers' 101 Ranch and worked along with Will Rogers (one day to become as famous as a personification of frontier wit as Mix was as a personification of frontier heroism). The two men also performed in the 101 Wild West Show. It was Mix's first taste of show business, but he was back on his ranch in Oklahoma when he was contacted by a pioneer movie maker by the name of Selig to help him in making some "documentary"-style films on the West. Soon Tom Mix was not only helping round up stock—horses and cattle, not celluloid—but was also performing in, writing and directing short films.

Some of these one-reelers—*Sagebrush Tom, Roping a Bride* and others—have miraculously survived and have become constant items on the home movie front. They are always casually dismissed by serious critics because they lack the somber realism of William S. Hart's films. However, Mix's films circa 1910 reveal a commendable amount of naturalism in style and a studied use of cutting from long shots to close-ups and medium close that make Mix a director worth marking in film history.

The great days of Tom Mix's popularity lay ahead of him, after he went to the William Fox studio and began starring in lavish feature-length vehicles designed for him, to display his riding and stunt work. His horse was Tony, bought for a few dollars (often quoted as nine) and trained and ridden by Mix. No press agent could exaggerate the bond between the two, or the times they risked death to bring a new thrill to the screen.

These Fox films of the 1920s were never shown on TV to my knowledge, except for brief clips from them on documentaries like *Wide, Wide World*. (This Sunday afternoon ninety-minute show hosted by Dave Garroway had in the 1950s the most breath-taking program ever done on Westerns with *live* in-person appearances by Gary Cooper, John Wayne, Gene Autry, Clayton Moore and Jay Silverheels as the Lone Ranger and Tonto, Bronco Billy Anderson, Gabby Hayes and others, as well as films of Tom Mix, William S. Hart, Buck Jones and others. It was one of those shows that was a historic event in itself.)

During the fifties it was the few Tom Mix sound films from the early thirties that made him a household name once more. Mix's non-actor-like voice and advancing years are often criticized in those nine Universal features beginning with the original *Destry Rides Again* and *The Miracle Rider* serial for Mascot. Despite these faults on the part of the star, this handful of films gained Tom Mix a very wide fan following.

Youngsters who did not know of Mix's death in a one-car accident near Florence, Arizona, in 1940 wrote him fan letters in 1952. Some of these were printed in the *Tom Mix Western* comic magazine issued by Fawcett and were dutifully answered by "Tom" in print.

For those of us slightly older, who had followed the Tom Mix radio show all during our childhood, it was a revelation to see the *real* Tom Mix. His voice was not as melodic as that of radio actor Curley Bradley, but here was the figure we had seen countless times in Ralston advertisements and comic strips come to life. Many were too young to have seen any Mix film in a theater. As with actually seeing Arthur Godfrey or Mr. District Attorney for the first time after hearing them for years, there may have been initial disappointment. But then all the mythic qualities instilled in this figure—by years of radio listening, reading Ralston's picturization of his life, by hearing our parents discuss his silent films—took over, and Tom Mix became The Cowboy.

Few stars in any genre have had the sheer presence of Tom Mix. The confidence, endurance, the promise of decisive movement were in every line of his body. He was probably the only Western star who was exciting standing still. One of the most thrilling moments of *Destry Rides Again* is a shot of Mix just standing at the rear guardrail of the train moving toward his destiny. At private showings, I've seen the feeling go through the audience at this moment—an almost physical sensation like the sight of the American flag or the playing of a stirring march. At this point, Tom Mix becomes more than a movie cowboy. He is the personification of the American West, or perhaps the spirit of adventure in all men of daring everywhere.

One of the typical Mix features run and rerun constantly in those early days of television was *Terror Trail*. Mix played Tom Monroe, a marshal called back to duty from his ranch by the state governor to round up the notorious Paint Horse Gang. Near the climax of the picture, Tom was trapped inside a ranch house by members of the gang, along with some of the good guys.

TOM: I'm going to make a run for it. If I can get away I can get help fast. If not, the ammunition will give out anyway.
(*He looks around the room carefully.*)
Looks like I would have the best chance through that back door. You would only have to hold them off on one side, letting those two windows go for a minute. . . . I'm going to call my horse. . . .
(*After all take their positions, Tom opens the door and whistles softly. We hear an answering whinny from off screen and then see Tony racing for the door. We hear a fusillade of bullets.*)
Shots to cover
Tom swings the door wide, and the horse races into the room, running right up to his master. . . . Tom mounts Tony.
TOM: Now when I give you the signal swing the door wide. When I get through it, slam it quickly, and barricade it. Keep on firing at intervals through the windows to make your ammunition last and keep off the gang.

The simple scene of the horse coming right into the house, and Tom mounting him and riding out, was very effective, having the impact of a spectacular stunt, although no particular skill or danger was involved. The original script called for Tom to use the top of a dining table as a shield against the outlaw's bullets, carrying it along with him. However, this device was not actually used in the film. Needless to say, Tom Mix and Tony could outrace any bullet and were able to return with help to round up the bandits successfully.

Some of the other Universal films had more unusual plots than *Terror Trail*. *Flaming Guns* was chiefly a romantic comedy, with a subplot about cattle rustlers disposed of halfway through the picture. In *Rustlers' Roundup*, Tom Mix played a costume hero vaguely akin to Zorro or the Lone Ranger, known as the Black Bandit. *My Pal the King* was not a Western at all but took place in a mythical European monarchy when rodeo owner Tom King (Mix) got involved with its boy king (Mickey Rooney) and those who intrigued against him.

The series was expensively mounted, and if not quite A pictures, they certainly looked like them when compared to Poverty Row Westerns starring the likes of Wally Wales and Bill Cody. No doubt Mix could have continued making routine B Westerns for minor studios despite the difficulties of age and voice, but he chose instead to tour with his own Tom Mix Wild West Circus.

Tom Mix returned to the screen only once more, in 1935, for the fifteen-chapter Mascot serial, *The Miracle Rider*. The film was not as bad as many critics who neither like nor understand serials in general have painted it, but it had its faults. It had the faults shared by all serials, and some peculiar to it alone. The first few chapters (the first three were the ones shown to the trade for reviews and bookings) are lively enough, offering a mature but still stalwart-looking Tom Mix as Tom Morgan, chief of the Texas Rangers, countering a plot by Charles Middleton (later Ming of *Flash Gordon*) as the sinister Zaroff who plotted to drive the Ravenhead Indians off their reservation lands (rich in minerals for X-94, a superexplosive) with the aid of a rocket-glider they mistook for their mystic Firebird.

Watching the movie serial unfold day by day (or week by week on some stations) was very much like seeing a TV picturization of the old *Tom Mix* radio show. The plot was similar to some used on the radio series, and there was Tom, a young girl (Jane on the air; the Indian girl, Ruth, in the film), and Rangers like onetime star Wally Wales vaguely resembling radio characters like Pecos. For faithful Tom Mix Straight Shooters, the serial was over all too soon.

There were many other Western movie serials on early TV—Buck Jones in *Roaring West*, Johnny Mack Brown in *Wild West Days*, Tom Tyler in *Battling with Buffalo Bill* among them. Most of these were merely excuses for fights and chases, often exciting in themselves, and vehicles for the personality of the star.

Because of their great length and repetitive elements, Western serials often became more palatable and interesting with the introduction of elements of fantasy and mystery. The Miracle Rider series did not have enough science fiction elements; the few it had in the beginning disappeared after only a few episodes and were replaced by nothing of equal interest. Science fiction elements were much more apparent in

Republic's *King of the Texas Rangers* with football star Slingin' Sammy Baugh.

The Singing Cowboy

There was plenty of super-science fantasy in Gene Autry's first starring film, *The Phantom Empire*. Autry's Radio Ranch, from where he broadcast his country music radio show, was located several thousand feet above the underground city of Murania. The interplay between the invading subsurface Thunder Riders and Autry's crew, including Smiley Burnette and the youthful pair, Frankie Darro and Betsy King Ross, supplied thrills enough for twelve chapters. Autry's acting left absolutely everything to be desired, but he revealed a certain boyish charm vaguely similar to that of Hoot Gibson, but unlike the Strong Man of the West image of earlier favorites Buck Jones or Tom Mix.

Gene Autry revealed an interesting sidelight in a recent interview in which he pointed out that the animal he first used in *Phantom Empire* as Champion was the very same horse Tom Mix rode in *Miracle Rider* and called Tony, Jr. The saddle of the top cowboy star of the screen was passed on literally as well as figuratively from Mix to Autry.

Autry, learning to act in a completely professional manner (if not one to evoke envy from Lord Olivier), went on to make countless Westerns at Republic (successors to Mascot) with rotund Smiley Burnette. The comedian played the role of Frog Millhouse and was a great asset to the appeal of the films. He was a man kids genuinely found funny and lovable. (Certain other "comics" such as Dub "Cannonball" Taylor were merely irritating or distasteful. In one Wild Bill Elliot starrer, Taylor spends much of the picture scratching for body lice. It was in the script, but a performer even of Taylor's rank could have influenced a change. Instead he wallowed in it.) One of Burnette's tricks was dropping his voice to a cavernous bass (giving him his character name of Frog). It was predictable yet amusing. He was a fat man but never helpless, making life a bit pleasanter for some fat kids.

Autry and Burnette were a team in a number of very successful Republic pictures such as *Mexicali Rose* and *South of the Border*. (Autry used a number of other comic sidekicks, predominantly Pat Buttram, also a genuinely pleasant and funny man, but somehow the chemistry never worked as well.)

The plots of Autry pictures were some of the most improbable (excluding some films written by star Ken Maynard, whose story lines were simply insane). In the prime years the stories were set in the "modern West" and were designed to offer up as much music as action (in some cases, far more music). They were not authentic or historical Westerns, but they had much of the same sense of fun as a rodeo or a Wild West show. They were not out of keeping with the frontier spirit. The grim William S. Hart would have disapproved of them, but there was room for more than his viewpoint.

The 1938 Republic film, *Public Cowboy No. 1*, was one of less frenzy, telling the story of modern rustlers with airplanes and high-powered trucks being fought by the old-time sheriff, veteran William Farnum, and his deputies, Autry and Burnette. Directed by Joseph Kane (who along with Lew Landers and Frank MacDonald directed most of the early Autry pictures), the film also featured Ann Rutherford as Autry's leading lady. (In later years, Gail Davis would hold the record number in this role.)

The two deputies received a lot of unwanted help from an Eastern detective named Quakenbush. Smiley Burnette as Frog sang a piece of special material, dedicated to the Easterner, while wearing appropriate costumes as Charlie Chan, the Thin Man, and Sherlock Holmes.

FROG: When it comes to crime prevention, I really ain't no fool,
    I took a dozen lessons from a correspondence school,
    When robbers start a-robbin', they find they're soon outwitted
    In fact, I solve a lot of crimes before they're committed.
    Now Hawkshaw was dumb and a trifle uncouth,
    And old Sherlock Holmes was an amateur sleuth.
    The greatest of all—well, I'll tell the truth,
    It's me—the Defective Detective from Brooklyn.

In another scene Gene goes to confront the editor who has been criticizing the sheriff's efforts to catch the rustlers and meets Ann Rutherford as Helen.

GENE: Where's the editor who's been making cracks about Sheriff Doniphan? I've come to give him a punch in the nose. He deserves it after today's paper.
HELEN: All right, go ahead. I'm the editor.
GENE: (*Reacts*): I'm sorry about the threat, but you have been printing some pretty mean things about the sheriff.
HELEN: The truth is frequently unpleasant.

Thus started the "friendly feud" between Autry and his heroine that was typical of many Autry pictures and much of the "light romance" stories in popular entertainment of the thirties and forties, when more sexual passions were not considered proper for presentation in a love story.

The romance and the singing were really not favored by the youngest members of Autry's audience in theaters or on television. The country music did have box-office appeal in rural areas, particularly the South, and the romantic elements may have influenced some mothers to take their children to Autry films, because the pictures were of some interest to the mothers themselves.

There was always a sufficient amount of action in an Autry film, most of it doubled for him. Yakima Canutt was his stunt man in the early films, and there were others after him, including Jock Mahoney, an excellent stunt man and good enough actor, but one who didn't resemble Autry in the least (being much taller and thinner) and was absolutely ridiculous "doubling" Autry in some of the last TV films.

Although Autry did not do the dangerous stuff himself, he learned to ride well and did the close-up stunt fighting convincingly. Even with all the doubling, Autry took quite a few risks climbing around high rock formations and the like, even into the 1950s for his half-hour TV films which featured more action and less music than the theatrical pictures.

It was Autry's pleasant personality and singing voice that made him a star, not cowboy skills such as those of earlier Western performers. He had spent some of his early years on a ranch but had moved to the big city to appear as a singer on the WLS *Old Barn Dance* in Chicago. When he talked producer Nat Levine into giving him his first screen appearances at Mascot, he had to learn to ride all over again.

In essence, Gene Autry was an idealization of the "average man." He was not larger, handsomer, more aristocratic than men we knew in everyday life. The goal was *obtainable*—as a grown-up "self" for boys, or a romantic object for women, to fantasize over.

Roy Rogers

Roy Rogers was brought in as Gene Autry's replacement as top cowboy star at Republic when Autry joined the Army during World War II.

Although he had made a number of successful Westerns, the budgets and promotion of Rogers' pictures were deliberately kept secondary to those of Autry's. But with Autry gone—and studio chief

Herbert J. Yates personally resenting Autry's enlistment—Rogers was boosted to the top.

Rogers was better-looking than Autry, tall and slender. He never had drastic difficulties with either acting or riding. A large fan following grew for him among small boys everywhere.

But not among all people everywhere.

In theaters that had been booking the last films of old-timers like Buck Jones and the contemporary ones of rugged stars like Bill Elliot, Rogers in his fancy flowered shirts was hooted off the screen. I must admit that Rogers was never at the top of my list of favorites. A star is often subject to the wishes of his studio, his personal manager, and his writers and director, yet he can influence his career in subtle ways reflecting his own personality. If Autry's films sometimes developed a circus atmosphere, Rogers' films seemed often like a cheap side show. Worse than that, they soon took on an incredible plastic look, so false on every note that even when on location the trees seemed to be papier-mâché.

His personal publicity reflected his screen image. After his marriage to his leading lady, Dale Evans, there were countless stories about his numerous children, natural and adopted. And about his dog, and his horse, and his deep religious convictions. It was sugary enough to make one's face break out.

Despite his religious convictions, Rogers' films—even his TV shows specifically designed for children—contained more relentless mayhem than those of any other star of his generation. A fist fight between Rogers and a heavy often ended with the villain out on his feet, barely hanging there, while Rogers smashed the poor wretch in the face time after time, sometimes dragging the man to his feet to do it all over again, often to the appearance of lavish amounts of Trucolor blood.

It's possible that Rogers was merely doing what the director told him, but a performer such as Buck Jones would simply have refused to do the scene that way. At the point where the heavy was barely hanging on, a man like Jones, with a sense of the reality and the propriety of the situation, would have shoved him back with the flat of his hand and ad-libbed, "Looks like you've had enough, *hombre*." Then the heavy would probably have had enough sense to collapse.

(Bill Elliot in some of his later films introduced the technique of the hero fighting as dirty as the villain. If the heavy slugged Elliot with a chair, Elliot picked one up and smashed the other man with it. But this was done from a desire for logic and realism, not gratuitous brutality.)

Roy Rogers must be credited with maintaining certain high professional standards. Even in his last few TV films, pushing fifty, Rogers routinely did dangerous jumps from his horse Trigger. But the series was so tricked out with the trick horse, the trick dog Bullet, the unfunny comic Pat Brady, and his trick jeep Nelliebelle, and Dale Evans in pants and a more dominant personality than Rogers' that it was difficult to appreciate Rogers' cowboy skills.

Violence and Style

Two important elements of the Western arise at this point: violence and personal style.

The critics of the Western are always obsessed with their violent content, but in reality the more important element is the personal style of the character or the leading man (usually synonymous in a Western). Quite acceptable Westerns have been done virtually without violence (or "action"). In the thirties, many small Westerns were successfully brought off with only a token fist fight or a single shot fired, wounding the chief heavy in the shoulder. In a somewhat offbeat picture, *Aces and Eights,* Tim McCoy, as Wild Bill Hickok, was shot dead in a prologue to the movie while holding his famous "Dead Man's Hand" of the title; but in the body of the picture he portrayed an honest gambler who never carried a gun.

In the silent era the action scenes in Westerns were seldom ones of the hero committing mayhem on another person. Rather, the action consisted of Tom Mix or Ken Maynard demonstrating his skill and courage in leaping his horse across yawning gulfs, climbing up a dangerous cliff, or perhaps expertly roping three fleeing bandits from their horses with one toss of his lariat. Cowboy stars of this era seldom —never in many films—shot anyone dead.

In reality men are often faced with situations where the choice is kill or be killed, but these innocent films were not meant to reflect reality. When William S. Hart did strive for realism and the hero he portrayed did have to shoot to kill, the sense of the scene was tragic; the killing was an act of good intentions defeated.

Children are formless creatures, searching for a pattern to live by. In years past children found a ready answer in the simplistic styles set by the heroes of Westerns. There was a variety of choices within certain defined limits. Bill Hart and Bill Elliot reflected the strong, silent man of the West; Allan "Rocky" Lane and Roy Rogers preserved at least their humorlessness. Buck Jones, Tom Mix, Tim McCoy and others were strong, solid figures, but their knowledge of the real West would not allow them to play it so straight, and their character was lightened with humor. Hoot Gibson, Ken Maynard, Gene Autry and others were basically fun-loving fellows. They and others differed from one another in the subtle ways that all human beings differ. On the screen, as in daily life, it is those subtle differences between people that decide to which ones go our love and our trust.

When the kids of the thirties or forties left the theater, or broke up the gathering around the television set in the fifties after a Western, they did not often discuss the way in which the hero killed some baddie but were interested in some detail of his costume—Hopalong Cassidy's seemingly all-black outfit—or some part of his speech—or Wild Bill Elliot's claim to be "a peaceable man." Cowboy stars had to have style, or they had nothing.

Perhaps because Western stars—and movie stars in general—began to present so little character or individuality, the action or violence steadily increased in content. By the forties, plot and characterization had virtually disappeared from B Westerns with the story line only a gesture on which to hang the fights and chases. The Buster Crabbe films for PRC became an endless series of fist fights between the former swimming champion and chunky Charlie King (with many comedy scenes—a few of them deftly done—by onetime silent comedian Al "Fuzzy" St. John). At present, theatrical Westerns often present unmotivated violence on a grand scale involving explosions, fires, hackings with swords and hatchets, as demonstrated by Clint Eastwood in *A Fistful of Dollars* and its sequels. The only purpose for all this gore is to gratify the imaginations of those people who take pleasure in fantasies of killing people.

The Western stars of the past would not have participated in this kind of film. The great ones—Hart, Mix, Jones and others—demonstrated that they would rather quit than lower their standards.

The soul of the Western film has been the B picture. It is the purest expression of the Western story. The A generally only succeeds in weakening or watering down the Western prototype by the intrusion of other elements. The big-budget film adds boy-girl romance—which often devolves into soap opera cliché. The major production adds psychological insight to characterization, but such psychological evaluations are more fittingly part of an affluent, leisurely society such as old Vienna or twentieth-century America. The frontiersman had to react, not analyze. The big epic—and the small-screen TV Western—

adds reels and reels of meandering dialogue. The dialogue is not for realism or for characterization—it is there because talk is a damned site cheaper to film than action.

Television has given us a chance to be admitted to the greatest theater of all time. Particularly in the middle fifties the selection was at its widest. Now stations frequently play it safe and only book the top few hundred films with proven drawing power. But in those days we could see the movies of three different decades competing with each other side by side. Younger viewers, without prejudice, could select their favorites out of virtually all the movies ever made. Very often their favorites were not by any means the newest product available.

In the fifties one could see for oneself the weaknesses of a film like Wesley Ruggles' *Cimarron* carrying Richard Dix and Irene Dunne through an all too faithful adaptation of the Edna Ferber novel. All the action was in the Oklahoma land rush sequence, and the picture soon bogged down in unrealistic oversentimentality. Dix went on through a handful of expensive A Westerns generally weighted down by romance and, because of his mature image, romance and/or domestic strife in marriage.

On through the thirties and forties, Hollywood offered only a handful of A Westerns, and time after time they were flawed by what surely must be an insult to womanhood, the movie studios' idea of "woman interest." These included Cecil B. de Mille's *The Plainsman* with lanky Gary Cooper, a great film prototype but a man who never really seemed to get material exactly right for him; another lackluster, actionless De Mille-Cooper film, *Northwest Mounted Police*; and the least offensive, *The Westerner*, directed by William Wyler and offering Cooper his best role as a larger-than-life yet still naturalistic cowboy (but nearly overshadowed by Walter Brennan as the charmingly corrupt Judge Roy Bean).

The big studios offered Westerns that were comedies (George Marshall directing Marlene Dietrich, reportedly the first sexy Western heroine, and James Stewart, not the first shy but deadly dependable Western hero, in *Destry Rides Again*; Gary Cooper again in *Along Came Jones*).

It was not until the movies returned to the stuff of the program Western, with John Ford, who had directed Harry Carey and Tom Mix, and with John Wayne, who had made countless oaters, and with a cast and crew native to small Westerns (plus a few imports), that the big cycle of sound Westerns began, more than a decade after the introduction of talking pictures in 1939 with *Stagecoach*.

The *Grand Hotel* on wagon wheels captured the interest of the general audience, but it was the sweeping majesty of the West itself in Monument Valley and the pounding hoofs, the flaming guns, the flying fists of Western action that had thrilled less sophisticated Saturday afternoon crowds for generations that made it more than a "classic"—it was a good picture.

Through the forties, fifties and sixties "adult" Westerns galloped across the movie screens. The ones that were most successful both artistically and commercially were the ones that stayed closest to the standards and values of the program Western.

High Noon was an anti-Western and an anti-people film. No longer was the hero (aging Gary Cooper) merely braver than the common man; the hero was apart from the common man because those of the common breed were completely without courage or principle. The townspeople of *High Noon* are total misrepresentations of historical fact—the people did rise up and help the lawmen against the bad men. (They even rose up against the lawmen when they were no good.)

High Noon may have expressed the topical and political views of producer Stanley Kramer and director Fred Zinneman but it did not accurately reflect the broader view of Cooper, who was old enough to have lived through the last of those days in person, and who defended the courage of the true Westerners. A dying man, he made one last television film, a documentary on how the West really was, almost as if to give answer to *High Noon*.

Despite many flaws, director George Stevens' *Shane* was a purer distillation of the Western film. Stevens was a cool craftsman rather than a warm artist such as Ford. Alan Ladd in the title role was a cool figure as well, untouched by past, present or future, his boyish face and glamorous buckskins unsoiled. After giving his all for the woman he loved (his friend's wife, not daughter, a modern touch), he did not even have a memorable death scene or screen, but merely rode off to, as is obvious except to the most optimistic viewers, die alone. Only the soil and the grimy little town and the stark black gun fighter figure of Jack Palance were real. Shane—the Western hero— remained a mythic figure, unreachable by the woman (Jean Parker) or the small boy idolizing him (Brandon de Wilde).

The Westerns of the seventies are no longer really Westerns. They try for something more, and occasionally succeed. But they are a thing apart. The horse opera is routine and predictable—as routine and predictable as ballet or grand opera. The story is old— good triumphing over evil—but it has always been the *style* with which the story was told.

It was television in the early days that let us see those men with style—Tom Mix, Harry Carey, Buck Jones, John Wayne, as well as John Ford and Spencer Bennet—their sources, their origins. Except for those persons with vast private film libraries at their call, this was—and probably will remain—the best time to gain the insight from those pioneers to really understand the meaning and scope of the Western film.

The Western film has created countless hours that were mixtures of excitement and contentment, given us dreams of right triumphant and of a life never devoid of color or of personal worth. These may only be dreams, but a man needs a dream if he is to do what a man must do. And he must.

And don't forget it, Pilgrim.

CHAPTER 14

Theater in Your Living Room

Live theater performed right in your own home. It was almost a Grecian ideal come to life. Through most of the fifties people in cities and small towns, rich, poor, middle class, could see some of the finest theatrical plays of a classic stature, and some promising new ones, right on their own TV sets. It was an incredible bonanza, too good to last, and it didn't.

Some of us in small towns had never seen a real play with professional actors before. High school plays, perhaps. Maybe even a few scenes performed in a carnival tent, but not a *real* play.

Actors meant *movies* to me back then. In the beginning I was disappointed in TV plays because they were not enough like movies. Where were the quick cutting, the constant shift of scenes and location, the chases, the exteriors? You seldom saw them on *Studio One*.

Strangely enough, in talking with my mother, aunt, cousins, I found that most of them really did not notice the difference between a live stage presentation such as the *United States Steel Hour* and a filmed presentation such as the *Schlitz Playhouse of Stars*. In fact, sometimes they could not tell the difference between the *Steel Hour* and a twenty-year-old movie offered under the banner of *Mystery Playhouse*. My family was not especially unobservant but, like most of the early television audience, they were not interested in *technique* but in entertainment. If the story was sufficiently entertaining they did not notice how long the actors stayed in one room or how many camera angles were employed. Perhaps it was my loss that I could not lose myself in the play. Then again, I enjoyed it on two levels—first, for the story itself, and secondly, with a somewhat detached part of myself, to see *how* it was done.

In the early days of TV the technique of how a TV play was presented was often painfully apparent. One did not have to worry about where the cameras were placed—you could see one of them picking up the other right over the actor's left shoulder. The way in which the sets were constructed became apparent when they fell down. You learned that the actors did not make up their lines as they went along—at least, not as a rule—and that they got them out of a script. At times you could see actors reading from a script that was supposed to be hidden behind a newspaper or a letter they were holding.

The script—ah, that was the thing.

Early television depended on the words of the script writer almost as much as dramatized radio had. Some shorter plays took place on one set—an office or a living room, not much different from the ones you saw each day in your own life. Two or three characters in business suits would walk in and out. The only possibility for imagination lay in the words they spoke, the only creativity in the words and the manner in which they were delivered.

Memorable performances came out of television's live period—sometimes. But often the demands of speed and economy made really polished interpretations impossible. The actors had enough trouble simply learning the lines well enough in a few days to be able to express them incisively. The script had to carry the story by itself very often.

As in radio, live television writers who were good enough became stars—Paddy Chayefsky, Tad Mosel, Reginald Rose, Rod Serling, Gore Vidal. The writers of today's episodes of *Gunsmoke* and *Cannon* do not become famous outside the industry. The range they can display is too limited to showcase their talents properly.

Despite those collapsible sets, flubbed lines and corpses walking off camera, live television did succeed in spotlighting some spectacular writing talents.

The development of early 1950s television theater showcases for writing and acting talents began when television itself was almost as much a subject for Sunday magazine supplement sensationalism as telepathy.

Plays were broadcast experimentally in 1929 (perhaps even earlier!) when only silhouettes could be recognizably transmitted and then only to another technician in another studio a few doors away. Historic "firsts" are a maze of disputes and are not the subject at hand—the shows that influenced our lives in the fifties.

But for the record, take a look at where *Marty* came from. In 1945 WCBW, the CBS station in New York, telecast a drama called *The*

Favor by Lawrence M. Klee. It was a wartime propaganda piece using a single set and four actors. The leads were well known in radio—Joseph Julian as Casey and Leslie Woods as Dottie, with Edith Tachna as Rita. None of the actors were glamorous Hollywood types. The set was starkly simple, a cozy bar, but one where the bar itself looked more like a huge clothes hamper than anything you would expect to find in a saloon.

The sketch concerned Casey, a soldier returning unexpectedly from the war front and finding his girl friend about to squander her money on a new coat.

CASEY: I want to ask you to do me a favor. Take that dough and invest it.

DOTTIE: A war bond?

CASEY: About 275 bucks' worth. I'm not askin' for myself. You know how Izzy got clipped? There was a pillbox holin' up our outfit. Izzy and me went after it with grenades and a flame-thrower. Maybe the cost of all that stuff came to—well, 275 . . . *Casey goes off. Rita enters.*

RITA: Sorry I'm late. I had to stop at Mrs. Bender's.

DOTTIE: Casey's mother?

RITA: You didn't hear . . . ? Casey was killed in France. . . . If you want that coat, we'd better hurry.

DOTTIE: I'm not getting the coat. I'm gonna buy myself a hand grenade and some bullets. . . . I've got to do a guy a favor. . . .

So the April 1945 issue of *Tune In* described this pioneering TV drama. (The ghostly soldier returning to urge us to buy War Bonds was a convention widely used in radio, movies, comic strips and even in television during World War II. In those days of fever-pitched emotion, its simplistic appeal could be effective. Often the dead soldier was not just a character to us, but someone we knew.)

In the very late forties more ambitious television drama began to appear. *Ford Theater* became the first *sponsored* dramatic anthology on television in October 1948, following its career on radio. Another radio favorite, winner of the Peabody Award (broadcasting's Oscar), *Studio One,* started on television November 7, 1948, as a biweekly sustaining program, but became the weekly, sponsored *Westinghouse Studio One* on May 12, 1949. (The many programs of this type that followed, including *Robert Montgomery Presents, Philco-Goodyear Playhouse* and *Playhouse 90* were not actually old radio titles but owed much to radio anthologies in format. Other shows were only slightly revised in titling from their radio counterparts: *Lux Video*

Theater from *Lux Radio Theater, Armstrong Circle Theater* from radio's *Armstrong Theater of Today, The United States Steel Hour* as a retitling of the record-length radio banner, *The United States Steel Hour Presents the Theatre Guild on the Air.*)

Even as we viewers fiddled around with our sets trying to bring in a clearer picture, the production staff was fiddling around trying to master the technique of live video drama. (The tragedy of it was that live drama was killed before it was ever perfected.) A 1951 *Radio Television Mirror* article told how *Ford Theater* got on the air.

The show's director was Franklin Schaffner, not long out of the Navy, with experience in summer stock and radio and documentary films behind him. With his script editor Lois Jacoby and producer Werner Michel, Schaffner decided on the proper script. Next he worked with set designer Al Ostrander on models of the actual sets. With casting director Marion Roberts, he sent out a call for actors to audition. The smaller parts were filled as Schaffner listened to actors reading for a part (and sometimes getting a part they had not aimed for).

The stars of the episode did not have to try out for the roles. Two grand old-timers, Walter Hampden and Dorothy Gish, were the leads for this play. They and the rest of the cast went through the plans Schaffner had blocked out for the placement of actors, cameras and cameramen, mike booms and technicians. There were always last-minute changes.

As the week of rehearsal went on, the director worked out the music cues with conductor-arranger Ben Ludlow. Costuming and make-up were established.

There was a dinner break at six-thirty, before the air time at nine. Miss Gish took a nap on one of the sofas on the set. The rest did the best they could. Then at nine the show went on the air *live*. There would be no retakes, no stopping of the tape, no mistakes to be wiped out magically. Everybody had one chance and only one chance to do his best.

The results were often terrific performances. TV drama sometimes had the quality of a live Broadway play. The best acting can only be obtained in a sustained, coherent presentation, with scenes in consecutive order, simulating real life as much as possible. For a few brief years television brought performances of this caliber to people who had never before seen acting as it was on the legitimate stage.

There were accidents, of course. Lloyd Bridges got so carried away by a performance on *Playhouse 90* that he accidentally said "damn," then *verboten*. Some of the accidents were funny—a "corpse" on *Climax* that could be seen crawling out of the scene, for instance.

Mistakes happened on live variety shows, too. Garry Moore went into a wild dance with his pants unzipped. Red Skelton brought on a very impolite cow, and while he was selling *Pet-Rich Pies,* the bovine delivered what folks in the farm country sometimes call "cow pies."

But whether variety or drama, the added element of the live performance often produced a memorable artistic event, a fact clouded over by the embarrassed jokes about the famous bloopers. Even the element of tape delay somehow lowered the intensity of feeling delivered by the performers. Unconsciously, they no longer felt that they had to give their all for this one time.

Without aid of reference materials, I can easily recall great moments from many outstanding television dramas. There was the sheer audacity of TV producers with limited budgets trying to match Hollywood multimillion-dollar epics. *Kraft Television Theater* sank the *Titanic* on its crowded sound stages. Bob Montgomery crashed the zeppelin *Hindenberg* all over again on *Robert Montgomery Presents* and afterward interviewed some of the actual survivors of the disaster. Cliff Robertson and Piper Laurie were unforgettable alcoholics in *Days of Wine and Roses,* a *Playhouse 90* presentation: the two of them cowering behind the door of their shabby apartment while the well-to-do couple from their former existence knocked for admittance; the anguished couple swigging down vanilla extract when their nerve failed them to get them through the dinner "party."

Practically every production on *Playhouse 90* was an event. One of the brightest came on October 11, 1956, when *Requiem* by Rod Serling appeared on *Playhouse 90.* In plays such as this Serling displayed his mastery of realism, which in the strange turns of video fate eventually led him to his own fantasy series, *Twilight Zone.* But the fantasy lay ahead. This night the note was stark truth.

The cast was flawless. Jack Palance, screen actor and, like playwright Serling, once a boxer himself, portrayed the aging Mountain McClintock. Beloved, delicate old Ed Wynn dropped his clown act of half a century to do his premiere character role, Arnie, the guy who fixed the cuts on Mountain's no longer fixable carcass. The old man's son, Keenan Wynn (in private life, admiring but rebellious like most sons), became the manager, Maish, whose heart was more calloused than Mountain's ears, and from the same business. They were live. The play was live. The audience was living it with them.

We saw a looming wall poster announcing the fight between Mountain McClintock and a very muscular, very young black man, Jack Gibbons. We heard the sounds of the crowd (a bit mechanical, dubbed in, imperfect, human). The sounds roared to a climax. The crowds spilled past the poster, laughing, talking. Gibbons danced into view. Well-wishers crowded in to touch him, to have some of his victory, his strength touch them.

The crowd dissolved like dust on a deserted road. A broken crucifix of a man came down the ramp from the arena, supported by two smaller men, Maish and Arnie. A sharp-faced man darted out of the haze of tobacco smoke, his pinched face demanding, insatiable. Money —money to pay off the syndicate for Maish's lost bet. Maish would get it. Both knew he had to get it.

The two men supporting McClintock dragged and coaxed him into the shower room, onto a rubbing table. He lay, trying to breathe with great effort. His face was layered with old pain, new pain, the same pain.

The ring doctor appeared. He did his business, trying to put Mountain's face back together. His work sickened him. He spoke of it. He told of how he hated the fight business, the fighters, himself. He put away his tools and left, leaving Mountain's death certificate hanging in the air. "He's through. A couple more punches and you'll have to get him a seeing-eye dog."

Maish was angered. His property had been denigrated. He complained of the unfairness of machinery wearing out. Mountain spoke of his pain then.

MCCLINTOCK: It hurts, Maish.

MAISH (*turns his back*): I don't doubt it. (*Then Mountain shakes his head, reacts with pain, touches the bandage on his eye.*)

MCCLINTOCK: Deep, huh, Maish?

MAISH: Enough. You could hide your wallet in there. Go lie down. Rest up a minute, and then take your shower. . . .

MCCLINTOCK: I'm coming around now. Oh, Lordy, I caught it tonight, Maish. I really did. What did I do wrong?

MAISH: You aged. That was the big trougle. You aged. (*McClintock looks at him, frowns. He tries to get some thread of meaning out of the words but none comes.*)

MCCLINTOCK: What do you mean, Maish? I aged. Don't everybody age?

MAISH (*nods*): Yeah, everybody ages. Everybody grows old, kid. Go ahead. I think a shower'll do you good. . . .

Under Ralph Nelson's direction, Serling's script showed us how a sport, an American institution, an American business, could be so corrupt that Maish would eventually rob Mountain of all human dignity—and only incidentally his eyesight—because that was the way things worked in the fight game.

Producer Martin Manulis continued to produce a brilliant series of *Playhouse 90* presentations. There were some misfires such as *Eloise* in the person of seven-year-old Evelyn Rudie, confronting Ethel Barrymore, Monty Woolley, Maxie Rosenbloom, Charlie Ruggles, Louis Jourdan and many others in a teleplay that reduced the charm of Kay Thompson's book to cuteness; and Melvyn Douglas as Stalin and Oscar Homolka as Khrushchev in *The Plot to Kill Stalin,* which succeeded only in killing all belief in a possibly true but not credible account.

In the end, the triumphs outweighed the mistakes. There was Mickey Rooney as the tormented star of *The Comedian* (was the inspiration Red Skelton? Milton Berle? Red Buttons?). *For Whom the Bell Tolls* was a two-part, three-hour presentation starring Jason Robards, Jr., and Maria Schell, who were less glamorous but more human than Gary Cooper and Ingrid Bergman in the same roles in the movie version. The adaptation was by author Ernest Hemingway's close friend, A. E. Hotchner. Papa Hemingway liked the show, although some critics did not. "For the most part, it was a worthy effort . . . more faithful than the movie version."

In the end, *Playhouse 90* triumphed over everything but the ratings. CBS resurrects the title of the show every few years for an annual or semi-annual presentation of something often absolutely uncommercial and sometimes absolutely unwatchable, but the true excitement of a new live play every week lies in the past.

However, anthology drama still thrives. Movies for TV are anthology stories, even if they are not called *Ford Theater* or *Studio One.* Plays done live—on tape, at least—are reappearing in late night and early afternoon slots where filmed presentations might prove too costly. New triumphs for anthology drama and "live" teleplays may very well lie ahead, but we will always recall the thrill of their superb beginnings.

Index